THE SIKH DIASPORA IN VANCOUVER: THREE GENERATIONS AMID TRADITION, MODERNITY, AND MULTICULTURALISM

D0771880

Canadian Sikhs have seen great changes in their communities, which are primarily concentrated in larger urban centres, especially Vancouver and the British Columbia Lower Mainland. In *The Sikh Diaspora in Vancouver*, Kamala Elizabeth Nayar illustrates the transition of Sikh social culture as it moves from small Punjabi villages to a Canadian metropolis.

The result of an exhaustive analysis of the beliefs and attitudes among three generations of the Sikh community, the book highlights differences and tensions with regard to familial relations, child rearing, and religion. In exploring these tensions, Nayar focuses particularly on the younger generation, and underlines the role of Sikh youth as a catalyst for change within the community. She also examines the Sikh community as it functions and interacts with mainstream Canadian society in the light of modernity and multiculturalism, exploring the change, or lack thereof, in attitudes about the functioning of the community, the role of multicultural organizations and the media, continuity in traditional customs, modifications in behaviour patterns, and changes in values.

KAMALA ELIZABETH NAYAR is a lecturer in the Department of Sociology and the Department of Humanities at Kwantlen University College.

THE SIKH DIASPORA IN VANCOUVER

Three Generations amid Tradition, Modernity, and Multiculturalism

Kamala Elizabeth Nayar

UNIVERSITY OF TORONTO PRESS
Toronto Buffalo London

ISBN 0-8020-8947-X (cloth)
ISBN 0-8020-8631-4 (paper)

∞

Printed on acid-free paper

National Library of Canada Cataloguing in Publication Data

Nayar, Kamala E. (Kamala Elizabeth), 1966–
  Sikh diaspora in Vancouver : three generations amid tradition,
  modernity and multiculturalism / Kamala Elizabeth Nayar.

  Includes bibliographical references and index.
  ISBN 0-8020-8947-X (bound)

  1. Sikh Canadians – British Columbia – Vancouver – Interviews.
  2. Sikh Canadians – Cultural assimilation – British Columbia –
  Vancouver.   I. Title.

FC3847.9.S55N39 2004   305.8′ 91412′ 071133   C2003-905492-6

This volume was published with financial assistance of the BC Foundation
for the Study of Sikhism.

This book has been published with the help of a grant from the Canadian
Federation for the Humanities and Social Sciences, through the Aid to
Scholarly Publication Program, using funds provided by the Social Sciences
and Humanities Research Council of Canada.

University of Toronto Press acknowledges the financial assistance to its
publishing program of the Canada Council for the Arts and the Ontario
Arts Council.

University of Toronto Press acknowledges the financial support for its
publishing activities of the Government of Canada through the Book
Publishing Industry Development Program (BPIDP).

For my parents,
Baldev Raj and Nancy Ann Nayar

Contents

Preface

This study examines the Sikh community's process of adaptation to Canadian society in Vancouver. It would be an understatement to say that the Sikh community in Vancouver faces serious problems in adaptation. After the first set of preliminary interviews with members of the community, it became apparent that the most productive framework for understanding the Sikh community's adaption process in Canada, in terms both of the advances made and their limits, would be the conflict between tradition and modernity. Especially so, because the Sikh community in Vancouver is unique among South Asian communities in that many of its members hail from an agricultural society. Thus, as a transplanted traditional community in Canada, the Sikhs face the challenge of integrating themselves into a modern, industrial society. In this study, considerable use is made of the associated concepts of *orality*, *literacy*, and *analytics* in examining the process of adaptation, especially as it manifests itself in the variant experiences of three generations of the Sikh community. The tradition modernity framework and the related concepts of orality, literacy, and analytics provide very useful insights into understanding the tensions among the three generations of the Sikh community. To some extent, multiculturalism seems to have prevented the community from interacting more effectively with the mainstream.

An analysis of the relations between the three generations of the Sikh community forms the centrepiece of this study and makes, I believe, an original and significant contribution to our understanding of the processes of adaptation and integration in the context of modernization and multiculturalism. To my knowledge, an analysis of the three generations of the Sikh community has not been attempted before. Besides shedding light on the overall process of adaptation and integration of the Sikh community in Canada, the analysis attempts to provide a clearer awareness of the issues faced by the third, Canadian-born generation.

The study should prove useful not only to members of the Sikh community in Canada but also to social workers, educators, counsellors, and policymakers who interact with that community. Most importantly, as an empirically based, in-depth analysis of one ethnic community, it should be of interest to social scientists making comparative studies of the integration of other immigrant communities in the multicultural environment of Canada and similar societies. Although this study focuses specifically on the Sikh community, the issues discussed in it are relevant to other ethnic communities as well, especially visible minorities and communities that have arrived in Canada from traditional rural or oral societies.

In the research and writing of this study, many people have provided immense help, and to all of them I am deeply grateful. First and foremost, gratitude is owed to all the interviewees, who took the time to share their thoughts, experiences, and insights. Without these interviewees this project would not have been feasible. The study was conducted under the auspices of the Centre of the Studies of Religion and Society at the University of Victoria, with which I was affiliated to pursue this research project. Its director, Harold Coward, was most helpful, both administratively and intellectually. Thanks are also due to Hugh Johnston of Simon Fraser University and John Wood of the University of British Columbia for their support, especially in the initial stages of the project, for networking with both the academic and Sikh communities. Nancy Waxler-Morrison of UBC was especially helpful in enlightening me on the challenge of researching a 'closed' community. Jaswinder Singh Sandhu, a graduate student in Counselling Psychology at UBC, aided me with his expertise in Sikh spirituality and in the psychosocial issues faced by the Vancouver Sikh community. Donald von Eschen of McGill University guided me in the intricacies of methodology in the social sciences; Jerome Black of McGill offered me his expertise on ethnic communities and multiculturalism.

Many members of the Sikh community assisted me in networking with the community, both through participant observation in community groups and by suggesting names of people to interview. It would have been difficult to pursue the study without their help. Deserving of special mention in this regard are Gurhimat Singh Gill, Preet Kaur

Pandher, and Sohan Singh Pooni. Their enthusiasm for the project resulted in many intense discussions on the community's social issues and concerns.

The Fonds pour la Formation de Chercheurs et l'Aide à la Recherche (Quebec) financed my research through a postdoctoral fellowship, and I am most grateful for this financial assistance. Thanks are also owed to the British Columbia Foundation for the Study of Sikhism, which shared its resources, including both access to Sikh research materials and the provision of a grant toward the publication of this manuscript. University of Toronto Press editors Virgil Duff, Lauren Freeman, Anne Laughlin, and Matthew Kudelka provided excellent support.

Thanks, too, to my parents, who have been good role models as academics, and who also ingeniously raised me as a Canadian without ever letting me lose sight of my Indian heritage. Finally, I am indebted to my husband for his genuine enthusiasm and loving support throughout the course of the project. And I want to express all my love for Shardha, whose gestation period coincided with the writing and completion of this book.

Although indebted to many, I alone bear the responsibility for the final analysis.

THE SIKH DIASPORA IN VANCOUVER

1 From Punjabi Villages to a Canadian Metropolis

A popular research theme among many scholars has been the diaspora – the fragment of an ethnic community that exists outside of its 'homeland.'[1] Studies on the diaspora have focused mainly on issues of migration and acculturation, especially the process of adaptation of immigrants and their children in the host country. This process is a complex one, during the course of which immigrants – who often carry the societal values of their homeland – face pressure to come to terms with a different set of values and to interact with a different set of institutions. Adaptation is not quickly accomplished because it involves a generational dynamic. The process is even more complex when the ethnic group comes from a traditional and economically underdeveloped society whereas the host country is a modern and developed one. To some extent the process is also moderated or influenced by the openness of some developed countries to multiculturalism – a feature that has been characteristic of Canada in the last quarter of the twentieth century.

In this study I seek to examine the process of adaptation and integration with respect to one diaspora group – the Sikh community in British Columbia. This community, which hails from the state of Punjab, India, has been an important immigrant group in Canada in the postwar era, though its roots in Canada go back to the early decades of the twentieth century. It is now the largest non-Christian group in Greater Vancouver, according to the *Vancouver Sun* (14 May 2003). In examining the process of adaptation and integration[2] in relation to the Sikh community in Canada, this study is distinctive in that (a) it analyses intensively the social interactions of, and tensions between, three generations in the community, and (b) it delineates the underlying multifaceted process of the community's transformation in the light of modernity and multi-culturalism.

Past research has focused on the 'East Indian,'[3] 'South Asian,'[4] or Sikh diaspora. For the most part, this research has provided the social or political history of the different waves of migration, with the primary interest being the relations – especially race relations – between immigrant groups and host countries.[5] In addition, some studies have looked at the relations these ethnic groups of the diaspora have with their homelands. The relations that Sikhs have with their homeland touch on issues such as the Sikh quest for an independent religious state.[6] More recent studies of the South Asian diaspora have focused on the growing importance of religion in the formation of group identity.[7]

The broader field of ethnic-cultural studies in the social fields of education, health, and counselling has also paid attention to the South Asian diaspora.[8] A common feature of these studies is that they lump all the different communities from the Indian subcontinent together as 'East Indians,' 'South Asians,' or 'Indo-Canadians.'[9] But this lumping of the entire Indian community into a single category does injustice to those communities' vibrant diversity[10] in the areas of religion, behaviour, and stage of development on arrival in the host country. As a result, the distinctive underlying processes of adaptation and integration and the specific issues arising within specific groups are often overlooked.

The Sikhs share certain features with the broader category of South Asians, but they are also different in important ways that must be taken into consideration. Since the Sikh community is the focus of this study, it is crucial to look at that community's distinguishing features, which play a large role in its adaptation to and integration into Western Canada. The following relevant factors seem important to consider:

1 The Sikh community as it has arrived in Canada – a modern capitalist society – has predominantly been an illiterate (or not very educated) farming community. Indeed, the community in the form it has arrived in Canada has been primarily traditional; it has not gone through a period of thorough going modernization and urbanization. Essentially, the Sikh community has been directly 'transplanted' into a modern society without having undergone the experience of industrialization. (In this respect, the Sikhs coming from the Punjab are very different from Hindu migrants, many of whom are from the urban, educated classes.)

That said, it is important to note that not all Sikhs living in Canada

have arrived directly from villages or from the Punjab; some have come from places such as the United Kingdom, Singapore, Hong Kong, Malaysia, and East Africa. Sikhs from these latter places have also been interviewed for this research project; for this reason, the analysis takes place of origin into consideration.
2 Like other immigrant communities, the Sikh community in Canada encounters modernity, in the context of a predominantly Western culture, notwithstanding that Canada is a diverse and multicultural society.
3 Sikhism, the religion founded and developed in the region of Punjab, faces issues of modernity (as well as the Western scientific world view); but on top of that, it is confronted by the issue of universalism. Although the Sikh scripture is universalistic, the religion has been followed mainly by people from the regional linguistic- cultural group known as the Punjabis.

There *are* white followers of the Sikh religion, who are referred to as Gora Sikhs.[11] Most of them are affiliated with the 3HO – the Happy, Healthy, and Holy Organization – under the leadership of Harbhajan Singh Puri (Yogi Bhajan), who is based in New Mexico. However, Gora Sikhs are few in number and have few connections to the Punjabi Sikh community. Two Gora Sikhs were interviewed for this research project. (A discussion of Punjabi-Sikh identity appears in chapter 5.)

The Sikh community in Western Canada has been encountering modernity, urbanism, and multiculturalism; at the same time, Sikhism has been emerging as a world religion. Thus, an analysis of the adaptation and integration process with respect to the Sikh community in Western Canada must be approached from this broader perspective: the Sikhs are a *group with a religious identity that is rooted in a traditional society, and they are facing pressure to come to terms with a modern society oriented toward multiculturalism.* Before we explore this issue in depth, I must set out the broader analytical framework, one with three key elements: the historic transition in human societies (the change from tradition to modernity), the ideology and policy of multiculturalism in Canada, and the issue of personal and group identity.

Transition: Between Tradition and Modernity

The meeting of two disparate cultures often involves – at least initially – one culture taking on 'technique,' or practices from the other without adopting its corresponding belief or value system. One can readily see this phenomenon in the way the West has taken on spiritual practices such as yoga without embracing at the same time their corresponding religious world views and higher aims. According to Indian religions or philosophies, the practice of yoga is not meant for mere 'relaxation' or 'stress management,' as one tends to see it presented in the Western context. Rather, yoga is simply one practice among many, all of which are meant to be pursued in the context of a religious world view, with the larger purpose of self-realization or God-realization.

Similarly, in the case of people from a traditional society who come into contact with a modern society, it is evident that they take on the techniques of social life more easily and quickly than they do the corresponding value system. A good example is the introduction of democracy in India: the formal structures of democratic institutions were easier to import and establish; the values associated with those institutions have not been adopted as easily. In effect, the institutions have been planted in a traditional value system that is often incongruent with them, and as a result those institutions often encounter serious functional problems.[12] In the case of the 'transplantation' of a traditional community into a modern, Western society (as is the case with the Sikh migrant community), there has necessarily been a time lag in working things out for the proper functioning of the community in its new homeland. Consequently, the movement toward the smooth operation of the community in its new setting is often an intergenerational process.

Since the mid-nineteenth century, there has been a great deal of scholarly discussion among sociologists about the impact of modernization on tradition. Ferdinard Toennies (1855–1936) posited a dual model of human will and action that leads to two different types of social organizations: *Gemeinschaft*, where the natural will is predominant, is the type of social organization that is living and lasting and is desired for its own sake (traditional community); *Gesellschaft*, where the rational will is predominant, represents the type of social organization that is artificial, mechanical, and transitory because it lasts only until the ends it serves are met (modern society).[13] Max Weber (1864–1920), who saw and valued rationality as the master key in societal and political progress, refined Toennies's dual model. He turned the historical facts of the French Revolution and its consequences into sociopolitical categories relating to the structure of authority: traditional domination versus legal-rational domination.[14] In the latter, there is a demystification of authority based on tradition or divinity, and human beings become the determinants of authority.[15]

The dichotomy between tradition and modernity was discussed extensively in the 1950s and 1960s. Talcott Parsons critiqued the nineteenth-century dual model on the grounds that it masked several distinctions. In his own elaboration, Parsons proposed five 'pattern variables':

1 *Affectivity* (for example, to love one's spouse) versus *affective neutrality* (to be 'businesslike' with one's secretary).
2 *Collectivity orientation* (that is, being oriented toward the collective group) versus *self-orientation* (that is, being oriented toward the individual).
3 *Particularism* (for example, to function according to kinship loyalties) versus *universalism* (to function without regard to the racial, caste, or religious backgrounds of others).
4 *Ascription* (for example, recruitment based on inherited characteristics or status) versus *achievement* (recruitment based on performance).
5 *Diffuseness* (for example, undefined range of obligations as in close kinship roles) versus *specificity* (bounded obligations as in a contract).[16]

Although Parsons himself did not use the pattern variables to distinguish traditional societies from modern ones, some social and political scientists did, for example, Francis Sutton. Sutton used Parsons's five pattern variables as a means of describing the role expectations and value standards in different social systems. According to Sutton, an agricultural society has the following features:

1 a predominance of ascriptive, particularistic, and diffuse patterns of behaviour.
2 stability and limited spatial mobility.
3 relatively basic and stable 'occupational differentiation.'
4 a diffused stratification system.[17]

By way of contrast, a modern industrial society has the following essential features:

1 a predominance of universalism, specificity, and achievement norms.

2 a high degree of social and spatial mobility.
3 a well-developed occupational system based on achievement and reliability.
4 prevalence of institutions or associations that are non-ascriptive as well as functionally specific (for example, hospitals, universities, government agencies, and business firms).[18]

Another important distinguishing feature of traditional society is that knowledge is largely constant, with elders being regarded as the best source of knowledge ('wisdom'). Conversely, in modern society, knowledge is understood as progressive so that the younger generation is regarded as the best source of 'up to date' knowledge. An emphasis on wisdom serves as a stabilizing factor and makes for a very slow rate of social change; an emphasis on up-to-date knowledge allows for and even encourages rapid social change.

More recently, Alex Inkeles has looked at modernity from the perspective of globalization, which he associates with an emerging world structure of modernity. Convergence in this world structure is to be found in the socio-economic arrangements that are compatible with the management of modern industrial societies. Yet divergence also exists, in the ways that cultural traditions and economic and political arrangements are adapted for such management.[19]

The tradition modernity dichotomy has been the object of much criticism – in particular, for its alleged ethnocentrism. That is, the dichotomy is said to identify modernity with the West, which perceives its features as normatively good and preferable.[20] Yet it cannot be denied that there are essential and radical differences between an agricultural society, and that the tradition modernity dichotomy is one useful aid to understandng that difference. Besides, other attempts to distinguish the two types of societies actually boil down to the same thing, even though they may employ different language.

It is important to note here that in this study I will make no attempt to prove or disprove any particular social theory or model. Rather, I will use certain theoretical concepts as tools for better understanding the phenomenon of adaptation. I am not dogmatic about the claims of the modernization theory; that being said, the tradition modernity dichotomy provides the most useful framework for explaining the Sikh community's adaptation to Canadian society. In any encounter between tradition and modernity, tradition faces strong pressure to give way to modernity. But modernity is not without problems of its own. Some of these problems have been highlighted by postmodern social scientists; they include ethnocentrism, the myth of progress and the scientific world view, social isolation, and community and family breakdown.[21] No doubt some social scientists regard the tradition modernity dichotomy as an old and outdated theory; however, the utility of any particular theory depends on the specific situation to which it is applied. Up until now, Indo-Canadians have been treated simplistically as a single category, and not enough attention has been paid to the diversity among them. The greater relevance of the tradition modernity dichotomy in this study stems from the fact that the Sikh community in Vancouver came predominantly from an agricultural society without having experienced life in an industrial society. In using these concepts, I am not implying any value judgment. In fact, it is quite plausible that by the fifth or sixth generation of the Sikh community, other theories or concepts will be more appropriate.

Furthermore, the tradition modernity model is not intended to parallel an India Canada model. Indeed, features associated with modern society exist in India as well, especially in its large cities such as New Delhi, Bombay, and Calcutta. Likewise, the characteristics of traditional societies were very much part of Canadian society as recently as the mid-1900s. But because the Sikhs who have migrated to Canada have come predominantly from traditional farming communities, the tradition modernity model serves as an important tool here in conceptualizing the research findings pertaining to a group in transition from tradition to modernity, and in understanding the transformative impact that modernity has on tradition.

The Sikhs in Canada may attempt to maintain an identity based on their religious and cultural heritage; yet in an overwhelmingly modern society such as Canada's modernity is bound to have a transformative impact on their traditional patterns of behaviour. James Chadney, one of the first analysts of Vancouver's Sikh community, found in the late 1970s that within that community there was continuity in values even while economic patterns were changing.[22] One question that I attempt to examine in the present study is whether Chadney's observation is still valid.

In the matter of societal transition, there are important questions to explore regarding the three generations in the Sikh community as they encounter and adapt to modern Canadian society. Some of the key issues this study attempts to address are as follows: What tensions are arising between the older and younger generations? Do these intergenerational tensions reflect an underlying process of adaptation? How do these intergenerational tensions among Sikhs reflect the transformative impact of modernity?

Multiculturalism: Western Culture amid Diversity

The Vancouver Sikh community is in transition from village Punjab to a modern city; significantly, it is also an immigrant community evolving in the context of a multiracial and multiethnic society. One cannot analyse the adaptation of the traditional Sikh community to modern Canadian society without also taking into account Canada's diverse ethnic makeup and the Canadian political value of multiculturalism. In an effort to distinguish itself from the 'melting pot' of the United States (although the notion of an American 'melting pot' has been falling out of favour),[23] and to grapple with the diversity of cultural groups within it, Canada has defined itself as – and taken pride in being – a multicultural society.

During the 1960s, the Royal Commission on Bilingualism and Biculturalism recognized the British and the French as the two 'founding' nations of Canada. The Canadian Liberal government under Pierre Elliott Trudeau made English and French the two official languages of Canada. The government, however, went further than this and in 1971 established the policy of multiculturalism within the context of official bilingualism.[24] Some have argued that the Liberal government instituted the policy of multiculturalism as a means to winning the 'ethnic' vote. Regardless, in theory the policy was established in order to provide Canada with the means to manage its racial and ethnic diversity without going in for full assimilation.

Before multiculturalism, Canada had followed a policy of assimilation – the process through which minority groups are absorbed into the dominant group ('Anglo-conformity') – as a way to manage the diversity of immigrant groups.[25] However, it was increasingly recognized that immigrants do not or should not lose their cultural distinctiveness, and as a result, assimilation had lost its popularity by the middle of the twentieth century. In the 1960s and 1970s it was replaced by the theory of integration, which held that ethnic barriers should be removed; the dominant and minority groups would then interact to create a new, integrated body. In practice, however, integration amounted to dominant-group conformity. Accordingly, the theory of multiculturalism became increasingly accepted. Following pluralistic principles (used to refute the theory of assimilation), multiculturalism refers to the 'management' of racial and ethnic diversity, chiefly through (a) explicitly acknowledging diversity, (b) positively valuing the benefits of diversity to society, and (c) recognizing that minority groups contribute to society.[26] At the same time, even though integration as an ideology or policy is not regarded as desirable, under multiculturalism some level of integration into the larger society is considered necessary for the smooth functioning of immigrant communities.

During the formative years of the Canadian government's multiculturalism policy, the focus was on cultural preservation and the 'celebration of diversity.' Later, after the adoption in 1985 of the Canadian Charter of Rights and Freedoms and the 1986 passage of the Employment Equity Act, the policy of multiculturalism was formally incorporated into the Canadian Multiculturalism Act of 1988, which focused on issues of discrimination in federal institutions. It stated:

> 3. (*i*) It is hereby declared to be the policy of the Government of Canada to: (a) recognize and promote the understanding that multiculturalism reflects the cultural and racial diversity of Canadian society and acknowledges the freedom of all members of Canadian society to preserve, enhance and share their cultural heritage ...
>
> (*ii*) It is further declared to be the policy of the Government of Canada that all federal institutions shall: (a) ensure that Canadians of all origins have an equal opportunity to obtain employment and advancement in those institutions ...

The Canadian Multiculturalism Act attempted to achieve its goals through affirmative action and institutional 'mainstreaming' – the integration of minority ethnic groups into the mainstream by ensuring adequate representation of, and equal treatment of, such groups. Meanwhile, multiculturalism also came to be viewed as a resource for political and economic pursuits: it has been used to appeal to the 'ethnic vote,' to mobilize support from ethnic organizations, and to advance international business interests.[27]

Although Canadian multiculturalism policy allows immigrant communities to live according to their traditional customs and practices, there has been much debate about the feasibility of that policy because it inevitably clashes with the modern Canadian values of individualism, equal opportunity, and merit.[28] Likewise, multiculturalism has been criticized as (a) potentially divisive, (b) a hindrance to the upward socio-economic mobility of ethnic minorities, (c) a form of tokenism (since it sanctions the preservation of cultural elements but does not attend to more pertinent issues pertaining to gender and class), and (d) impractical.[29]

The most common criticism of multiculturalism relates to its potential to encourage or reinforce multiracial and multiethnic divisions in Canada. In his passionate but one-sided discussion, Neil Bissoondath views the Canadian policy of multiculturalism as promoting a 'government-sanctioned mentality' that is divisive and that 'encourages a feeling of ethnic pride and belonging in narrowed communities' by asking 'immigrants to conserve their past and make it their only identity'.[30] Similarly, Arthur Schlesinger, in his critique of multiculturalism in the United States, underscores that the lack of a national identity in Canada is related to its policy of multiculturalism: 'Unlike Britain or the USA, inclined for generous reasons to a policy of official multiculturalism, Canadians have never developed a strong sense of what it is to be Canadian.'[31] In response to the critique that divisiveness and the ghettoization of ethnic minority groups are encouraged by the multiculturalism policy, Will Kymlicka argues that multiculturalism in fact calls for the *integration* of ethnic groups into a common 'societal culture' (common language and social institutions), thus creating a national identity.[32]

Another important criticism of multiculturalism is that it hinders upward socio-economic mobility among racial and ethnic groups. In his monumental work *The Vertical Mosaic*, John Porter linked social inequality to ethnic pluralism in Canada. According to him, ethnic pluralism encourages insular and isolationist patterns, which in turn prevent upward social mobility for ethnic groups. Ethnic groups should not be bound to inherited (ascriptive) qualities; rather, they should have the chance for economic advancement based on achievement. Porter contends that multiculturalism, with its emphasis on the promotion of group culture, diverts attention from social and political control and economic advancement, which remain the privilege of the dominant groups. In sum, instead of promoting equality and meritocracy, multiculturalism reinforces the superimposition of ethnicity and class.[33]

Both the debate over multiculturalism and the actual process of adaptation and integration of minority groups in relation to the host culture have to do with the degree to which one has a unified identity with fellow citizens and, correspondingly, the degree to which one keeps one's inherited culture. The balance between the two is inevitably affected by the nature of the interaction between minority groups and the 'host' country. In Canada, this is undoubtedly influenced by multiculturalism policy. Conflict is likely in relations between minority groups and the host country when ethnic groups are expected either to remain distinct or to assimilate into the mainstream involuntarily. And because integration can be defined in various ways, the official 'sanction' of cultural preservation can be a source of much conflict, especially between generations – in particular, between Canadian-born children and their immigrant parents.

Although politicians use popular slogans such as 'celebrating diversity' and 'living in diversity' to express Canada's spirit of multiculturalism, there are at the same time popular references to different generations being 'caught' or 'sandwiched' between the home culture and the host culture.[34] Indeed, while in the literature on the Sikh diaspora there are references to the 'conservative' and 'strict' nature of the social or ideological orientation of Sikhs[35] relative to other groups in the South Asian community, there has been little exploration of why that particular community is in a sense more insular. Nor has there been any serious examination of the social consequences of that insularity.

In this study, in analysing the underlying process of adaptation and integration among three generations of the Sikh community, I explore the policy and practices of multiculturalism (including institutional 'mainstreaming') and their effect on the Sikh community. I do this with a particular focus on the traditional and changing attitudes that the Sikh community manifests toward social issues. I consider the following questions: Has the Sikh community's process of adaptation been influenced by Canada's policy of multiculturalism? What are the societal consequences of 'transplantation,' and what are the effects of Canada's emphasis on diversity? What effect is multiculturalism having on the Canadian-born youth as they integrate themselves into mainstream society? What role does multiculturalism play in the progress or betterment of the Sikh community? What effect does multiculturalism have on the Sikh community in social areas?

Identity: Group and Personal

The study of a visible minority – especially one whose religion is rooted in a traditional society – invariably brings issues of identity to the fore. The meaning of identity varies, but most often it is defined in terms of the psychosocial identity of people: 'the condition of being identified in feeling, interest, etc.' (*Oxford English Dictionary*). Identity designates one's association with a particular group, ideology, religion, social role, or career. Although psychosocial identity is a popular theme in the West, it is important to note that the concept does not exist in traditional cultures.

In traditional societies, religion and its associated customs are the foundations of culture. Most philosophical or religious systems are concerned with the notion of the self in relation to the universe or God. In traditional societies, the concept of the self is derived from one's religion. In turn, the religious concept of the self can be considered the foundation of identity. However, in traditional society one's identity is ordinarily 'collective,' largely dependent on one's familial relations. Indeed, in a traditional society the most important and central dimension of one's identity is the family (or clan), within which roles are diffuse, status is ascriptive,[36] and there is a collectivity orientation. Religious identity is thus rooted in tradition; the emphasis is on the community and its role in social control.

In a modern and developed society, one's sense of self is more complex, because the basic orientation is toward the individual and the developmental process of self-differentiation, wherein one distinguishes oneself from others, including one's family. The concepts of self-differentiation and personal identity emerged in the works of modern thinkers like Friedrich Nietzsche (1844–1900) and Sigmund Freud (1856–1939). These notions, which have been in play since the beginning of the twentieth century, were popularized by psychologists during the 1950s and 1960s. Jean Piaget highlighted the self-differentiation process with regard to cognitive development.[37] Erik Erikson popularized the concept of ego-identity and the individuation process with regard to adolescent psychological development.[38] Psychologists have also extended the concepts of collectivism and individualism to traditional and modern groups, respectively.[39] Thus, in a modern society self-orientation is understood as a characteristic of the individual, and the individual's status is seen as a function of personal achievement rather than of racial, caste, or religious background.[40] And because in modern society there is an orientation toward the individual, as well as a rise in secularism and the expansion of choice, religion – when it exists at all – becomes more of a personal matter; the emphasis is on the individual's personal relationship with God.

The issue of identity is even more complex when individuals belong to a visible ethnic minority. Ethnic identity has been defined as 'that part of an individual's self-concept which derives from his knowledge of his membership of a social group (or groups) together with the value and emotional significance attached to that membership.'[41] Whether individual or collective, 'ethnic identity can arise, flourish or decline depending on the lived circumstances, and be expressive or instrumental, voluntary or imposed, uniform or situational.'[42] Ethnic or minority identity, however, is often explored from the perspective of the majority group, instead of from the perspective of how people of the minority group see themselves or how they would like others to see them. In societies that encourage cultural preservation and that emphasize difference, the issue of identity is multifaceted, since individuals belonging to immigrant minority groups have multiple interactions. These individuals interact with (a) their homeland, (b) their host country, and (c) their ethnic community within the host country.

The question of identity becomes especially complex for children of immigrants who are raised in the host country and hence interact more with mainstream society. Some studies have argued that the younger generations do not see the host culture and their own ethnic culture in conflict and that in fact they successfully integrate the two.[43] However, these conclusions are based on very limited data and can hardly be used to make generalizations about the broader Sikh or South Asian communities.

Although the literature on identity definition and formation is considerable, for the purposes of this study I will look at identity from the perspective of (a) the personal level – which is taken here to mean the individual and family – and (b) the group or community level. This approach involves asking questions about the changes among three generations in relation to both family and the 'host' country. Examples: How do Sikhs who come from traditional Punjab perceive themselves as they live in Canada? How do children develop when parents provide a traditional home within a modern society? How do the members of a Canadian-born generation identify themselves? How do they see themselves in relation to their parents' homeland and ethnic background?

Since this study is concerned with the multifaceted transformation of the Sikh community in Vancouver, Canada, it is important to provide an overview of the history of the Sikhs in Western Canada, and to discuss the definition of the Sikh community used in this study.

Overview of Sikh Migration to Western Canada[44]

A term often used at the beginning of the twentieth century to describe those migrating to Canada from the Indian subcontinent was 'Hindoo.'[45] Yet most of these early arrivals were, in fact, Sikhs from the Punjab, most of whom belonged to the farming Jat caste. Sikh immigration to Canada can be seen as having occurred in five waves: (1) the early arrivals, in the first half of the twentieth century; (2) white-collar professionals, who immigrated in the 1950s; (3) blue-collar labourers, who immigrated during the 1970s; (4) family members who arrived through sponsorship or arranged marriages beginning in 1951 and continuing to the present; and (5) immigrants arriving after Operation Bluestar in 1984 on the basis of being 'political refugees.'

The first wave of East Indian migration to Canada, in the early 1900s, is often connected to a story about a Sikh regiment of the British Indian Army, which travelled through Canada in 1897 on its way home after celebrating Queen Victoria's Golden Jubilee in London.[46] As a result of this trip, Canada became known in India as an attractive place for economic advancement. Reflecting the 'gutsy' Punjabi character, East Indians (predominantly Punjabi) were willing to traverse unknown territory under incredibly difficult conditions in the hope of finding more lucrative employment. Most of these early immigrants were young Sikh males seeking employment to earn money to send back home, and came to Canada with the intention of eventually returning to India.[47] East Indian migration began when Canada was in need of manual labour. The East Indians found jobs mainly in lumber camps and saw mills, but also in railway construction, in salmon canneries, on cattle farms, and in fruit orchards.

By 1903 there were only about three hundred East Indians in Canada.[48] Between 1904 and 1908 – a time when immigration was unregulated – the numbers increased to 5,185 (5,158 men [99.5 per cent], 15 women [0.3 per cent], and 12 children [0.2 per cent]).[49] In 1908, however, the Canadian government erected a barrier against Asian immigration, part in response to the 1907 anti-Asian riots in Vancouver against the Chinese, Japanese, and East Indians. This new barrier resulted in a sharp drop in the number of East Indian immigrants. Between 1909 and 1913, only 101 immigrants were permitted into Canada from India: 93 men (83.8 per cent), 6 women (5.4 per cent), and 12 children (10.0 per cent).[50]

The early period of East Indian immigration was marked by considerable racism. The East Indian community (Sikhs, Hindus, and Muslims) often banded together to fight racism, poor working and living conditions, and immigration restrictions. This is most evident in the Sikhs' founding in 1906 of the Khalsa Diwan Society. In 1908 the society built a *gurdwara* (Sikh temple) in Vancouver, which served as a place for religious practice as well as for social and political activities.

East Indian immigrants contested the racial discrimination they experienced in Canada. In 1909 the congregation, guided by Sant Teja

Singh, at the Vancouver *gurdwara* rejected a government proposal for East Indians to immigrate to British Honduras; they saw this proposal as simply a scheme to expel East Indians from Canada. The Khalsa Diwan Society also protested against the Canadian immigration requirement of 'continuous journey.' The 'continuous journey' rule required every ship to arrive in Canada directly from its home port; this made it impossible for an Indian ship to dock in Canada, since a ship leaving distant India had to stop at a foreign port en route for refuelling. In effect, this rule meant that no immigrants could conceivably come from India. This angered and dismayed many East Indians: even though they were from a colony under the British Crown, they were forbidden to migrate to another part of the empire – Canada.

The discrimination against East Indians in Canadian immigration law became most evident in 1914. A Japanese ship, the *Komagata Maru*, had been chartered by Gurdit Singh to bring 376 Punjabi immigrants to British Columbia. Gurdit Singh had chartered the ship from Hong Kong in an attempt to get around the 'continuous journey' restriction. However, the attempt proved unsuccessful: by a court order, the ship was prevented from docking at Burrard Inlet in Vancouver.[51]

During the First World War there was a sharp decline in East Indian migration: between 1914 and 1918, only one East Indian man entered Canada.[52] After the war, only a few East Indians were permitted to migrate to Canada – some women and children. Between 1919 and 1947 the number of East Indian immigrants remained quite low. In response, the Vancouver Sikhs established the East Indian Canadian Citizens Welfare Association (EICCWA) in 1947. The EICCWA lobbied to change government policies especially immigration policies.[53] For example, in 1949 the Sikh community began demanding the right to bring fiancées to Canada; in 1951 they were extended this right. By the mid to late 1950s a generation of Canadian-born East Indians, mostly Sikh, was beginning to emerge.[54]

Only after 1951, following changes in Canada's immigration law in the wake of Indian independence (1947), was there a real change in immigration patterns. The early 1950s were marked by increased East Indian immigration to Canada based on the sponsorship system – a system that worked in favour of Sikh immigrants, since most of the earlier East Indian immigrants were Sikhs. During the same period there was another change in Canadian immigration policy, based on Canada's need for educated white-collar professionals.[55] This change opened the door to white-collar professionals from India, in contrast to earlier times when East Indian immigrants found work mainly in mills or on farms. In terms of the Sikh community, some educated army veterans were permitted to immigrate to Canada. However, the majority of Sikh immigrants during the 1950s and 1960s came under the family sponsorship program.

The largest influx of East Indian immigrants occurred during the Trudeau era in the 1970s, especially after the multiculturalism policy was initiated in 1971. During this time, many Sikhs immigrated to Canada, and found work as labourers or machinists. The many Sikhs who were permitted to immigrate into Canada around this time encountered a great deal of hostility and racism. As a result, many East Indians formed socialist movements to fight against racism, for example, the B.C. Organization for Fighting Racism (1975–80). While the leftist organizations were at their height in the mid-1970s, the Sikh community became divided. Unlike the earlier generations of Sikhs, who gave up many of their customs, some of the newer immigrants wished to maintain the traditional orthodox practices they had brought with them from the Punjab. This resulted in ongoing tensions between the earlier and the more recent immigrants, between the less orthodox and the more orthodox Sikhs.

During the 1980s the sentiment grew among Canadian Sikhs that the Indian government was marginalizing their co-religionists in the Punjab. On 3 June 1984, in Operation Bluestar, Indian government troups stormed the Golden Temple at Amritsar, in response to armed separatist activity taking place within its walls. Although many Sikhs continued to immigrate through the family sponsorship program and arranged marriages, a considerable number of immigrants arrived after the assault as political refugees. As the political climate in the Punjab cooled down and elections resumed, Sikhs migrated to Canada mainly through the family sponsorship program.

Because it includes so many waves of immigrants, ranging from new immigrants to those who have been living in Canada for over fifty years, the Sikh community in Western Canada is not a single, monolithic entity. Besides, there is a wide spectrum of religious affiliations within Sikhism. In sum, the community is quite heterogeneous although all Sikhs are linked to some degree by their Punjabi ethnicity and Sikh religion.

Aims of the Study

In this study I examine the complex transition of the Sikh community as it moves from Punjabi villages to a Canadian metropolis. I also delineate the wider processes of continuity and change in a traditional religious-ethnic group in the context of a modern society with an official policy of multiculturalism. Accordingly, I first investigate the community's issues from within, at the personal level: the relations between the generations as they live in Vancouver, Canada. In doing so, I highlight the differences and tensions between three generations with regard to the role of religion and familial relations, including child rearing and personal development. In exploring the relations and tensions between the three generations, the study focuses particularly on the younger generation. In other words, I investigate the generational changes within the Sikh community as they relate to modernity and multiculturalism, emphasizing the role played by Sikh youth as a catalyst for community change.

Second, in this study I attempt to analyse the Sikh community as it functions and interacts with the broader Canadian society, in the light of modernity and multiculturalism. The analysis of continuity and change is based on investigations of community and social life. With respect to this community and to social life, I explore the change or lack of change in attitudes toward the functioning of the community as a whole, focusing on interaction with the mainstream, the role of multicultural organizations, and the role of the media. I also examine continuity in traditional customs, modifications in behaviour, and changes in values and customs within the broader Canadian social environment of diversity. I then attempt to show what Canada can learn about itself in light of multiculturalism.

In brief, the chief aims of the study are these: (1) to analyse the tensions among the three generations of the Sikh community, and the implications for youth; (2) to understand the development of the Sikh community as a whole in terms of continuity and change, using the following as focal points in the analysis: the role of the community in a multicultural context, issues regarding interaction that the Punjabis have with the mainstream, the role of multicultural social organizations, and the role of the media; and, importantly, (3) to evaluate the general place of the Sikh community in a multicultural Canada.

I must preface the discussion of these issues with a warning. There is always a danger of generating overly broad generalizations and stereotypes by looking at a single ethnic community in the light of modernity and multiculturalism as that community adapts to, and integrates with, the host society. No single study can aim to cover all facets of the community or to include every point of view. This study nonetheless attempts to explore important questions, and I hope it points toward at least tentative answers. The goal is to come to a general understanding of some of the major issues that the community is confronting as it adapts to and integrates with Canada.

Methodology

The research involves two elements. The first is an analysis of traditional Punjabi-Sikh perceptions, beliefs, and practices. This includes a textual analysis of Sikh scripture – the *Sri Guru Granth Sahib* – and the Sikh code of ethics – *Sikh Rahit Maryada*. The second and more important element is a sociological analysis of the beliefs and attitudes among three generations of the Sikh community in the Greater Vancouver area. The sociological analysis is based on the following: eighty semistructured interviews with three generations of Sikhs (see below for definitions of the three generations); twelve semistructured interviews with professionals in the medical and social fields (one doctor, one police officer, two counselors, five community and social service workers, and three educators); and (c) six semistructured interviews with public figures involved in the Punjabi community (one judge, three media people, two politicians). Besides conducting interviews, I engaged in active participant-observation at several social and religious events and programs for seniors and youth.

The analysis is based on standard qualitative methodology. Semistructured interviews were vital as a means to uncover the issues that members of the Sikh community consider most pertinent to their lives. Earlier studies on Indian communities have tended to use rather crude variables to measure integration and assimilation. These variables have limited value in enhancing our understanding of the integration process. For example, how can measuring the frequency of wearing Punjabi clothing shed light on the younger generation's tendency to engage in role playing or live a double life? And, how does analysing assimilation and integration based on citizenship as an indicator elucidate the third generation's experience of ethnic insularity and the 'Punjabi bubble'? In this study, instead of using superficial indicators for quantitative analysis, I have relied on qualitative data drawn from the experiences of the members of the Vancouver Sikh community – data that have been gathered through a hundred face-to-face interviews using open-ended questions. Punjabi, English, or both languages were used during the interviews, depending on the interviewee's capability or preference. The interviews conducted in Punjabi were translated into English, with particular care for nuances. To avoid awkward constructions, in some places I have provided a loose translation that does not follow strictly the literal pattern of the Punjabi grammar.

The interviewing process is discussed in chapter 2; however, it is important to note here that I tried hard to ensure that the entire community was represented. The Vancouver Sikh community has many layers, for example, different waves of migration and different religious orientations or subsects. It is also a rather closed community, quite wary of outsiders. To find individuals to interview, I employed the 'snowball sample' method.[56] However, I sought out different types of people so that the field research could follow, in a sense, several snowballs landing in various circles within the community, from baptized Sikhs to non-baptized Sikhs, and from new immigrants to those who have been living in Canada for several decades. That said, most of the people interviewed were from families that had come to Canada in the late 1960s and early 1970s.

In the field research, I tried to include as broad a spectrum of the Sikh community as possible; I also tried to include several individuals who described themselves as having been 'marginalized' by the community, mainly because of mixed marriages or divorce in the family. Finally, the research also included interviews with several third-generation men who were raised as orthodox Sikhs but had since moved away from living according to the Sikh code of conduct.

The three generations are delineated basically as follows: grandparents, parents, children. This departs somewhat from the conventional understanding of generations among immigrant groups, where the first arrivals constitute the first generation, their children the second generation, and their grandchildren the third generation. The delineation applied in this study takes the household as the unit of analysis and distinguishes the generations on the basis of stages in life, mainly because most immigrant grandparents were not in fact the first family members to immigrate to Vancouver; rather, they were sponsored by their children late in life. However, the analysis considers other important criteria as well, such as gender, year of migration, and level of education. The categories are differentiated in terms whether the individuals lived in India during their formative years; however, this demarcation is not absolute. For purposes of comparison, I also interviewed Sikhs who do not fit the descriptions of the three categories (see below); for example, although most of the younger generation were Canadian-born and raised in Canada, I also interviewed two third-generation Sikhs who were born in India, and whose formative years were spent in India, and who had come to Canada in the past five to ten years.

First generation consists of the 'elders' who were fifty-six or older (up to eighty-eight). They are grandparents or even great-grandparents. The people in this group are all Indian-born, spent their formative years in India, and came to Canada as adults. Most Sikhs in this group came through sponsorship by family members, typically their children; thus, they arrived in Canada after their children. Eighteen members (ten males, eight females) of the first generation were interviewed for this study.

Second generation consists of people who are 'middle age,' that is, from thirty-one to fifty-five. Some members of the second generation were born in India, some in another country (e.g., Britain), but they have spent most of their adult life in Canada. Most of them are married and have families. Most Sikhs in this group came to Canada from India in their late teens or early twenties during the late 1960s and early 1970s. Some were born in Britain, East Africa, or Southeast Asia. Twenty-one members of the second generation (ten males, ten females, and one Gora [white] Sikh female) were interviewed for the study.

Third generation consists of the younger generation, who range in age from eighteen to thirty. Most members of this generation are studying in pursuit of careers. Some are married, but none has started a family. Two Sikhs from this group were born in India, but most are Canadian-born. Thirty-eight members of the third generation (nineteen males, fifteen females, one Gora [white] Sikh male, and three males who have moved away from Sikh orthodoxy and have engaged in rebellious defiant behaviour) were interviewed for the study.

As it turned out, fewer interviewees from the first and second generations were necessary for the research because the information relayed in the responses seemed highly repetitive. In contrast, in the case of the third generation, more interviews were conducted because there was more variation in their answers. When cited in this study, the interviewees are identified by a code for the sake of confidentiality. The codes reflect both gender and generation: male interviewees are referred to as Singh, whereas female interviewees are labelled as Kaur; the three generations are marked by the number of the generation (i.e., 1, 2, or 3), followed by a number given to the specific individual. For example, Singh 2.6 refers to a Sikh male belonging to the second generation, who is number 6 on the list of second-generation interviewees.

Likewise, Kaur 1.14 indicates a Sikh woman belonging to the first generation, who is number 14 on the list of first-generation interviewees. Unless otherwise indicated, the generalizations and statements included in this study draw on the interviews and on participant observation.

Since this is a social study of the community, questions about politics were not pursued. However, people invariably brought up political issues when discussing their religion, the role of the media, and the Sikh community in the context of multiculturalism. Since the study is based on interviews on the Vancouver mainland, its conclusions cannot necessarily be generalized to the Sikh community throughout Canada. However, many Sikhs in Vancouver have moved to the area after living for a time in other parts of British Columbia.

Summary of Chapters

The study has eight chapters. This one has introduced the study by providing a theoretical background on the three themes of societal transition, multiculturalism, and identity as well as a brief history of the Sikh community in Western Canada. This chapter has also discussed the aims of the study and the research methodology employed.

Chapters 2 to 5 are based on intensive field research and focuses on the process of transition from tradition toward modernity as the Sikh interviewees have experienced it at the personal level. In the light of the theoretical framework of 'orality, literacy, analytics' (elaborated in the next chapter), this part of the study analyses the transition process as it has occurred among the three generations of the community in Vancouver. Chapter 2 looks at the changes in communicative patterns I discovered when interviewing individuals in the three generations. It demonstrates how the interviews actually reveal the underlying transition experienced by the Sikh community itself. The interviewing process not only reflects the transformative impact of modernity on tradition, but also provides the foundation necessary to understand the tensions between the older and younger generations – the focus of Part B of the study.

Chapter 3 explores changes in attitudes toward familial relations and lifestyle. It includes a discussion of the tensions between keeping redefined yet traditional family values in the household and the younger generation's exposure to modern values. Chapter 4 looks at the traditional approach to child rearing and its effects on the third generation as they are raised in a modern, Western environment. Chapter 5 investigates the transmission of religion and religious practices from one generation to the next. It, again, explores the tensions between the older and younger generations with respect to religious values. It also discusses the younger generation's growing problems with the traditional pattern of transmission of Sikhism, and underlines the need for new and different approaches in teaching the Sikh religion to Canadian-born Sikhs.

Chapters 6 and 7 focus on the functioning of the Sikh community in relation to Canadian society. Chapter 6 examines the experience of a traditional community as it encounters diversity, and explores the consequences for a traditional community living in the context of a Western cosmopolitan environment. In doing so, the chapter looks at the changing role of social control. Chapter 7 studies the nature of interaction that the three generations have with mainstream society by examining how each of the three generations relates to Canadian society, the role of multicultural social organizations, and the role of the media. This inquiry, in turn, reflects the impact of multiculturalism on the Sikh community.

Chapter 8 provides the main conclusions of the study regarding the tensions between the three generations of the Sikh community in Vancouver in the light of multiculturalism and the tradition modernity dichotomy. The chapter discusses both the external and internal influences on the transformation of the community as a whole, with special attention paid to the third generation. The study concludes by looking at what Canada can, in turn, learn about itself in the light of the experience of the Sikh community in Vancouver.

2 Communication among Three Generations: Reflections on Orality, Literacy, and Analytics

The subject of relations among the three generations of the Sikh community is a complex one. The heart of any human relationship is communication – the act of transmission of verbal or non-verbal expressions, opinions, and information; this means that communication is the foundation of any study of relations between the members of any given community. Past literature[1] on communication within immigrant groups has often focused on the language barriers they face in the host country. In this study, we are concerned not with the problem of language barrier as commonly understood, although it is certainly experienced by immigrants in relation to the host country, and between immigrant relatives and Canadian-born children; rather, our concern is with certain other barriers to communication that seem to require close attention. One such potent barrier reflects changes in forms and patterns of thought – changes associated with the different stages in the historical development of society. Thought forms express the kind of society the person comes from; for example, traditional and modern societies have their own distinctive modes of thinking, or mentalities. The nature of change in modes of thinking can thus provide valuable insights into the process of adaptation and integration that a traditional immigrant group undergoes when living in a modern, developed society.

In this chapter I focus on communication among three generations of the Sikh community, and the limits and constraints in this communication. This particular aspect of the research emerged during the interviews; I had not anticipated it. The interviews did more than provide factual and attitudinal information; they also revealed distinctive thought forms prevalent among the generational groups. The different

modes of thinking of the generational groups can be seen as an important source of tension between the three generations, tension that goes
beyond language or cultural differences.

This chapter has two parts. The first discusses the analytical framework, which is organized around three concepts: *orality*, *literacy*, and
analytics. The second applies this framework to the three generations of
the Sikh community on the basis of the interviews' responses. It
explores the distinctive thought forms or modes of thinking found in
the three generations.

Orality, Literacy, and Analytics

The theoretical framework organized around the categories of orality,
literacy, and analytics is useful for conceptualizing the development of
thought forms and patterns generated by the process of modernization.[2] These concepts capture important aspects not only of the distinction between tradition and modernity, but also of the transitional
process from the one to the other. The first concept, *orality*, refers to the
mode of thinking that is part of the oral tradition, a tradition that is
characteristic of traditional society. Orality pertains to a traditional
mentality in which speech consists of the telling and retelling of ideas
and stories that have been passed from one generation to the next.
Associated with it is the notion of limited reflection on and exploration
of the validity of the voiced ideas that have been handed down. For
this reason, the thought form is aggregative – that is, ideas are agglom-
erated without being prioritized or discerned. Furthermore, the
thought pattern in orality tends to be conjunctive – that is, ideas and
thoughts often merge into a continuous stream. To the 'modern mind,'
what is said or expressed often seems copious or repetitive covering, a
wide range of ideas (see below for the definition of *analytics*).

Orality reflects a collectivity orientation; the individual identifies
strongly with the group to which he or she belongs. The self's differentiation from the collectivity tends to be very weak. As a result, communication is subjective, in that the speaker mostly speaks out of his or
her own personal experience. The orality mode of thinking is also
empathetic and participatory; that is, comprehension is achieved only
when the speaker has experienced and actively participated in what is
being voiced.[3]

The thought form associated with orality is both concrete and situational.[4] Expressions are about concrete things in the sense that they are

about human life or the physical world – that is, objects actually experienced by the five senses. Simultaneously, expressions are situational in that they refer to one's immediate life situation – the 'here and now.' As a consequence, the person's sense of the past (i.e., before he or she was born) and the future is minimal. Instead, speech either expresses the present situation or is based on memories that are relevant to the present.

Literacy, the second concept, refers to the transitional mode of thinking. This mode is influenced by the ability to read and write; however, it still operates within the context of traditional society. The thought forms and patterns of literacy reflect many of the characteristics associated with orality even as they make possible the change to analytics. As Walter Ong points out, during the early stages of printing the printed texts were of what had originally been oral works, and they thus retained the essential characteristics of orality.[5] There is no doubt that literacy goes beyond orality, in the sense that it comprises the ability to read and write; that being said, it is still within the context of oral culture and conditioning. Literacy – the ability to read and write – thus remains only at the literal level.

As a consequence of the ability to read and write, certain distinctive developments emerge in thought and speech. Although literacy is still marked by a strong traditional mentality with its concrete thought form, there is a clear shift toward *some* comprehension of the abstract. This comprehension is evident in the development of the ability to *translate* (i.e., cast a communication in other terms or into another form of communication[6]) statements or questions that contain one level (e.g., abstract) to another level (e.g., literal or concrete). In addition, there is the development of the ability to *interpret* – that is, to 'comprehend the relationships between the various parts of the communication, to reorder or rearrange it, and to relate it to one's reservoir of experiences and ideas.'[7]

The speech form associated with literacy is still continuous with orality in that it remains close to human life and to the material world: it verbalizes knowledge that relates to familiar life situations. But, although such speech often relates to one's life situation, it is also influenced by what 'one has read,' and as a consequence there is some distancing from the directly known. It follows from this that speech is not necessarily empathetic or participatory.[8] Likewise, although there is a continuing collectivity orientation – a feature of orality – there is some movement toward differentiating the self from the collectivity.

The last category – *analytics* – refers to the mode of critical thinking that emerges out of the culture of reading and writing and that breaks away from traditional mentality to mirror the essential characteristics of modernity. It carries the marks of a 'modern mentality,' which includes the capacity for self-reflection. It goes beyond the category of literacy, since written texts no longer represent oral works, but rather are the result of deeper thinking and conditioning. Analytical thought involves intellectual experimentation and exploration. The thought form is thus focused, and it prioritizes ideas. Analytics also incorporates a self-orientation, whereby one is able to differentiate the self from 'others' or from the directly 'known.' In the process of self-differentiation, there is a personal distancing from the expressed idea or thought; this makes objectivity possible.[9] In contrast to orality, one is able to speak or comprehend thoughts or ideas without 'experiencing them.'

The mode of thinking associated with the concept of analytics typically includes abstract and theoretical thought forms[10] that extend beyond the directly perceived human life situation or physical world. The mentality that goes with analytics is explorative and inquisitive; it transcends the sphere of concrete things. It evidences the ability to comprehend universals and to conceptualize knowledge. Furthermore, it allows a heightened awareness of time (both past and future) that extends beyond one's life situation.[11]

These concepts of orality, literacy, and analytics constitute an highly useful framework for understanding the changes that occur in thought forms and patterns among the first, second, and third generations of the Sikh community.

The First Generation and Orality

Most members of the Sikh community newly arrived in Canada have just left an oral community in rural Punjab. Most of the first-generation interviewees for this study were illiterate or nearly so. Accordingly, they reflected orality – the mode of thinking particular to a traditional society's oral culture. As mentioned before, the interviews with people belonging to the first generation did more than provide factual and attitudinal information; they also revealed a distinctive concrete thought form based directly on the interviewees' life situation and collectivity orientation. This was most evident in how the interviewees told stories in concrete thought form about themselves and their families while responding to questions.

Facilitating the Interview Process

Many of the people of the first generation were accessible through seniors groups connected with community centres or *gurdwaras* (Sikh places of worship). The interviews were conducted in private and lasted two or three hours each. The first-generation interviewees seemed highly intrigued by my own background – especially by my stories about one of my parents, who is from the Punjab – and by my account of the places where my family and I had lived in India. This shared connection with the Punjab broke down cultural barriers and made the seniors more willing to talk about their own background and life situation.

The members of this group understood and accepted that the interview was for 'a university study.' However, they showed no indication that they understood how the information was going to be used, nor did they ask. Although I discussed the issue of confidentiality with them, they did not show any real concern about it. In fact, several of them pointed out that confidentiality is not valued in Punjabi culture – for example, 'We don't have this [confidentiality] in the Punjabi community. I know they have this here [in Canada]' (Kaur 1.14). On the whole, however, members of the first generation were relieved that their names were not going to be revealed in the study. Interestingly, during an initial interview session at one of the *gurdwaras*, several Sikh men feared that I might be investigating their eligibility for pension (Singh 1.5 and 1.9). This concern undoubtedly reflected the mentality they had brought with them from their homeland; in India, local bureaucrats and police are generally distrusted, and there is always the fear that such officials are likely to report back to the government against the common people.

Storytelling the Biographical Information

The interviewees from the first generation responded to requests for biographical information by narrating extensive stories of the major events in their lives. This very much reflects orality: concrete thought form with many aggregated facts and details. For example, a seventy-nine-year-old Sikh who had been a farmer in the Punjab responded to a specific question about his educational level – 'How much schooling did you have?' in Punjabi: 'I studied up to the fifth class and then left. I studied privately with another person at another place. I had to do farming, my father got me two oxen and I started farming. I had land, 130 *bighas*[12] [roughly 70 acres] of land. I started with two oxen, then made it to three oxen. Then I bought a camel, and started having two servants, before I only had one servant. Then I bought a tractor. There was land consolidation [in 1955]. I bought a tractor [in 1960]. I bought an engine and got two motors [generators] after we got electricity' (Singh 1.9).

The interviewees gave elaborate descriptions about their lives, yet often they did not mention dates unless specifically requested. Members of the first generation, most of whom had little or no education, were rarely able to give the precise year for major life events, though they found it easy to give their own age, the ages of their children, and their age on arrival in Canada. Often, the seniors had to look at their health care card in order to give the actual year of their birth (Singh 1.5, 1.9; Kaur 1.8, 1.11, 1.14). It was as if dates were not relevant. Rather, their focus was on the stories they wanted to tell.

Concrete Answers Relating to a Collectivity Orientation

Orality was also reflected in the interviewees' responsiveness to the particular types of questions asked. More conceptual questions such as 'How have attitudes toward the elderly changed among the generations of the Sikh community in Canada?' were not likely to be useful in eliciting responses. The questions had to be more concrete and related to their life situation – for example, 'How did you treat the elderly in the Punjab?' or 'How are the elderly treated now in Canada?'

Answers given by the first generation to the interview questions demonstrated additive thought patterns, with ideas joined or combined together. Often used was the conjunction 'and' (in Punjabi, *te*) – a thought pattern associated with orality. Orality thought form has the tendency to accumulate thoughts without much prioritization. During the interviews, the members of the first generation found it difficult to provide focused answers; they needed to be constantly redirected.

Also, the answers given by first-generation interviewees were concrete and close to their life situation. For example, a sixty-eight-year-old Sikh widow of forty years explained the treatment of the elderly in this way:

'*How are the elderly treated in Canada?*'
   There is lot of difference in Canada. Here seniors have a pension and enjoy life. There [in India] one is under the control of children. The seniors

have benefits, there are no problems here. If no one gives you food, you go wherever you like here ... Pensions are good for seniors. There is no problem; one can spend. In India, seniors who have husbands, they have no pension; only one who has a job gets a pension. Only people with jobs get pensions. Here people who do nothing get a pension when they are sixty-five. Women who have jobs in India have income. But [otherwise] they are dependent on their children. (Kaur 1.10 trans.).

This quotation reflects a concrete thought form relating to the respondent's particular life situation – her concern about economic independence as a widow. This reflects not only a concrete thought form, but also a collectivity orientation.

A distinguishing feature of the orality mode of thinking is its collectivity orientation; thus, the interviewees spoke in general 'collective' terms when discussing an issue from the perspective of their own specific life situation. Even though first-generation interviewees spoke from their own life situation, they rarely differentiated themselves from the collectivity. Another instance of a concrete thought form close to one's life situation, that also expresses a collectivity orientation, was an answer given by a seventy-six-year-old Sikh widow who had chosen to live independently:

How are the seniors cared for in Canada?
   After coming to Canada, the children are busy and people like me who stay at home want to rule [over the rest of the family] because we have the habit from India ... The problem is that when those who work come home [at the end of the day], [if] we criticize them, they are not going to take it well. That is the root of the problem. (Kaur 1.8, trans.).

The preceding quotation reflects the woman's experience of the tensions between the first generation and the younger generation, but she expressing it in general terms and in the third person. Here again, a member of the first generation is speaking with a collectivity orientation; although she is talking about her specific situation, she is speaking as if it is the collective experience of the community.

The telling of stories is the traditional form of transmitting knowledge or information; it is a distinguishing feature of orality. At the same time, storytelling is a mode of expression that is concrete, close to one's life situation, and oriented to the collectivity. Narrating stories seems to involve active participation with the known, through observing or reliving it. Typically, the first-generation interviewees reflected a traditional mentality in the telling of popular folk stories that teach lessons about life and human nature. After narrating two popular Punjabi folk stories, a Sikh woman of eighty told a story about her neighbours in response to this question: 'Are parents taken care of by their children in their old age in Canada?'

> In [a town in Northern B.C.] there is an East Indian old guy. His kids are grown up but I had never seen them before. This old man had a ritual – every garbage pick-up day he would leave a beer on top of the garbage can because he wanted the garbage man to have a beer. Then one day the garbage man came and there was no garbage can and no beer. He thought something must be wrong. So he went knocking on the man's door. No one answered. He went to the neighbors who did not know. Then he called the police. The police came to the house and found the man lying dead. The very next day the kids appeared in a van to take what they needed. One son said he will live in the house until it gets sold. (Kaur 1.14, trans. Punjabi)

Without explicitly answering the question, the interviewee was telling a story about how children are *not* taking good care of their parents. Many of the first-generation interviewees, especially the widows like the ones cited above (Kaur 1.4, 1.8, 1.13), expressed joy at being interviewed – they were delighted to have their many stories 'told' and 'heard.' It seemed that by telling their stories, they were able to relive them.

As mentioned earlier, most of the interviewees of the first generation were illiterate or minimally educated, and their interviews reflected orality. But several interviewees reflected literacy, in part because they had received secondary or higher schooling in the Punjab. One educated Sikh man of seventy-one explained that there was a gap in thinking between him and the ones who were not educated: 'The elders occupy themselves with talking about what they have done, discussing politics according to their knowledge, playing cards, and gossiping (*gup shup*). I don't participate with the seniors. I attended the seniors committee but went one or two times ... It is difficult to make uneducated people see things differently. Like they say, "[You] can't tame an old person, [you] can only tame a young one"' (Singh 1.15).

Similarly, a Sikh woman of eighty – who was extraordinary in having studied up to grade ten – read newspapers and books and attended seniors groups. She often took newspaper clippings to the seniors groups to read to the illiterate women. Yet, in talking about how she brought reading material to one of the groups, she commented on the limited interest of the non-educated people: 'I come to [the senior group to] read newspaper stories to the other women. But they have no interest. They have no interest in history. They want to talk about cooking, clothing, their children. It is because they did not go to school. School gives you the interest' (Kaur 1.4).

Kaur 1.4 recognized the difference between illiterate groups – who are more preoccupied with their daily lives – and those who are literate; furthermore, by her comment she was also demonstrating her own shift to literacy. She made critical observations about others, while still expressing her thoughts in concrete terms. She also indicated some self-orientation, distinguishing herself from the collectivity. Indeed, her statement sheds light on the transition from orality to literacy.

The Second Generation and Literacy

Some Sikhs were educated in India and thus were literate on arrival in Canada; however, most members of the second generation spent their formative years in an oral culture. As they become more educated, there inevitably took place a shift from orality to literacy. Since literacy is a transitional mode, it shares some of the characteristics of orality even while faciliting the move to analytics. The second generation tends to be more able to articulate ideas in concrete terms according to what its members have either read, or experienced close to their life situation (orality). Emerging at the same time, however, is some distancing from the collectivity – a distinguishing feature of literacy – even as members remain rooted in traditional culture. Interestingly, members of the second generation were eager and willing to provide historical-biographical accounts, devoid of the storytelling style of the first generation. Furthermore, they also demonstrated an ability to translate from the abstract to the concrete and to interpret at the literal level.

Facilitating the Interview Process

Unlike the first generation, the interviewees from the second generation did not particularly need to be told about my personal background and link with India. In fact, they were more interested in knowing about the university degrees I held and where I had studied. Because they had agreed to be interviewed at the request of a friend or acquaintance, the legitimacy of my study and of the interviewing process itself was not an issue for them.

They understood that a study was being done, yet they showed little real curiosity about its nature. Only a few of the interviewees expressed adequate comprehension of the study or the need for it (Singh 2.10, 2.11; Kaur 2.17). The interviewees of the second generation understood the issue of privacy, but their concern over confidentiality varied widely, from indifference to outright appreciation for it. Most of the interviews were conducted in the interviewer's home. The female participants chose a time when they could be interviewed in private; in contrast, the male participants opted to be interviewed with their family in an adjoining room. During the course of these latter interviews, other family members sometimes joined in – especially the interviewee's parents and wife. The interviews were two to three hours in duration.

Literal Biographical Accounts

The biographical accounts of the second generation largely reflected literacy. The interviewees provided answers – without elaboration or explanation – to the open-ended questions asked about the major events in their lives. Note, for example, the following exchange with a Sikh man of forty-nine:

> *When and where were you born?*
>   I was born in [...] in the [...] district.
> *How much education did you receive?*
>   I was educated up to grade eleven.
> *When did you come to Canada?*
>   I came to Canada in 1969 when I was [...] years old. I worked on farms at first and then got a mill job in 1971. (Singh 2.9)

In contrast to the first generation, the educated people belonging to the second generation willingly offered straightforward facts about their lives; they provided chronological accounts of the major events in their lives. While answering, these interviewees (unlike the members of the first generation) included the dates of the major events (migration, marriage, birth of children), and the certificates or diplomas they held, along with the names of the schools they had attended and their employment history.

Literal Responses with Some Distancing from the Collectivity

The most obvious feature of literacy noted during interviews with the members of the second generation was their ability to translate questions containing some degree of abstraction to a concrete level. But at the same time, they did not demonstrate an ability to translate communications in a concrete form to an abstract level or from one level of abstraction to another level of abstraction. Unlike the first generation, the second generation was able to comprehend simple conceptual or abstract questions even while answering those questions in concrete thought form. Note the answer given by a forty-eight-year-old Sikh woman to this conceptual question: 'What is the source of tension for the younger generation?' 'Every family has to talk with the[ir] kids. [In] the ten houses on my street, parents do not communicate with their kids. Parents are [like] "birds out of a cage." When they left India, they thought they were free in a place of good fortune. They did not keep some of the routines they needed to in order to keep the children on the right track. They changed, thinking things would be okay in North America' (Kaur 2.18).

While the above response is expressed in concrete thought form, it answers the conceptual question. Also, the interviewee uses the expression 'like birds out of a cage' to articulate an abstraction. Occasionally, some interviewees used proverbs to express conceptual thought: 'Every grain you eat has your name written on it' (Singh 2.22) or 'While in Rome do as the Romans do' (Singh 1.1).

The answers provided by the members of the second generation were more focused; these people needed less redirection. However, probing was necessary in order to validate information. For example, one fifty-seven-year-old Sikh man pointed to his father during the interview and said, without any elaboration, 'He is both my mother and my father' (Singh 2.2). After some probing, he explained that his mother had died when he was very young and that his father had never remarried.

Because answers remained at the literal level, it was usually necessary to ask further questions in order to flush out the austere answers. Consider, for example, the following exchange with a forty-seven-year-old Sikh woman from Jullundur city, who had been educated up to grade eight:

Do you take ayurvedic or homeopathic medicines in Canada?
    I don't believe in ayurvedic doctors.
But you said that in the Punjab you went to an ayurvedic doctor?
    I don't trust ayurvedic doctors here.
Why do you trust them in the Punjab, but not in Canada?

In India, we do but it is different there because you know everyone and you know who is the right one to go to. Here you don't know.

Why don't you try to find out a good ayurvedic doctor here?

We don't go because it is not covered by medical coverage. If they [doctor's fees and medicines] were covered we would go to both and see which one helps. It gets expensive having to pay for fees and medicines. (Kaur 2.3)

The above quotation demonstrates the need to probe with respect to literal answers; doing so can lead to completely different information. There may be other ideas and issues underlying the literal answer – ideas that cannot be adequately developed without further questioning. Literal answers do not explore or elaborate, and as a result important information can be missed.

Another distinguishing feature of literacy is its ability to express thoughts with some distancing from the known. This reflects some movement toward the differentiation of the self from the collectivity. While discussing the pros and cons of multiculturalism, a forty-two-year-old Sikh mother demonstrated literacy in using concrete terms to explain something more conceptual. Specifically, she pointed out the reasons why parents prefer to send their children to a Punjabi school: 'Parents [who] send their children to [...] School are not interested in academics, not even in aspirations or even goals. You see, the parents like [...] School because there is no alcohol, or drugs, and because tradition from India is there. They fear their daughters dating ... It is like India, and the parents want this' (Kaur 2.21).

In the above citation, although the thought form is concrete and aggregative, it is also interpretive of the reason why parents send their children to a Punjabi school. This requires the interviewee to be able to distance herself from the known.

Another feature of literacy evident in this run of interviews was the interviewees' ability to literally interpret thought – to comprehend the relationships between the various parts of the communication, to reorder or rearrange them, and to relate the communication to their reservoir of experiences and ideas, even as the latter remained at a concrete level. As an example of interpretation expressed through concrete thought form, a forty-nine-year-old Sikh man, noted that living on one's own makes one develop more than if one remains in the extended family: 'I grew more when I left my family [parent's home] and was on my own. You have to learn fast about budgeting and mortgages' (Singh 2.9).

Another example: a fifty-four-year-old Sikh man spoke about how the *gurdwaras* remain isolated from the larger community, with which they ought to be engaging: 'Our people go to the *gurdwara*, take *langar* [food at the community kitchen] and socialize with each other and then they come home and feel *razi* [fulfilled]. They don't teach anyone outside the *gurdwaras* about the [Sikh] community and religion' (Singh 2.11).

Although in the last two quotations the thought forms remain concrete, they are interpretive even while alluding to something conceptual.

The ability of simple interpretation is there, but it is limited in that it is rooted in concrete thought form. Consider the statement of a fifty-seven-year-old Sikh who explained the relationship between the Sikh community and the mainstream:

> *What do you think about the Sikh community interacting more with the mainstream?*
> Sikhs are not fanatic like the other religions. Sikhs are not against other religions. We recognize other religions. But we should remember Sikhism and teach about the gurus. You don't see Jews or Muslims putting up Christmas lights. Sikhs do. They [the Jews and Muslims] know their religion. If people come [to the *gurdwara*] we should welcome anyone, but not [just in order] to convert them. (Singh 2.22)

At this statement, the man's son intervened and started to 'interpret' his father's concrete thought form, raising it to a more conceptual one:

> Did you understand what my father is trying to say? What he is saying is – how can we expect to teach others about our religion if we do not know our own religion? We don't convert, but we should know about the religion, the gurus. Sikhs take on the tradition of Christmas, but don't know their own religion. We should teach others. But how can we teach others about the religion, if we are not even loyal to [teaching] our own [people]? (son of Singh 2.22)

Indeed, the son's rejoinder reflects a move beyond literacy toward analytics; this is characteristic of the conceptual and critical mode of thinking found in modern society.

The general tendency in the second generation is toward literacy, which is directly related to the individual's educational level and also, importantly, to whether that person spent his or her formative years in a traditional society. This is most evident in the ability of the members of the second generation to report literally – that is, to articulate ideas according to what they have read and to repeat sayings or proverbial platitudes in relaying information or answering questions. The second generation reflects literacy but with strong residues of orality. Although most members reflect literacy, a few professionals interviewed from this generation have made the transition to analytics.

The Third Generation and Analytics

It became clear during the interviews that communication patterns differ with respect to the children of immigrants who have been raised in the host country and have been educated in Western schools, and who are living within the mainstream society and interacting more with it. Most parents of Canadian-born Sikhs range along the continuum from orality to literacy; their children have been interacting with the culture and mode of thinking associated with analytics. Among the members of the third generation, the general tendency is away from literacy toward analytics. This movement is manifest in their self-reflective biographical accounts, their ability to articulate analytical responses, and their self-orientation (as opposed to collectivity orientation). While many third-generation interviewees have not completely crossed over to analytics, they are at very least in a state of transition to it from literacy.

Facilitating the Interview Process

As with the second generation, members of the third generation evinced an interest, before being interviewed, in the degrees I held. However, this aspect was secondary to their curiosity about the research project itself. Unlike the first and second generations, the third generation, for the most part, showed that they understood the purposes of a social science study. Many interviewees asked if 'a book was going to be written' (e.g., Singh 3.4, 11, 14, 15, 16, 24, 26, 34, 37, and Kaur 3.7, 9, 18, 19, 23, 25, 27, 32, 35). In fact, some interviewees asked me to contact them after the project had been written up so that they could read it (Singh 3.14, 24; Kaur 3.7, 19, 25).

Many third-generation interviewees told me there was a need for such a book about their community. This sentiment was not directly related to education level. In fact, two of the three third-generation males that had moved away from Sikh orthodoxy and engaged in rebellious-defiant behaviour, had dropped out of school (the third interviewed [Singh 3.30] had returned to school). Yet in separate interviews, the two men stated that they had agreed to be interviewed because they thought it would help to have their ideas and experiences reported in a book (Singh 3.34 and 3.37). One interviewee went even further, commenting that he had agreed to be interviewed because he believed something good would come out of it, because 'not much usually happens with the spoken word in the community' (Singh 3.24). Unlike the first and second generations, members of the third generation for the most part valued the norm of confidentiality in the interview process; also, they preferred to be interviewed in private, neutral areas such as in a coffee shop or on a university campus. The interviews were conducted in private and were two to four hours in duration.

Self-Reflective Biographical Accounts

In providing biographical accounts, third-generation interviewees reflected analytics in the way they gave 'facts' along with interpretive commentary. While they willingly answered questions about the major events in their lives, they also provided comments about the events; this demonstrated a high degree of self-reflection. They mentioned dates but, unlike the second generation, this was not an important aspect of their biographical accounts. Rather, the real significance lay in their interpretation of, and commentary on, the different aspects of their lives. For example, a twenty-seven-year-old woman, in response to the question about educational level, answered: 'I finished high school ... I had a love marriage when I was nineteen years old ... I wanted to go to school but he [my husband] did not encourage it because he was not that educated ... My parents supported me throughout the episode [divorce]' (Kaur 3.22). The comments offered while giving biographical data demonstrated not only interpretive abilities but also self-reflection.

Analytical Responses with a Self-Orientation

Many of the questions asked of interviewees were abstract, and their answers likewise reflected of a modern mentality; that is, the answers were conceptual and analytical. An example of a self-reflective and analytical answer is one provided by a twenty-three-old university Sikh woman:

What are some of the issues in the community that affect the youth?

The problems of the culture are: (1) The treatment of women ... Girls' careers are affected because it is a big issue for girls to leave the city. It is a huge deal to not live with parents until marriage. Girls are not reaching their goals ... (2) Adults keep control rather than trust ... Trust is not in their way of thinking. It is co-existence in the home, everyone has to do their role ... (3) Alcohol ... (4) The notion of son caring for them ... and (5) *Izzat* [honour]. (Kaur 3.23)

Not only does this quotation reflect the analytical thinking characteristic of a 'modern mentality,' but Kaur 3.23 was able to answer a general highly conceptual question in an elaborate way, prioritizing her thoughts according to what she viewed as critical even while giving examples of what she had noted in the community. Another example of an answer that gets to 'the point' in an objective and critical manner is that of a twenty-two-year-old university Sikh man:

What are your final thoughts on the community? What is needed in the community?

I think what is needed is some sort of organization with strong, positive leadership. There are a number of organizations, which do exist, but I don't think they are having the impact they have the potential to have. Really, what is needed is a lot of thankless effort on the part of dedicated individuals to offer some sort of service or organization to which the youth can always turn to for help and direction as far as culture is concerned. (Singh 3.4)

Besides manifesting an objective and critical mode of thinking, many of the interviewees of the third generation expressed conceptual and theoretical ideas.

Among the third generation, conceptual and abstract thought form seemed to be related to the individual's level of education. This was most evident among those who had studied the social sciences or humanities at the university level. These students demonstrated the ability to articulate theoretical and abstract ideas and to manifest a strong self-orientation. In contrast, the high school graduates or college dropouts interviewed for this research project had more difficulty articulating their abstract and conceptual insights about the community. Nevertheless, the self-oriented mode of thinking (analytics) – the ability to differentiate oneself from the 'other' – was clearly evident among them. One college dropout male, when discussing how he had gone off track, dropped out of school, and used to be involved in drugs, stated: 'Some live in fear and do what their parents want them to do. Then others go off track with drugs. I would rather be in fear of parents, than in fear of the streets that someone will shoot me ... Oh, it seems big to you because you are in a good environment, but people are in worse shit than me' (Singh 3.34).

This third-generation male was less able to express abstract thought than a university student; even so, he had a developed self-orientation, evident in how he differentiated himself from the interviewer.

Many interviewers told me after the interviews that they had enjoyed the activity of exploration – another feature of analytics. Many stated that discussing issues in their lives helped them clarify their own views. This desire to explore issues during the interview was not related to educational level; rather, it reflected the increase in emotional needs during the self-differentiation process among the third generation (see chapter 4). Some said the interviewing process was like 'therapy' (Singh 3.24, Kaur 3.27); others said they enjoyed exploring such issues because they had never really had an opportunity to do so before (Singh 3.10, 11, 36; Kaur 3.18, 25). Some even commented that they did not talk to people in their community – even their friends – about these things because it would become source material for gossip (*gup shup*) (Kaur 3.19, 22, 23). Regardless, being interviewed was for the members of the third generation a unique opportunity to talk about what was on their minds.

In sum, the third generation reflects the presence of analytics, which is associated with modernity, in that its members are self-reflective and manifest the analytical thought form and self-orientation. Although a move toward the analytics mode of thinking is evident in the third generation, occasionally some literacy is also noticeable, especially for those few who have not had a university education.

Communication Barriers among the Three Generations

The concepts of orality, literacy and analytics provide a framework for understanding the changes that occur in thought forms and patterns with modernization; they also, by and large, correspond here to the modes of thinking of the first, second, and third generations. The distinctive thought forms or modes of thinking become especially evident when the comments on similar issues made by interviewees belonging to each of the three generations are placed alongside one another. Given below in quick succession are comments from one interviewee from each of the three generations. Although they expressed similar views on the economics of the care of seniors in Canada (a neutral topic, unaffected by cultural barriers), they reflected quite distinctive thought forms:

First Generation. A seventy-year-old Sikh widower who lives alone and depends on a pension.

Do you think the traditional attitudes of the children caring for parents in old age are changing in Canada?
[unable to answer]
How are the elderly treated in Canada?
I know nothing about getting old. I did not go to school ... Canada, here, life is easier. The government gives money to spend. Here, if the children do not do it, the government takes care. There is nothing wanting here, they get money here. Since there is not enough there [in India] people fight over food in the family. But that is not the problem here. (Singh 1.5, trans. Punjabi)

Second generation. A fifty-four-year-old Sikh man who was educated in India and has been living in Canada for more than twenty years:

Do you think the traditional attitudes of the children caring for parents in old age are changing in Canada?
Yes, it depends on the family.
Do you expect your sons to care for you in old age in Canada?
[My] son will care for me in old age, but it is not necessary to be [given] financial support here because of the good system. In Punjab, there is no system. Here people have pension and RRSP. The extended family is not a need, economically. (Singh 2.11)

Third generation. A thirty-year-old Sikh man raised and educated in Canada:

Do you think the traditional attitudes about children caring for parents in old age are changing in Canada?
Yes. Everything has to do with economics. Perhaps previously there were some traditional values of love, but most things are dependent on economics. Families in India were financially interdependent, now people

are economically independent. People want to be able to have their independence and space. (Singh 3.1)

The comments of all three men have to do with the economics of the
extended family, but they reveal thought forms that are distinctive to
the particular generation to which each individual belongs. The man
from the first generation is illiterate; he answers the question with a
concrete thought form based on his own life situation, and he
expresses a collectivity orientation (orality). The man belonging to the
second generation is literate; his literal interpretation is expressed in
concrete thought form, too, but with some prioritizing of, and distancing from, the known (literacy). The man from the third generation has
been educated in a modern milieu; his mode of thinking is conceptual,
and he articulates his views in a self-reflective manner (analytics).

It is clear that the three generations largely correspond to the distinctive modes of thinking associated with the concepts of orality, literacy,
and analytics. This finding found confirmation in interviews with educators, who spoke on the basis of their interaction with Sikh students
and their parents. One elementary school educator emphasized the
presence of a gap in communicating with the parents of the students.
This educator found it difficult to explain things effectively to parents
because 'there is the lack of ability to communicate, the ability to reason' on their part (educator 2). Likewise, another educator, who teaches
at the college level, noted that although there was not the problem of a
language barrier with the Punjabi students (as found with some other
ethnic minorities), the Punjabi students often had difficulty conceptualizing the material in the social sciences. The real problem lay in the lack
of conceptual and abstract thinking: 'The kids on their exams and
papers would write concrete things. I had no idea how they came up
with these concrete ideas. Many were not able to conceptualize what
was taught' (educator 3). This educator pondered how to teach theoretical and conceptual subjects to such students.

The comment made by educator 3 may seem at first blush to run
counter to the findings about the third generation, who have been
described here as moving toward analytics; in fact it does not. First and
most importantly, the interviewees categorized as belonging to the
third generation were mainly university students (whereas high school
or college drop-outs reflect more of literacy). Second, the educator was
speaking from the perspective of teaching college students in a predominantly Punjabi area. This area is commonly referred to as a 'Pun-

jabi ghetto' by non-Punjabi workers interacting with Punjabis; it is even characterized as such by interviewees of the third generation who had lived outside it. On the whole, the third generation perceived the 'Punjabi ghetto' as having a negative impact in the sense that it delayed the acquisition or development of the skills needed to interact more and better with the mainstream society; it thus hindered the process of adaptation and integration. (The role of multiculturalism and the effects of the Punjabi ghetto on the younger generations of the Sikh community are discussed in chapter 6).

Conclusion

Beyond the issue of the language barrier – which is often experienced by immigrants in relation to the host country or between immigrant relatives and Canadian-born children – there are, indeed, other communication barriers that reflect the particular thought forms and patterns associated with traditional and modern societies. The distinctive thought forms express the kind of society the people come from. The concepts of orality, literacy, and analytics provide a framework for understanding the changes that occur in thought forms and patterns with modernization; interestingly, they also correspond with the modes of thinking of the first, second, and third generations.

The interviews with members of the three generations of the Sikh community shed light on the distinctive features of each of the generations. The particular thought forms, in turn, constitute indicators about the process of adaptation and integration of a traditional immigrant group in relation to the modern host society. The first generation is predominantly oral. Its thought form is concrete, close to the life situation, and oriented toward the collectivity. All of this is characteristic of the orality mode of thinking. The second generation is predominantly literate yet strongly conditioned by orality; it demonstrates the ability of literal interpretation that is typical of the literacy mode of thinking. The third generation, which has been educated mainly in a modern society, shows the ability to engage in self-reflective, self-oriented, and conceptual thinking; this points to a shift to the modern, analytics mode of thinking.

The different mentalities – traditional, modern, and the transitional – represent highly distinctive ways of thinking and of viewing the world. This provides insights into the sources of tension between the three generations in the Sikh community as it faces pressure to transform itself from a traditional society into a modern one. Rooted in the historical process of development from one type of society to another, this source of tension exists without anyone deliberately willing it. At the same time, the concepts of orality, literacy, and analytics, in turn, provide a valuable framework for understanding the differences and tensions between the three generations at the personal level, specifically as they pertain to family relations, child rearing, and religious practice – the topics treated in the next three chapters, respectively.

3 Family Relations among Three Generations: Duty, Role Playing, and Independence, Part 1

The distinctive ways of perceiving and thinking about the world on the part of the first, second, and third generations of the Sikh community are rooted in the larger historical process of societal development. The impact of modernity on the traditional mode of thinking raises barriers to communication between the generations; the communication barriers, in turn, become the source of unintended tensions. These unintended tensions inevitably have serious effects on family relations. Thus, we need to explore, continuity and change with respect to the household network and the roles of family members in order to better understand the intergenerational dynamics within the Sikh community.

In any investigation of family relations among immigrant groups, we must heed the fact that immigrants (the first and second generations) carry family values and customs from their traditional homeland even while they face pressure to adjust to a different set of values in the modern host country. In traditional societies the extended family is marked by a collectivity orientation, in which roles are diffuse and status is inherited (ascriptive). In contrast, in a modern society like Canada, the nuclear family is marked by self-orientation, in which roles are specific and status in the broader society is established as a result of achievement.[1] Attitudes toward the family are an expression of what kind of society a person comes from; that is, traditional and modern societies have different understandings of the household network and the various roles of family members. The distinctive approaches of the two societies to the functioning of the family provide insights into the tensions that exist between the three generations, and help delineate the process of adaptation and integration of a traditional group in relation to its modern host society.

This chapter focuses on family relations among three generations of the Sikh community, including the gap between the traditional and modern understandings of the household network and the various roles of family members. The different approaches to family functioning correspond to the distinctive generational modes of thinking; they also shed light on the tensions between the older and younger generations. Grandparents and parents bring their traditional Punjabi values to Canada and then attempt to adapt to a modern society; their children and grandchildren are raised in that modern society and have considerably more interaction with it.

This chapter has three parts. The first provides background material on traditional Indian family values and on the roles of the different family members. The second analyses each of the three generations of the Sikh community, identifying the main themes regarding the family that emerged from the interviews – themes that, reflect the tensions between the first, second, and third generations. The third analyses the intergenerational tensions that arise as a traditional community adapts to modernity in Canada in the context of family dynamics.

The Indian Tradition of Duty and Honour

Most Sikhs arriving in Canada are coming from a traditional agricultural society. Their community's culture is strongly rooted in Indian tradition, with its values of *dharam* (duty) and *izzat* (honour). The literal definition of the Punjabi term *dharam* (*dharma* in Sanskrit and Hindi) is 'duty,' 'virtue,' or 'action,' but it also has a broader meaning: the moral or ethical order of nature. In common usage, *dharam* refers to the performance of proper action according to the moral and ethical rules of nature and society.

In classical Indian thought, all deeds – good or bad – have repercussions in terms of one's own *karam* (*karma* in Sanskrit: 'action, merit and demerit'), which binds one to *sansar* (*samsara* in Sanskrit) or the cycle of birth, death, and rebirth. The religious ideal is for one to perform one's duty or action (*dharam*) for the maintenance of social order while at the same time striving for the ultimate goal of liberation (*mukti*; *moksha* in Sanskrit) from the cycle of rebirth. *Dharam* is a central religious concept for Hindus,[2] but it is mainly a cultural concept for Sikhs. For Sikhs, it is important for one to fulfil one's social duties as a grandparent, parent, marital partner, or child, within the context of being a *grhasthi* (*grhasthin* in Sanskrit: 'householder'). One should attain material comfort and raise children, even while following the Sikh religious rules (see below)

in pursuit of the Sikh path of salvation (*mukti*), through which one real-
izes the true nature of the Guru.

Guru Nanak and the succeeding nine Sikh gurus, as well as the *Sikh
Rahit Maryada* ('Sikh Code of Conduct'), denounced the Hindu caste
system,[3] which is based on *varna* (the order of social divisions or
classes).[4] Nevertheless, many Sikhs, who primarily follow Punjabi customs, identify with it, especially at the time of marriage (Singh 1.1. 1.2,
1.5, 1.6, 1.7, 1.9, 1.12, 1.15, 1.16, 1.17; Singh 2.2, 2.3, 2.4, 2.9, 2.14, 2.22;
Kaur 1.4, 1.8, 1.10, 1.11, 1.13; Kaur 2.12, 2.16, 2.18). The *khatri* caste,
which is associated with the Hindu *kshatriya* ('warrior') class, has been
associated with the Sikh tradition from its very beginning.[5] The
founder of the Sikh religion, Guru Nanak, and the nine succeeding
Sikh gurus were born into the *khatri* caste, although they themselves
rejected the notion of the caste system. Although the founders of the
religion were from the *khatri* caste, most of the converts to Sikhism
came from the lower, *jat* caste. Over the course of time, the *jats* became
the dominant caste among the Sikhs, both socially and politically.[6]

The value of honour (*izzat*) is pan-Indian – and a common feature of
traditional societies in general – but it is particularly esteemed by the
warrior castes, including the Punjabi Sikhs. Warrior culture typically
elevates fighting in the protection of one's honour as a value at both
the personal level and the level of the community. Consequently, the
value of honour (*izzat*) is extremely powerful among Punjabi Sikhs.

Duty (*dharam*) and honour (*izzat*) are widespread cultural values in
India and also integral to the culture of the Sikhs of Punjab. According
to Harjot Singh Oberoi, during the early nineteenth century the boundaries between Sikhs, Hindus, and Muslims in the Punjab were
'blurred'; it was not until the formation of the Tat Khalsa in 1873 that a
distinct Sikh identity became crystallized.[7] Regardless, the *Sikh Rahit
Maryada* issued by the Shiromani Gurdwara Parbandhak Committee –
which had been set up in 1925 by the Sikh electorate to administer the
principal *gurdwaras* – was developed in order to distinguish the Punjabi Sikhs from other Punjabis (the Sikh identity is discussed further in
chapter 5). The *Sikh Rahit Maryada* requires Sikhs to abide by three fundamental religious principles: (1) meditation on God's name (*nam
japo*); hard work and honest living (*kirt karo*); and sharing one's earnings with the needy (*wand chako*).[8]

The First Generation and Family Duty

A distinguishing feature of orality and traditional society is that knowledge is largely static and is passed down from generation to generation. This means that elders are regarded as the best sources of knowledge ('wisdom'); it also means that there is *only one way of doing something*. In this situation, people are apt to be averse to changing their ways and views, which makes social change a very slow process. So when members of the first generation, most of whom embrace the orality mode of thinking, attempt to adapt physically to living in a modern society, they are generally unable to comprehend or take on its corresponding value system.

In terms of the family, the first generation has been transplanted to a situation where it must adapt to change in the family structure – change that inevitably occurs with migration to Canada (unless the family lives on a farm in Canada). In the process of adapting to the new family structure, the first generation experiences tension with the second generation regarding changes in lifestyle relating to economic independence and women joining the workforce. As well, the first generation experiences tension with the third generation with respect to the changing values of the youth.

Traditional Family Structure

The family pattern in the Punjab is that of the joint family.[9] Traditionally, the extended family in the Punjab is patriarchical; that is, the father is the head of the family and the home includes his family and his sons' families. The household may or may not include the father's brothers and brothers' families. If it does, the eldest brother is the head. Sons most often take on the trade of their fathers, which in the Punjab has been predominantly farming. Daughters, on the other hand, leave their childhood home after a marriage has been arranged for them, to join the husband's extended family. Sons also have arranged marriages; such marriages are social compacts between two families. Often the bride and groom do not have the right of consent, and do not even meet beforehand.

Thus, the first generation has grown up in an extended patriarchical family network. During this study I interviewed only one member of the first generation who had not been raised in a traditional extended family. This person had lived in a boarding house in a Punjabi city after losing her father at a very young age (Kaur 1.4). Another interviewer (Singh 1.1) lost his mother at a very young age, and still another (Singh 1.5) lost both parents. The father of the former remarried; the latter was raised by uncles and aunts.

Difficult circumstances, such as losing a parent or the partition of India in 1947,[10] often reinforced a high regard for the extended family; many interviewees cherished the tightly knit extended family as one that 'gives support' (Singh 1.1), especially because 'only the people of the house care, others do not care' (Kaur 1.11). Most of the first-generation interviewees grew up in the company and care of their grandparents. The only exceptions were when the grandparents died before the interviewees could remember them (Singh 1.7, 1.17; Kaur 1.8, 1.14). Otherwise, most first-generation interviewees had vivid memories of their grandparents.

Most of the first-generation interviewees were illiterate, but some of the men among them had attended school. Women in traditional Punjab are required to conform to *pardah* ('veil'), that is, the custom of placing a *chunni* ('scarf') low over the head so that eye contact in public is unlikely. Women of the first generation have typically not gone to public school. A seventy-six-year-old Sikh woman commented on her not having been allowed to attend school: 'I had a tutor for class five. Women had tutors in the home because of *pardah*. There was a lot of *pardah*. There was too much [of it] in the house. I was admitted to a hostel in Amritsar to study, but my parents changed their mind because of *pardah*' (Kaur 1.13, trans.).

Since women could not freely go to public school, only a couple of the first-generation women I interviewed had acquired some reading and writing skills, from a tutor in the family home (Kaur 1.10, 1.13). There were a few exceptions; astonishly, one of the women interviewed had gone to secondary school (Kaur 1.4). But the rest had followed Punjabi tradition[11] and had not received any formal education (Kaur 1.8, 1.11, 1.14).

Traditional Family Values

As the children grow up in the traditional family and take on increasing responsibility as contributors to the household (familial duty), especially after having their own children, they gain more respect. Respect manifests itself in the giving of orders (*hukam*), which other household members (such as the wife and children) comply with.[12] Most of the first-generation interviewees had vivid memories of their elders 'being the boss' (Singh 1.6). A Sikh man of sixty-eight remembered the family structure in the Punjab: 'Parents had full control of the house, and they had the money and the land. When the son or son-in-law or daughter [wanted something], they would say, father, I need this thing.' (Singh 1.6, trans.)

Likewise, an eight-year-old Sikh woman remembered how the household was run, with the elders exercising control: 'They [grandparents] had power and duty in the home. The children follow grandmother's orders or advice. And son would seek permission or advice from mother or father before doing something. The grandparents had the duty of caring for the house, running the house, giving guidance in the house' (Kaur 1.4).

The Punjabi value of fulfilling one's 'duty' is central to the smooth functioning of the traditional family household. Oriented to the collectivity, the members of the household perform 'their' duty. The Punjabi custom of performing one's duty was the aspect of familial relations most often noted during the interviews. The interviewees often alluded to it in biographical accounts: 'I came [to Canada] when my *dharam* was finished with the kids' marriage' (Kaur 1.14). At other times, duty was discussed in response to questions about the family in the Punjab and Canada: 'A child is an experience-less individual and the parent is a well-experienced individual, and it is the duty of parents to impart that experience, groom, tutor and coach their kids to become good citizens of this world' (Singh 1.1).

Duty is the fulfilment of one's wide range of responsibilities within the household; it is also directly linked to 'respect.' One shows respect by fulfilling one's duty, and one expects respect for having fulfilled one's duty. Even more important, it is the duty of children to show respect to their elders. An eighty-year-old Sikh woman discussed the relationship between duty and respect: 'Elderly people have to be respected. We were always expected to cover the head with *chunni*, and especially with elders and in-laws when first married, we were expected to touch [their] feet. When they arrive at the house we had to bring a bed, and give food. Giving a lot of respect. We say *ji* to God when we pray, kids should say that also to elders, who are above you. Mother and father – mother mainly – taught them this' (Kaur 1.14, trans.).

Respect is a central feature of traditional Punjabi culture and a very important aspect of life to the first generation; that said, duty and respect are expressed solely in concrete terms, such as 'touching the feet,' 'serving food,' and addressing elders with the honorific term '*ji*'. All of this reflects the orality mode of thinking. A sixty-seven-year-old Sikh woman explained that respect is the absence of quarrelling or swearing, and provided an example of the understanding of respect in concrete terms (orality): 'Treatment was good. No fighting. The people were so nice, they did not even swear. Only the people of the house care, others do not care. They did not have land. The sons serve their parents there' (Kaur 1.11, trans.).

In traditional Sikh families, duty and respect are central to family relations; they are also values that correspond to one's position in the family structure and that are intended to ensure the smooth functioning of the household.

Perspective on Change

Since the first generation has, in a sense, been transplanted to a modern society, it inevitably has had to adapt to the change in environment. The family patterns have undoubtedly changed, since the extended family dwellings typical of village and farm life in the Punjab are not easily sustainable in Canada. For example, brothers do not generally live together in Canada as they did in the Punjab. Nonetheless, the tradition of grandparents living with one of their children remains quite strong in the Sikh community in Canada. Essentially, the members of the first generation live in a 'modified extended family'; that is, grandparents often live with one of their children and his or her spouse and their children. Most members of the first generation presently live with one of their children, but at the same time they recognize that changes are occurring in the traditional values of duty (*dharam*) and honour (*izzat*).

Not surprisingly, the aspect of modernity that seems to be doing the most to bring about change in family dynamics is economics. The first generation's children (that is, the second generation) are economically independent as a result of being employed in the Canadian economy. Their economic independence undermines the traditional power structure of the family household, wherein the elders had previously possessed the family wealth (often in the form of land or gold jewellery). The first generation's loss of economic control and the second generation's acquisition of economic independence often disrupt the traditional lifestyle: duty and honour no longer function as smoothly as the first generation expects and remembers being practised back in village Punjab. Even in the case of those first-generation members who had worked in Canada, their work experience did not transform their family values so as to lead them to acquire the values associated with economic independence and modernity – self-orientation, expansion of personal choice, and the notion of earned respect.

Every member of the first generation I interviewed – except for one Sikh man, who talked of how his children treated him the same in Canada as they did in the Punjab (Singh 1.7) – thought that attitudes toward the family had changed in Canada. This change was most often seen in the shift away from the collectivity orientation of fulfilling one's duty, within the context of the extended family, toward the Western notion of 'independence.' A sixty-eight-year-old Sikh man linked the change to economic independence: 'Ten years before, when I came here, people respected elders. But people seeing TV and Western culture here, they now are thinking in other terms ... Parents had full control of the house, they had money and land. When the son or daughter-in-law [spoke] they would say, father I need this thing. When parents were happy [in a good mood] only then children would dare to ask. Now it is changing. Everybody is in service [working]. The young people think that father knows nothing. They think they know' (Singh 1.6, trans.).

The above quotation reflects the material effects of economic independence; it also shows that a change in mentality is intertwined with this independence. There has been a shift away from the traditional understanding that knowledge is inherited – making elders the best source of knowledge ('wisdom') – toward the modern notion that knowledge is progressive and that the younger generation is the source of 'up to date' knowledge.

Another frequently mentioned aspect of attitudinal change in the Sikh community in Canada relates to the dominant motive of making money and the simultaneous weakening of the 'traditional' value of *izzat*. An eighty-year-old woman said, 'When someone gets to Canada from India, they forget about *izzat* – we are free to do what we want. *Izzat* is respect for others. That is, if someone comes, [then] ask how are you? Care for people as your own, *izzat* is when others respect you for respecting them. You can't have *izzat* based on the house or money because material possessions can come and go.' (Kaur 1.14, trans.).

Similarly, a seventy-seven-year-old Sikh man commented on how the Punjabi value of *izzat* has changed in Canada; however, he related it to social isolation and the impersonal nature of relations within the community after migration to Canada: 'Here, after coming there is some change in the relationship. The cause is that there [in Punjab], we live in brotherhood [a community], but here there is no fear of what other people will say (*izzat*). There people will say, such and such person's son is not serving his parents. But here people do not know who their neighbour is' (Singh 1.7).

Although many of the first generation speak of the differences they have noticed in family life, between the Punjab and Canada, those who regularly travel back to the Punjab talk about how the family structure is changing there as well (Singh 1.9, 1.15, 1.16, 1.17; Kaur 1.13). A seventy-one-year-old educated Sikh man, who returns to the Punjab every winter, explained that changes are occurring within the family and community in his Punjabi village:

> In Punjab in the olden days, people in general respected elders more than they do now there. Communication between families has changed with radio and television. People don't have the link. [People] took a break in village, sitting together in a common place to gossip. People are busy now. People go home and sit together to listen to the radio instead of talking with the people of the village. People watch the shows, but at least because families only have one TV, they sit together. Young children used to ask *dadiji* [father's mother] to tell stories, now kids get the stories from the TV. (Singh 1.15)

In brief, the first generation as it lives in Canada experiences a change in family life. This change in family life, resulting mainly from economic independence, is a source of tension between the first and second generations.

Tensions with the Second Generation

The main tension between the first and second generations is that, while the first generation has a great deal of responsibility in modern life (e.g., taking care of the grandchildren and household), it no longer has control over the family, nor does it receive the respect from family that it did in the Punjab. This loss of respect and control is due, no doubt, to the fact that they are economically dependent on their children, even as they have more responsibility for maintaining the household and for bringing up the grandchildren, since both children (son and daughter-in-law) often work outside the home (Singh 1.1, 1.2, 1.6, 1.12, 1.15; Kaur 1.4, 1.10, 1.13). The members of the first generation acknowledge that there are strong tensions between the first and second generations, especially because the second generation often does not have time for them because its members are gainfully employed (Singh 1.2, 1.6, 1.9, 1.12; Kaur 1.13, 1.14). A seventy-year-old Sikh man, who is responsible for looking after his grandchildren, stated: 'We feel sometimes that we cannot go anywhere; we have to watch the children. There is too much responsibility on the elderly because the sons and daughters-in-law are working' (Singh 1.12, trans.).

Among the second generation, women have also achieved economic independence. However, the notion of women working in the public sphere has disrupted the traditional lifestyle, which requires women to work only in the home and to serve the elders. The absence of women from the household because they are working outside it gives rise to much tension: outside employment prevents women from doing their traditional duty at home, and the first generation is not used to this. There is resentment among the first generation that working women do not always listen to their elders the way women of the first generation listened to their mothers-in-law in India. The attitudinal change among members of the second generation – that is, their failure to heed those of the first generation – is often interpreted as a lack of respect. An eighty-year-old Sikh woman explained that although it is good that women are now receiving education and working, they should still not lose the traditional value of respect:

> In Canada, everyone is doing their own thing and are like monkeys jumping around in a zoo. The ladies in India, they know how to treat elders and in-laws, and they are taught to be nice to anyone, no matter who. In Canada, they have become overtaken by the desire for money, and are only nice if they need something from you. If they don't need anything, they act like you don't exist. Their motives are based on the desire for money. Yes, women have to work to maintain the house, but the money should not be primary – you should use the money to show gratitude. (Kaur 1.14) [translated from Punjabi]

The change occurring in the household, including the practice of respect, is here related to the earning of wages and the rampant consumerism associated with the West. Similarly, a sixty-eight-year-old Sikh woman noted that children who are born and raised in Canada take on Western customs, while those born and raised in India tend to carry on Punjabi customs: 'The custom continues to be to stay with the children. Those that are born here [Canada], like that [living independently]. But those [children] who have come from there [India], they do the same as they did before. Those who are born here have different ideas' (Kaur 1.10, trans.).

The second generation continues with the traditional customs even while simultaneously adapting to the modern lifestyle; in contrast, the Canadian-born third generation is undergoing significant changes in its value system. This is the main source of tension between the first and third generations.

Tensions with the Third Generation

The tensions experienced between the first and third generations are many. The sources of these tensions are language, communication, and cultural barriers. First of all, there is the language barrier, which exists because most members of the first generation do not speak English, while few of the third generation are fluent in Punjabi. Many in the first generation experience the language barrier with their Canadian-born grandchildren (third generation): 'Punjabi language is a problem with the grandchildren' (Kaur 1.13). Many grandchildren have learned some Punjabi, but lack a native facility with the language beyond what is required for mundane, everyday interaction. One eighty-year-old Sikh woman emphasized the limited nature of the third generation's knowledge of Punjabi: 'Kids, even though they may know some Punjabi, they don't know Punjabi in depth ... The kids don't learn it fluently because the only one who speaks it in the house is the old lady. No one responds to me. Kids [speak] only for small talk' (Kaur 1.14, trans.).

Members of the first generation express a great deal of sorrow that their grandchildren are unable to communicate with them in Punjabi: 'The elderly are very sad because of the language barrier with [the] grandchildren. Kids speak back in English' (Singh 1.17). Members of the first generation find it difficult to speak with their grandchildren because they themselves do not speak or understand English very well: 'Then there is the difference of language, we cannot speak English as thoroughly as the younger generation does' (Singh 1.7).

The language barrier apart, the first generation also encounters another major communication barrier: it dislikes children asking the question 'Why?' For the first generation, it is a sign of disrespect to ask elders the reasons for things; elders see themselves as having accumulated life experience and wisdom, which should not be questioned (Singh 1.1, 1.7, 1.15; Kaur 1.4, 1.8, 1.13, 1.14). A seventy-seven-year-old Sikh man noted that the first generation does not like the children to question things: 'There is no problem with the first and second generations. [But] kids ask "Why?" and parents say, "because mom says so," which is all they have to say' (Singh 1.1).

Another Sikh man of seventy-one commented: 'The young generation questions ... They are always asking 'Why?' and want an answer' (Singh 1.15).

Those of the first generation experience disrespect as a result of the inquisitive nature of the third generation; they also feel that the children do not address them respectfully, as tradition demands. This was mentioned very often in regard to the third generation failing to use the honorific *ji*. Several interviewees mentioned that they perceived disrespect in the manner in which the third generation addressed them. Only one 76-year old Sikh woman stated that people she knows are now used to it: 'People have gotten used to kids not talking with *ji*' (Kaur 1.13). One third-generation Sikh man explained that many of the children only know the 'rude' or 'condescending' form of Punjabi. Apparently, the Canadian-born children copy the manner in which their parents speak to them – the main exposure they have to the language. The children therefore speak in the manner their parents do (Singh 3.14).

Many in the first generation perceive the younger generation as 'rude' to parents or grandparents; however, some are making efforts to adapt. One eighty-year-old Sikh woman observed: 'The young don't listen because they want to be independent; this makes them rude to parents. However, I believe that the mother-in-law should not interfere with her son and daughter-in-law unless they approach the mother asking for advice or because things have gotten very bad. But even then, they should give their advice or opinion nicely and politely. This is something that has to be worked on by the elderly to improve relations' (Kaur 1.4).

As noted earlier, the cultural barrier that is most often experienced by the first generation relates to Western notions of independence. The first generation sees the act of independence solely as selfish.

The positive aspects of independence and self-orientation, such as equality and succeeding on merit, are not often acknowledged by elders. The first generation's inability to comprehend self-orientation or independence reflects an orality mode of thinking. Many in the first generation also believe that they cannot change – and why should they since their way is the right way, or the only way? Having been raised in the Punjab, most of them believed that they would remain traditional for the rest of their lives, whether they were living in the Punjab or somewhere else, like Canada.

In sum, the first generation emphasizes the traditional values of duty and respect. But it understands these values in very concrete terms and articulates them in the context of a collectivity orientation. The first generation, which functions according to the traditional norms and customs of the extended family system, experiences much tension as a result of the shift in the locus of economic control within the family network. Its members continue to expect respect from the other family members by virtue of their seniority. Even as they experience the effects of economic independence within the family household, they are unable to comprehend or accept the social impact of modernity. Besides feeling discontented at not getting the respect or attention they had received 'automatically' in traditional households in the Punjab, members of the first generation feel overworked in the home as grandparents, since both second-generation parents work outside. They miss the support of the full extended family structure at home as it exists in the Punjab.

The Second Generation and Role Playing

The second generation of the Sikh community has largely adapted itself to the 'techniques' of modern society; for the most part, however, it has failed to embrace the corresponding value system. At the same time, even though the second generation continues to uphold traditional Indian practices and values, it has to a certain extent redefined them, as a result of distancing itself from the collectivity, and also because economic independence has changed the family structure. The continuity in traditional values has done more than generate tensions between generations; it has also affected gender relations.

The 'Modified Extended Family'

Like many other immigrant groups, the Sikhs have come to Canada largely for economic reasons – to earn a better income. Whatever their reasons for coming, the act of immigration to a different society has generated social and psychological changes in their community, as it has in other immigrant communities. James Chadney, who was one of the first to study Vancouver's Sikh community, found in the late 1970s that changes had taken place in economic patterns within the community even while its values remained more or less stable.[13]

With regard to the family, Chadney found that the joint family system persisted. Eighty per cent of Vancouver's Sikh families conformed to the traditional joint family; only 20 per cent were in some modified form of a joint family or some supplemented form of a nuclear family (fewer than 1 per cent of the families could be included in this last category).[14] By the late 1980s, however, this seemed to have changed. In their study of the Sikh community in Canada between 1965 and 1987, Norman Buchignani and Doreen Marie Indra concluded that it would be difficult to offer any sweeping generalizations about the Sikh experience, including the family system, because the community was so diverse. However, they did advance two generalizations about the Sikhs in Canada: (1) the family is the central element of Sikh social organization and, although the extended or joint family is uncommon, many households are still larger than simply a nuclear family; and (2) kinship is a principal feature of the informal but intensive community networks, and this is related to 'heavy' immigration.[15] They also emphasized Sikhs found it difficult to maintain the joint family system in the context of Canada's social structure.

The findings of Buchignani and Indra are confirmed by the present study. In the many interviews I conducted, I found that the most common form of Sikh family organization is the 'modified extended family,' which no longer incorporates all the members that the traditional Sikh family in the Punjab does. The basic pattern is that of a nuclear family supplemented – though not always – by grandparents. When any other member lives in such a household, it is for special reasons. The stay is only temporary when a new immigrant is settling in the host country; however, the stay is more permanent in cases of divorce or the premature death of a spouse. Beyond that, the nuclear family, with or without elder parents, now seems to be the most common household pattern. This development reflects the impact of modernity on socio-economic arrangements; the traditional Sikh family is incompatible with modern industrial society.

Most members of the second generation were born in the Punjab and raised there in a traditional (patriarchical) extended family, have been living in Canada for many years. However long they have lived in Canada, a strong kinship network exists among them. In part, this is because of the 'chain' of immigration. Most second-generation males came to Canada to find work. However, some from this generation followed their parents or another relative to Canada (Singh 2.8; Kaur 2.12, 2.19). Many of them – especially the women – came to Canada after marrying someone already residing in Canada (Singh 2.2.10, 2.11; Kaur 2.6, 2.13, 2.16, 2.17, 2.18, 2.20, 2.21).

Many second-generation immigrants sponsored their parents to join them once they had settled in Canada (Singh 2.2, 2.4, 2.5, 2.9; Kaur 2.6, 2.12, 2.20). Because the Sikh family setup in Canada has changed – with the married siblings living independent of one another – parents usually live with one of their children's families (Singh 2.9; Kaur 2.12). Although many children have sponsored their parents, some of the parents have chosen not to settle outside their homeland. Even so, many parents who have stayed in the Punjab visit their children in Canada regularly (Singh 2.3, 2.8, 2.11, 2.14; Kaur 2.13, 2.16, 2.17, 2.21).

Despite the change in family organization, many of the second generation – especially those who lost a parent at a very young age – value the extended family because of the support it has always provided (Singh 2.2, 2.8, 2.10). Difficult circumstances faced by the members of the second generation in the Punjab (such as the partition of India) have often reinforced the value of extended family networks (Singh 2.10). One Sikh woman, who came to Canada after marrying a Canadian resident, told me that the extended family in the Punjab is one's sole support: 'In the Punjab there are no community resources [like in Canada]; the family is the only resource people have to depend upon' (Kaur 2.17).

Change in Lifestyle, Continuity in Values

The traditional Indian values of fulfilling one's duty (*dharam*) and respecting and honouring one's elders (*izzat*) have been carried over from the Punjab by the second generation and remain quite pervasive in the second generation's mode of thinking. But, because of the impact of modernity on the family structure and lifestyle (economic independence), the second generation's *practice* of these traditional values has changed. Nowadays, respect is often based on achievement rather than simply seniority. Members of the second generation demand respect from others for what they have achieved personally in building and establishing the 'modified extended family' in Canada. They are aware that they have worked hard to earn an income in order to provide an 'economically better life' for the family. At the same time, second-generation parents remember how they respected their elders when they were growing up in the Punjab. They tell stories about this tradition to their third-generation children in an effort to obtain the same form of respect.

Although there has been a shift to the 'modified extended family,' the traditional family as a social institution controlled by the elders is a very powerful construct in the minds of the second generation (Singh 2.1, 2.2, 2.3, 2.4, 2.5, 2.8, 2.9, 2.10, 2.11, 2.14, 2.22; Kaur 2.6, 2.12, 2.13, 2.16, 2.17, 2.18, 2.19, 2.20, 2.21). For example, a Sikh man of fifty-nine remembered that by tradition, it was the duty of family members to follow the orders of the elders: 'The oldest figure was the one who controlled the household and made the decisions. They also controlled the finances. It was one's duty to follow the orders [*hukam*] of the elders' (Singh 2.3).

This quotation reflects the traditional power structure of the household; it also shows the importance to the Indian value system of fulfilling one's duty. Yet, even after settling in Canada, many in the second generation expect to exercise control over the home that they have built. The traditional value of performing one's duty remains very strong. All those of the second generation that I interviewed for this study mentioned – at the very least – the Indian value of doing one's duty. One fifty-seven-year-old Sikh man explained the value of duty; his explanation is broadly held among the second generation:'Parents work hard to raise children and then it is the duty of the children to look after their parents [when they are old]. It is their duty to take care of the elderly. When the elderly are very old, the son takes over decision making. The old people have control over the money and govern how it is spent' (Singh 2.2). The value of duty remains strong in the thinking of the second generation; however, that value has been somewhat redefined in order to incorporate economic achievement through hard work. Nowadays, those who govern the household demand respect by virtue of the economic independence they have achieved, as well as by virtue of their seniority relative to the third generation.

Though generally speaking, the second generation settled in Canada many years ago, most have found it difficult to adapt to some of the societal differences between the Punjab and Canada – especially to the change from an agricultural society to a modern one. These people have encountered in Canada a different lifestyle in terms of the requirements of efficiency and the importance of time, and this has affected the functioning of the household. In an agricultural society, economic life is less structured than in modern society, where one works in wage-paying jobs. The adjustment alluded to most often by the interviewees, and the one they found most difficult, related to the different notion of time. One man told me: 'Everyone is working here where there is no time. It is totally different from village life. If someone is sick they can care for him/her at home but [not here] ... because of less time and more pressure – they cannot leave work for too long. If someone is old they need more attention – they need people to talk with – but people [here] are bound by time. [They are] limited in terms of the amount of time they can give' (Singh 2.1).

The attitude toward time is different in the farming culture of the Punjab. Life is not as rigidly structured as in Canada, and the women are often at home to care for the children, the elderly, and the sick. A forty-six-year-old Sikh man described the change in lifestyle as he experienced it: 'There is not much flexibility here with the system. On the farm you were flexible to do things. Here if you don't work you have nothing. Everything is dependent on money. In India one could be more self-sufficient and self-reliant even if out of a job. And when working on the farm you had flexibility with time. Here there is little time. (Singh 2.4; also Singh 2.2; 2.3, 2.8, 2.9; Kaur 2.6, 2.12, 2.16, 2.18, 2.19, 2.21).

Another important aspect of lifestyle change relates to the practice of women working outside the home, whether permanently or for shorter periods of time (wives of Singh 2.1, 2.2, 2.3, 2.4, 2.5, 2.8, 2.9, 2,10, 2.11; Kaur 2.6, 2.12, 2.16, 2.17, 2.18, 2.19, 2.21). In their study of the Vancouver Sikh community in the early 1970s, Michael Ames and Joy Inglis found that some of the changes in attitudes were related to contact with industrialization and urbanism. There was a decrease in satisfaction for women in the home, because unlike in the Punjab, they had limited links with the larger community; in contrast, the men continued to behave in a traditional manner in the home even while developing links with the outside world through their jobs.[16]

The general argument by Ames and Inglis on the partial impact of modernity on the Sikh family finds support in the present study. That said, the situation of women having only limited links with the community had changed by the late 1990s. Many Sikh women are now in the workforce. This has given them a taste of economic independence; it has also exposed them to Western customs. The experience of economic independence has, however, increased tensions between mothers-in-law and working daughters-in-law as well as between husbands and wives. One Sikh woman of forty-six has worked most of her life in Canada; as a result of economic independence, she eventually rejected her duty as a daughter-in-law:

In Canada, parents have money and independence ... In India there is no choice, no place to go, and no money. Every woman has a problem with the in-laws. In India, the parents have the attitude that the daughter-in-law has to respect them. The elderly want the son to marry [so as] to have someone to care for them in old age, they want a 'slave for the house.' There is no real relationship with the wife. I worked hard and then had to give the money to [my] husband. I used to have to give the money, and [then] ask for money from my husband when I wanted to buy something. It was like this at the beginning, but now it has changed. My mother told me before my marriage that you have to listen to your husband and in-laws. I did not listen to my in-laws, which is why there were problems. (Kaur 2.19)

A thirty-six-year-old Sikh woman described herself to me as having been independent, living in a Punjabi city, before coming to Canada, where she married into a 'traditional' environment. She spoke about the tensions between daughter-in-law and mother-in-law that she had experienced here in Canada: 'However, most people [in India] are economically dependent. I feel so frustrated because I find that coming to Canada has changed my situation to being dependent. I have no car to go outside freely. My mother-in-law views things differently than I do. My mother-in-law is traditional and not educated, but I compromised and stepped back. There was no point in creating tension. For the first year, I kept quiet and respected my in-laws. But then I felt I could not live like this' (Kaur 2.17).

Whether the women first experienced economic independence while living in Canada, or whether they arrived from modern city life in India to a more traditional family environment in Canada, the experience of economic independence has undermined the traditional power structure of the family and has thus become a source of tension between the generations.

Another consequence of economic independence – one that disrupts the traditional customs of the household and causes problems for second-generation parents – is that the sons usually want to move out of the parental home after marriage. Interviewees discussed the difficulty they encountered in adjusting to such changes, which they saw as the result of Western influence. A fifty-seven-year-old Sikh man discussed the role played by economics and by Western notions of independence in the context of the hardship he faced after his son moved out after marriage: 'People in Canada are living independently. They like their privacy. The system here is not that of a joint family system. People earn money and want to live on their own. I feel sad about my son moving out ... I was with my son for twenty-seven years and now he has gone. I don't care what others think but that it is a big loss. My son wants his space with his wife, so I have to accept this ... I find it very hard to adapt to this, but it is part of this culture' (Singh 2.2).

The second generation finds it difficult to accept self-orientation and the nuclear family, both of which are associated with modernity.

Tensions with the First Generation

The second generation's experience with economic independence has resulted in the expansion of personal choice (especially as between wife and husband and between daughter-in-law and mother-in-law). This expansion of choice has become a major source of tension between the second and first generations. The change in the family power structure in Canada has created difficulties in adjustment for the first generation. A Sikh daughter-in-law explained:

> I remember that in the Punjab, when I was growing up, the elderly were very much respected. The elderly managed the whole house – like a busi-nessman manages a business – in terms of groceries, finances. They were the boss of the house, made all the decisions and controlled the money ... I live with my in-laws and it was difficult at first because they did not know how to do anything, did not know how to speak the language, and did not have any money. It took my husband and me ten to twelve months to educate them in these things. The elders feel they should be respected because they are seniors but they have to be educated about liv-ing in Canada and [take] time to adjust to the different way of life ... I find that the more educated one is the more one is able to adapt to Western customs. The less educated or uneducated people do not learn or want to change. (Kaur 2.12; also Singh 2.8; Kaur 2.6, 2.)

Another member of the second generation emphasized the role of education – or rather the lack of it – in generating tension with the first generation: 'I am aware of the bad stories about grandparents and their children in the community. I believe it is the fault of both parties, not just the younger generation. I believe that getting along with the family in an extended setting is dependent on personal choice. People can choose how to be. But then it also has to do with education. Many are not that educated and this affects their way of dealing with change in setting or culture' (Singh 2.8).

The encounter with a different lifestyle has made it hard for the first generation in another way. Traditionally, daughters-in-law remain at home, where they perform the household duties and serve and care for the elders and the children. Since daughters-in-law in Canada now often work outside the home to earn money, there is little time for them to attend to the in-laws and the children.

The change in lifestyle in terms of women joining the workforce has been a source of much tension in still another way. Employment in the workforce has made it possible for them to sponsor their *own* parents to Canada and to care for them. Traditionally, once a Sikh woman is married, she belongs to the husband's household and is no longer responsible for caring for her own parents. Likewise, the parents of a married daughter are not supposed to take anything – not even a cup of tea or a drink of water – from her home.[17] Yet some daughters, after arriving in Canada, have been sponsoring their parents to immigrate and looking after them once they get here – a custom unheard of in traditional Punjab. This continued bond between daughters and their parents even after marriage has created considerable tension between women and their in-laws, as well as between the married daughter's new family and her birth family. A Sikh woman commented on all of this: 'Traditionally, the girl's parents are not welcomed in her home. So many girls came [to Canada] after marriage and then sponsored their parents. There were many problems in the household ... There is tension between marriage [duty] and [loyalty to] parents. Both sides need to compromise with each other. The elders [here] need to realize that this society is different, busier, and they need to adapt and cooperate. The kids need help at home because life is busier. Both parents are working' (Kaur 2.16).

The tension between the first and second generations is aggravated in situations when the parents live with their daughter, and the daughter helps support them.

Tensions between Husband and Wife

Clearly there has been change in the family structure and in Sikh lifestyles generally, reflecting the impact of modernity, in the sense that socio-economic arrangements have adjusted to modern industrial society. That said, the assimilation of the corresponding values that go with modern society is not as evident. The second generation has largely maintained a traditional mentality and a collectivity orientation. Several scholars, such as Michael Ames and Joy Inglis, contend that in adapting to life in Canada, South Asians welcome modernity but not Westernization: 'They ideally desire for themselves a modernity devoid of the more corrupting influences of Western civilization.'[18] Similarly, according to Josephine Naidoo, South Asian women do not feel that they have been influenced by Western values regarding their place in society, marriage, and family.[19] In the present study I found that second-generation Sikhs approve of *modern* 'economic' practices, such as being employed in the industrial sector, but disapprove of *Western* 'cultural' values, such as individual independence. They see the former (earning wages) as 'good' and readily take to it, whereas they perceive the latter (independence) as 'bad.' Indeed, there is a general fear that women or children will embrace too tightly the cultural values of learning and become too independent. The second generation rationalizes this selective adoption by defining Canadian economic practices as *modern* and Canadian cultural values as *Western*. However, this approach to Canadian society is too simplistic when viewed from the perspective of tensions between the generations and the smooth functioning of the community.

The difference between modernity and Westernization is not as clear-cut as the second generation understands it. There seems to be a general failure on the part of the immigrant groups to understand that the cultural values associated with Western society – such as self-differentiation, equality, and the exercising of personal choice – actually follow from Western economic practices and the related independence. This failure leads to personal disorientation; it also causes tension between generations and genders. These consequences become obvious when second-generation males discuss issues regarding their wives and children (especially their daughters). Evidently, most second-generation males have not accepted the modern values of equality and self-orientation, especially when it comes to women and daughters.

Even though the fulfilment of one's duty to family remains a key value among the second generation, economic independence has resulted in some distancing from the collectivity orientation. Women's familiarity with economic independence – whether or not they have to hand over their salaries to their husbands – is one aspect of modern life that seems to have disrupted the traditional value system. Women, now that they are participating in the workforce, seem to be 'playing the role' of the ideal daughter-in-law or wife without actually feeling fulfilled by the notion that they are doing their duty. One consequence of this role playing is that second-generation mothers often find themselves following the beliefs or orders of their husbands, whether or not they agree with them. This becomes a source of emotional distress: they find themselves caught between their traditional husband and their more modern children who are attempting to fit into Western society. For example, in order to placate her husband, a mother will act distressed about a son who has cut his hair, even though she in fact sympathizes with her son. In some cases the experience of role playing extends as far as admitting that they would have liked to have had a friendship with their husband instead of just playing out the *role* of a wife (Kaur 2.19, 2.21): 'I think it is nice if people can have a relationship instead of playing the wife-role' (Kaur 2.21).

Some Sikh women who do not work outside the home, and who do not enjoy economic independence, still experience alienation when they continue to play their familial roles as wife, daughter-in-law, and mother after all the children leave home. (When the children continue to stay at home, Sikh women tend not to suffer alienation, because they believe they are continually to do their duty for the collectivity.) Because most second-generation women were raised with a collectivity orientation, such that their identity is rooted in their defined roles in relation to the collectivity, they experience alienation when the collectivity breaks down. The alienation is often triggered later in life when their children leave home. A twenty-two-year-old Sikh man, the only son in his family, explained the situation: 'Changes are occurring because of economic independence in the first place. On the farms with landowning, people don't want to split up the land ... Many parents are pretty rich here but they don't want to let go of the kids. I have my own theory that mothers and fathers don't often get along because the relationship is based on doing roles. The parents need other people around like children and grandchildren' (Singh 3.33).

The experience of alienation as a result of role playing is especially difficult for second-generation women. They have been raised and molded to have the skills to fulfil wifely and motherly duties for the family (according to the orders and wishes of their husbands); later, these women's skills can become an obstacle for them in term of reaching out or building a network for themselves beyond the extended family. Not having developed a self-orientation, they lack the confidence to make the adjustment. Some Sikh women whose children have left home adjust by babysitting the grandchildren. Interestingly, third-generation members who spoke of leaving home later in life often stated that their only concern or regret was leaving their mother alone with their father (Singh 3.16, 3.24, 3.33; Kaur 3.23, 3.25, 3.27).

Another aspect of modern life that seems to have disrupted the traditional family structure and its value system is the choice or opportunity for the woman in Canada to leave a marriage and seek a divorce. Divorce was almost unheard of in the Punjab until recently. The situation is now different with the Sikh community in Canada. Three of the second-generation women I interviewed for this study were divorced (Kaur 2.6, 2.20, 2.21); one third-generation interviewee was divorced; two third-generation interviewees had divorced parents. In the 1980s and 1990s, drinking (and abuse) by the husband was the most common cause for divorce. One Sikh counsellor explained:

> The 1980 to 1995 period was very hard for women when they married because in 1972 a big influx of immigrants came. It took about three or four years to settle and be able to sponsor family [members]. These people went to India to get married with a dowry. They were able to get wives more educated than themselves because they lived in Canada. It brought a hard time for the women because 85 per cent of the men were drinking. The ladies were upset because of the [mental and physical] suffering. Eventually, they started to call 911 [the police] ... on the radio show, [Rhim Jhim] was involved with the problem of husbands drinking and beating wives. Some put up with it, but some stood up against it. (counsellor 1)

Although divorce has become more common in the Sikh community, it has been difficult (in varying degrees) for the women to risk it, especially because of the stigma associated with it and the dishonour it brings to the family. The degree of difficulty the woman faced in pressing for divorce was inversely related to the support she received from her own parents or other 'blood' relatives. Undoubtedly, economic independence has also played a role in enabling women to go through a divorce and to survive on their own. One divorced Sikh mother stated that even though there is stigma attached to divorce in the community, she had the strength to leave a mentally abusive situation because of economic support from the government and emotional support from her family:

> There are more choices here as a single mother. In India, I could not have survived as a single mother. My brothers [in India] may have helped for a

short period of time but would not have wanted to do it all the time. Some women may have a good job, so it is okay for them to leave their husbands and their families, but most don't have the money to be independent. I get money support from the government and emotional support from my family. In my culture, parents tell you that you have to respect your in-laws and husband, and that, if you leave, it will look bad. In India, women are scared if no one is around. However, if you are in a relationship where you are not treated nicely [i.e., abused], you should not get stuck in the situation, don't be passive. One has to be active. You have to give attitude back [stand up to them], and if people don't change then you have to leave the situation. You can't get stuck. It is not an issue of destiny (*kismat*). God does not say to stay stuck in the situation. The Sikhs have to be for social justice. God is not going to take you out of the situation. People have to get themselves out. (Kaur 2.20)

According to the interviewee, her comments about the religious interpretation of destiny actually came from her supportive cousin, who belongs to the third generation. Indeed, the cousin's interpretation of *kismat* reflects a move beyond *literacy* toward *analytics*, in the sense that it is conceptual and self-reflective rather than a literal interpretation of the traditional belief.

Tensions with the Third Generation

The tensions experienced between the second and third generations relate mainly to communication and cultural barriers. The modes of thinking of the older generations range along the continuum from concrete thought form based on a collectivity orientation (orality) to literal interpretation expressed in concrete thought form, with some distancing from the known (literacy). Thus, there naturally occurs an unintended communication barrier between the older generations and the third generation, which has the capacity for conceptual thinking along with a self-reflective manner (analytics). Similar to the first generation, the second generation dislikes the inquisitive nature of the third generation, because it is traditionally seen as disrespectful to question comments or orders from elders, who perceive themselves as having accumulated life experience and wisdom.

The communication barrier apart, the cultural barrier that is most often experienced by the second generation with respect to the third generation pertains to Western notions of independence. As mentioned earlier, second-generation parents accept economic independence and expect respect based on their achievements in Canada, yet at the same time they see acts of independence on the part of the third generation as 'selfish.' This is because they see Canadian economic practices as 'modern' but Canadian cultural values as 'Western'.

The general orientation of the second generation corresponds to *literacy*. Some degree of distancing from collectivity orientation has undoubtedly taken place; this is evident in the second generation's generally negative experience of 'role playing.' At the same time, even as the second generation experiences the effects of economic independence within the family household, it refuses to accept, or is incapable of accepting, the corresponding modern values of equality, self-orientation, and expanded personal choice. The second generation continues to believe in the traditional Indian values of duty and respect; however, the change in lifestyle has forced a redefinition of these traditional values. The second generation demands respect for its hard work in establishing the 'modified extended family.' It also acknowledges that tension exists between it and the third generation. Even so, its traditional mentality and its inability to intellectually justify redefined traditional values are major communication and cultural barriers vis-à-vis the third generation.

The Third Generation and Independence

Unlike the second generation, the children of immigrants (i.e., the third generation) were raised in the modern host country of Canada, and they tend to interact more with the mainstream society. As a consequence, there is tension between the traditional values that members of the third generation learn at home and the modern values and practices they learn at school or absorb from the society at large. The third generation was raised mainly in a traditional setting, but it interacts on a considerable scale with a society that embraces the modern values of personal choice, self-orientation, and success by merit. The process of living in both milieux (i.e., traditional and modern) inevitably results in tension with regard to arranged marriages, family obligations, and the questioning of authority.

'Modified Nuclear' Family Household

As discussed earlier, the Sikh community's tradition of extended families was forced to change in Canada. Unlike earlier generations, most members of the third generation have been living in nuclear families, consisting of parents and siblings; thus, they see the household as nuclear. Many in the third generation, however, know what it is like for grandparents to be living with them either intermittently (Singh 3.1, 3.4, 3.6, 3.14, 3.16, 3.26, 3.37; Kaur 3.2, 3.3, 3.8, 3.20, 3.23) or more or less permanently (Singh 3.10, 3.24, 3.29, 3.30; Kaur 3.27, 3.31).

A more recent phenomenon is the presence of divorce, giving rise to the single-parent family. Two third-generation interviewees came from divorced families: one lived with the mother and *nanaji* and *naniji* (mother's parents) (Kaur 3.3); the other lived with his father until he was eighteen (Singh 3.14). Another interviewee had recently divorced her husband, at the age of twenty-four, and was living with her brother (Kaur 3.22).

Most members of the third generation, even as young adults, still live with their parents or other relatives. Normally in mainstream Canadian families, after high school or college children live independently; many even move to another city to build their lives. The most common pattern among the Sikh children is to stay at home until marriage, if not permanently. Even the three interviewees who had engaged in rebellious-defiant behaviour (including involvement in drugs) were living with their parents. Several others among the third generation lived with their parents until they got married (Singh 3.1; Kaur 3.12, 3.22, 3.25, 3.35). However, two Sikh men continued living with their parents even after marriage (Singh 3.13. 3.17). Several interviewees had married siblings who were still living in their parents' homes (Singh 3.5, 3.34; Kaur 3.31). In contrast, there were only two Sikh men who had moved out of the parents' home in order to pursue their life as they wished 'without strings attached' (Singh 3.14, 3.24). Although the family structure has changed so that the second generation has become masters of the house (regardless of whether elders live in the household), there is a continuation of the tightly knit network within the supplemented form of the nuclear family, with the parents trying to ensure that children belonging to the third generation continue their traditional roles within the household.

Altered Form of Arranged Marriages

One important change relates to the tradition of 'arranged marriages.' In his study of the Vancouver Sikh community in the early 1970s, Chadney found continuity in the custom of arranged marriage; spouses were 'recruited from India so that at least one of the parties was born in

India. This practice reflected one strategy for preventing total assimilation into Canadian society and for ensuring that Punjabi family values and Sikh religious identity were retained.[20]

The general observation by Chadney finds support among the second generation in the present study; that said, the pattern had changed among the third generation by the late 1990s. First, most second-generation parents believe it is more practical for their children to marry people raised in Canadian society, since they have been educated in Canada (since, a spouse educated in Canada can easily enter the workforce). Second, the second generation – in light of some sponsorship marriages ending in divorce in the 1980s and 1990s – has come to realize that, because of the cultural gap between children raised in the Punjab and those raised in Canada, it is better to arrange marriages between Canadian-born children.

It is now recognized that there are disadvantages to arranging marriages with partners from India; even more significantly, changes are occurring in the custom of arranged marriages. In their study on gender role socialization among adolescent South Asians, Aziz Talbani and Parveen Hasanali found that arranged marriages remained quite prevalent; this preserved the traditional parameters concerning the role of the family and the status/role of the girl (as caretaker of the family and child bearer). At the same time, they found that 45 per cent of the twenty-two participants in the study[21] felt that their parents would ask for their opinion and might respect their wishes, and that 30 per cent of them believed that their parents would probably not object if they chose their own mates.[22] Michael Angelo, in his study on professional Sikh families in New York state, found that although both sexes expressed 'a strong preference for some form of an arranged marriage,' there was evidence of a shift toward 'a more Western pattern of love marriage' (albeit slower among women than among men).[23] In the present study I found that although there is a range of opinion among the third generation regarding arranged marriages, the general movement is away from the traditional arranged marriage toward the Western custom of love marriage. A few favour arranged marriage, and a few others favour love marriage, but most Canadian-born third-generation interviewees favour a modified form of an arranged marriage, which I will refer to as 'semi-arranged marriage.'

The 'semi-arranged marriage' is different from the traditional form in that the man and woman already know each other (to the extent that they may already have been 'secretly' courting). In order to appear to be behaving according to traditional norms, one of the two individuals asks a family member or friend to initiate the 'arrangement' of the marriage by bringing their families together. This creates a sense among the second-generation parents that their children's marriage is being arranged between the two kin groups; it also allows the Canadian-born children to exercise considerable choice with regard to their life partner.

This new form of arranged marriage has emerged among the third generation as a means for managing the tensions they confront between the pressures of traditional parents and exposure to the modern life-style. 'Semi-arranged marriage' is a coping mechanism that enables the third generation to appease their parents. It allows for the preservation of *izzat* in that it conforms, in a sense, to the tradition of arranged marriage even while reflecting the third generation's attempt to expand its choices.

Changing Attitudes

The third generation has a general and continued appreciation for the close-knit family – 'our parents don't kick us out at eighteen years of age' – but it also has a critical approach to family dynamics as they are based on the traditional Indian values of duty and honour. For example, quite a few members of the third generation were vociferous in their esteem for their grandparents (Singh 3.10; Kaur 3.2, 3.3, 3.27, 3.31). At the same time, they offered critical comments about the traditional tensions between members of the household – 'my father blames my mother for not getting along with my *dadiji*' but 'my grandmother does not give my mother a chance' (Kaur 3.2, 3.7, 3.23, 3.27, 3.31). Even when members of the third generation uphold the Indian tradition of living with parents after marriage in high – or at least some – esteem, they disapprove of the traditional practice of families keeping problems hidden in the household in order to preserve family honour. For example, a twenty-eight-year-old Sikh man wanted attention to be given to problems within the family: 'It is good that Punjabis have maintained their tight-knit families. However, there are things to address, like drugs and physical or sexual abuse' (Singh 3.13).

More fundamentally, the third generation has begun to question the traditional family values of duty, respect, and honour. This questioning of traditional values reflects the impact of modernity on the third generation's mode of thinking (*analytics*). With it, there also occurs a change

·in attitude toward the roles of specific family members. They recognize the importance and benefit of the traditional Punjabi value of duty (*dharam*), but many – both men and women – feel there is too much emphasis on duty. They even see this value as an instrument of control. A twenty-four-year-old Sikh woman stated:There is a lot of control present in the family ... I don't understand why everything with parents has to be "duty"' (Kaur 3.2; also Singh 3.14, 3.24; Kaur 3.3, 3.23, 3.27)

This notion that duty is used as a means of control arose repeatedly in interviews with the third generation (Singh 3.14, 3.16, 3.24, 3.24, 3.38; Kaur 3.2, 3.3, 3.23, 3.27). A Sikh woman of twenty-one, asserted that duty was linked to financial support, which was used as an instrument of control: 'There is too much about duty. Parents use financial support as a way to control children. They [parents] help educate kids so as to control their choices.' (Kaur 3.3).

Of course, in Western families, too, parents use economic support as a means of control. However, in the eyes of the third generation of the Sikh community it is used to control *all* aspects of life. What is true of duty applies also in the case of *izzat*. The general consensus is that *izzat* is not working in Canada and that it is hurting the community and family (Singh 3.13, 3.14, 3.16, 3.21, 3.26, 3.33. 3.34, 3.37; Kaur 3.9, 3.18, 3. 3.19, 3.22, 3.23, 3.27).

As noted earlier, the first generation sees duty as simply indicative of respect for elders, who are entitled to it by their seniority. That said, the third generation approaches the custom of duty within the extended household network more analytically. It sees duty as being determined by economic conditions. A thirty-one-year-old Sikh man remarked: 'Everything has to do with economics. Perhaps previously there were traditional values of love, but most things are dependent on economics. Families in India were financially interdependent, now people are economically independent. People want to be able to have their independence and space' (Singh 3.1). Similarly, a twenty-six-year-old Sikh man – who had moved out of his parents' home so that he could make his own life decisions, and who continued to live apart from the parental home after marriage for reasons of privacy – underlined the importance of economics and independence: 'I like privacy for my wife and me, although we live close to my parents. People want to live separately because of economic independence. With economic independence one can make choices. There are always problems between the in-laws living together [mother-in-law, sisters-in-law and daughters-in-law]. My wife does not have [to contend with] this, as there is [more] space. It is also hard for the girl coming into a new family.' (Singh 3.24).

Not only is respect perceived as linked to economics, but the third generation sees respect as something that should be deserved or based on the behaviour of those being respected. A Sikh man of twenty-five stated that the reasons sons stay or do not stay at home after marriage are related to whether or not parents interfere with the son's space and independence: 'It depends on the parents how interfering they are. A lot of people want to be on their own for their personal space. There are competing interests – son torn between parents and wife – privacy and freedom. People often live nearby parents if they see it is better to move out for privacy' (Singh 3.17). In other words, a son is willing to stay with his parents so long as there is mutual respect and the parents grant the son and his wife privacy and space.

The relationship between duty and economics works both to constrain the children, but also to provide them with ease and comfort. The parents' main fear is that the children will leave home (which goes against the traditional value of *izzat*), so they do not encourage their children to develop a self-orientation. Rather, they shower many luxuries and comforts on the children so that they will continue to stay at home and bring *izzat* to the family – specifically, to the parents. Some among the third generation who still live with their parents ostensibly out of a sense of duty, really do so in part because of the financial support or comfort that comes with it. A nineteen-year-old Sikh woman commented on the linkage between duty and comfort: 'Kids should stand up for what they want and who they are. Parents are giving too much to the kids – the cultural way is to give the best life to kids that they can afford. Kids don't stand up because they don't want to let go of this. Parents complain that kids don't listen, but the parents need education on how to rear children in the West ... Parents should see that culture is something that evolves and is not fixed. Parents cling to it in fear of losing it' (Kaur 3.20; also Singh 3.14, 3.24; Kaur 3.2).

The second generation's inability to let go of traditional customs encourages them to keep material comforts on their children in order to preserve the traditional values of *izzat* and family collectivity orientation (as opposed to the modern values of equality, self-orientation and success by merit).

Alienation from Role Playing

Quite a few second-generation women 'play the role' of the dutiful daughter-in-law or wife without exactly feeling fulfilled by it, but are not aware of what they are doing, or feel too guilty to say as much.

However, a number of the third-generation women I interviewed – especially those who are moving toward a self-orientation – articulated more openly their problems with living according to the values of duty and family honour within the household; they saw it clearly as nothing more than 'role playing.' A thirty-year-old Sikh woman commented on her experience of role playing in her in-laws' home after marriage and its negative effects: 'I lived with my in-laws for one year but could not take it. The difference between a mother and a mother-in-law is that a mother will forgive you no matter what, but a mother-in-law does not forgive. I did not feel like myself in the house. I did not argue because I was taught to respect elders. [However,] I did not feel like myself. I was very unhappy because I wanted more out of life. I was just living a role, as an extension of the family, dressed up to look nice. I felt like a trophy for the family, even more so after having a son' (Kaur 3.18). Not only did this young woman interpret fulfilling the family duty as role playing, but she also expressed a keen desire for a self-orientation.

The issue of being pressured to play a role for the sake of the family's honour underlines the absence of 'real' relationships within the Sikh family in the sense of mutual respect and sharing. From the vantage point of observing the interactions within their homes – especially between their parents – many of the third generation overwhelmingly believe that their own parents are simply role playing without any sense of a 'real' relationship (Singh 3.14, 3.16, 3.21, 3.24, 3.33; Kaur 3.7, 3.18, 3.19, 3.22, 3.23. 3.25, 3.27, 3.32). A twenty-year-old Sikh woman stated that her criterion for marriage was to 'click' with her partner-to-be; the implication was that she wanted to have a genuine relationship with her future husband: 'I have not really discussed marriage yet with my family, but there is pressure within my family to get married. I am not traditional. Living with in-laws would depend on who my in-laws would be and how they would treat me. I want to marry [someone] who I click with ... even if he is not a Punjabi' (Kaur 3.19).

Questioning Authority

The very act of questioning is a great source of tension between the generations. Traditionally and according to the orality mode of thinking, one does not question elders, who are assumed to possess accumulated wisdom. A child is simply expected to respect those in authority based on seniority and to follow their orders (*hukam*). The

violation of this norm inevitably generates tension between the generations. And because the traditional elders interpret questioning as disrespectful, they often neither entertain questions nor answer them. The
difference between the traditional approach and the modern approach
to communication was underlined by a Sikh woman of twenty-three, a
teacher by profession, who was concerned about the lack of encour-
agement to inquisitiveness among Punjabi children in their homes:
'The kids need to be motivated by having their questions answered. If
one is able to shed light on their questions it will increase their curiosity' (Kaur 3.27).

In voicing this thought, she was expressing the communication barrier between the first or second and the third generation. Indeed, the
third generation's inquisitive tendency, which is encouraged or fostered in Western schools, is viewed by the first and second generations
as undermining authority. A thirty-year-old Sikh man suggested that
the older generations need to adapt to the ways of Canada, while
simultaneously following their culture, in order to bridge the differences in the modes of thinking: 'Culture should be practised to a certain extent. However, the elders are not able to answer the questions of
the younger generation. Respect of elders is traditional. The younger
generation knows more, which threatens the older generation' (Singh
3.16). Not only are parents not used to questioning, and not only do
they find it disrespectful, but they also feel threatened by it when they
do not know how to answer the questions.

In sum, the third generation reflects a move toward, as also the presence of, the *analytics* mode of thinking, in that its members show the
capacity to conceptualize and to analyse in abstract terms the trends
they experience in their families and personal lives, especially with
respect to the relationships between the three generations. The contradictory situation of Canadian-born members of the third generation –
who interact more with mainstream society, yet are pressured to live
according to the traditional norms of *dharam* at home – is a real source
of tension. Because they were born and raised in Canada, the members
of the third generation are exposed to the values of a modern society.
With modern society comes economic independence, which leads to
an expansion of choice for individuals. By way of it also come a self-
orientation and the capacity to treat others as individuals. Furthermore, modern society has 'taught' the third generation to determine
other people's status on the basis of personal achievement rather than
racial, caste, or religious background.[24] A member of the third genera-

tion seeks respect from the other family members by virtue of being an individual; however, this quest clashes with traditional values. While most members of the third generation see duty as a control mechanism, some of them believe that some traditional values should be internalized instead of being imposed on them by the collectivity for the sake of saving face or displaying honour. The third generation's desire for an expansion of choice and its appreciation of the value of self-orientation undermine the traditional value of fulfilling one's duty in honour of the collectivity – the family.

Tensions between Punjabi Values and Canadian Lifestyles

Although changes in economic patterns and in the nature of the family organization indicate 'partial adaptation' to Canada, the present study on the tensions experienced among the three generations of the Sikh community points to the continued presence of considerable 'social insularity' in the sense of the persistence of traditional values, which in turn are the source of tension between the generations. No doubt the change in economic patterns among the older generation – which reflects its partial adaptation to Canadian society – has had repercussions for the traditional customs and value system, the most obvious being in terms of the role of the family. However, in the 'transplantation' of any traditional community into a modern-Western society, there is always a time lag before the community fully adapts and begins to function more smoothly. The Canadian Sikh community, which came from a traditional society to a modern or Western society, has obviously adjusted better in economic terms than in terms of value systems.

Initially, many immigrants came to work in Canada with the intention of returning later to India. Since then, most of them have realized that they are not going to return (see chapter 6). However, in establishing themselves in Canada, many of them still intended to maintain their traditional beliefs and values. Meanwhile, their Canadian-born children went to Western schools, and were there exposed to Western social values, among which the key one is the importance of the individual and his or her opinions and choices. Canadian-born Sikh children are expected by their parents to absorb the 'techniques' of the West – for example, to have an education in pursuit of a well-paying job. As a result they struggle with the clash between modern techniques which are linked to a system of Western values and attitudes, and traditional Punjabi Sikh mores. For instance, parents expect their children to behave in accordance with the tradition of duty, even while the Canadian value system calls for individuals to make their own choices. Neither the older generation nor the younger is to be blamed for the tension that has resulted from this: at base, this tension is simply the result of the clash between tradition and modernity.

The meeting of the two value systems is unintendedly transformed into tension between the generations, which becomes manifest in cultural and communication barriers between them. To illustrate, Canadian-born children (third generation) are taught at school to question what they have heard and read and to use reason as a means to acquiring knowledge. This learned value creates an unintended conflict: parents belonging to the second generation (and even more so their grandparents, i.e., the first generation) expect the children to follow the Punjabi culture of respect toward, and obedience of, their elders, but when Canadian-born Sikh children ask 'Why?', as they have been taught at school, the parents perceive them as being disrespectful.

Similarly, the tension between the traditional Indian value of 'prescribed' duty and the Canadian emphasis on rights results in conflict between generations:

> Kids do what they want to and don't communicate the same way as we had to with our elders. I told my son to only watch television thirty minutes a day, he said, 'This is not a jail.' They speak up to parents. The younger generation doesn't have the concept of 'duty' – they want to build their own castle so they can be the boss. The younger generation also know the system and take advantage of it. For example if there is a problem they will call 911, seek financial aid to be independent, move out if they don't want to stay home ... If they get through twelfth grade without getting into the problem of drugs and the law then it should be okay. Middle-aged people see the problems of younger generation [as arising from] too much emphasis on rights. (Singh 2.5)

The tension between the three generations is thus a result of the conflict between (1) the traditional value and custom of duty, in the context of economic interdependence and collectivity orientation, and (2) the modern value of the individual, in the context of economic independence and self-orientation. Members of the older generations often interpret the latter pattern as 'selfish'; for their part, members of the third generation sense that something is 'missing.' The missing element is most often perceived to be communication. All of this relates to the fact that physiological needs are more easily met in modern society, and that once they have been met, other higher needs come to the fore that require attention.

Modernity and People's Emotional Needs

Abraham Maslow (1908–70), a child of immigrant parents from Russia who faced his own intense parental conflicts throughout his lifetime,[25] is widely recognized for having made humanist psychology a legitimate branch of psychology. Maslow developed a hierarchy of human needs (see Figure 3.1). At the base of the hierarchy is the 'lowest' need, the physiological, which he saw as the most basic. At the peak of the hierarchy is the highest need, self-actualization, which he defined as the most 'human' need, and which he saw as involving the realization of one's full potential. Once a person's most basic needs are adequately satisfied, that person sets out to satisfy the next most basic ones, and so on through the hierarchy until he or she is in a position to become self-actualized.[26]

The hierarchy of needs toward self-actualization is founded on the modern ideals of self-differentiation and success by merit. Furthermore, it can be used, as I use it here, to illuminate the gap between generations as the Sikh community encounters modernity and is forced to come to terms with it. In traditional society the family develops economic interdependence in order to fulfil the physiological needs (hunger, thirst and sex) and safety needs (protection from pain or danger) of individuals in the collectivity. The family members meet these basic needs by functioning smoothly on the basis of the values of duty (*dharam*) and honour (*izzat*) in the particular context of an integrated community. A system like this works in the traditional milieu of village life; however, it breaks down in a modern society, which functions as a meritocracy and is heavily based on achievement. The members of the second generation have readily absorbed the 'technique' of earning a living according to the modern ideal of meritocracy, but they have not absorbed to its corresponding belief system, which is predicated on self-differentiation and self-actualization.

The transformative impact of modernity on tradition is evident in the changing attitudes toward the 'belongingness and love needs' of Maslow's hierarchy. No doubt, the traditional way of life provides a strong sense of belonging to family, clan, religion, and community. This collective sense of belonging may be very strong for the first and

Figure 3.1

Hierarchy of Human Needs[27]

Self-Actualization Needs

Need to live up to one's fullest and unique potential.

↑

Esteem Needs

Need for self-esteem, achievement, competence, and independence;
need for recognition and respect from others.

↑

Belongingness and Love Needs

Need to love and be loved, to belong and be accepted; need to avoid
loneliness and alienation

↑

Safety Needs

Need to feel that the world is organized and predictable; need to feel safe,
secure, and stable

↑

Physiological Needs

Need to satisfy hunger and thirst.

second generations; however, this orientation toward *only* the good of
the group does not find support among most third-generation Sikhs in
Vancouver, nor does it satisfy their sense of belonging. In fact, most
third-generation Sikhs attempt to fulfil the need to be loved and
accepted at the *individual* level, and this leads to tension between the
older and younger generations.

Furthermore, the more abstract and conceptual needs of the highest two stages of Maslow's hierarchy – esteem (to be a contributor to other human beings or society) and self-actualization (to reach one's full potential)[28] – have not been attended to by the first and second generations, because they are not incorporated into the orality and literacy modes of thinking. This does not mean that traditional people do not love, nor is it to say that they don't want what is best for their children; it simply means that for them, love means something different and so must be offered in a different way, through the concrete actions of feeding, providing for survival needs, and helping the individual *as a member of the group*. Such concrete actions are regarded as the fulfilment of a parent's duty. In terms of meeting the needs of the family *as a group* at the physiological and emotional levels, the ideal has been to fulfil one's duty to the collectivity. In contrast, Maslow's goal of self-actualization is a goal of personal development in the context of modern ideals. For Maslow, reaching one's full potential is the ultimate goal. In this view, many members of the third-generation Sikh community, especially the women, are concerned that 'something' is not being allowed to them, or is not being attained by (see chapter 4).

Conclusion

The differences in the modes of thinking between the three generations of the Sikh community shed considerable light on the intergenerational dynamics within Sikh families. Two inherited values and customs – duty and honour – have allowed traditional Punjabi family networks to function smoothly. However, as the predominantly traditional Sikh community encounters modernity in Canada, invariably tensions arise between the three generations – tensions that are related to the gap between tradition and modernity, and to the drift away from economic interdependence within families toward individual economic independence. The first generation expects respect by virtue of tradition and seniority. In contrast, the third generation seeks respect by virtue of simply being human (and also on the basis of merit). Meanwhile, the second generation demands respect for having worked so hard to achieve economic independence (and also on the basis of seniority).

Tensions within Sikh families in Canada are generated as a result of the clash between tradition and modernity, and also as a result of the communication and social contradictions that emerge when Canadian-born children living in traditional Punjabi households attend schools where they are encouraged to explore and ask questions about the world. It is not that the third generation rejects the value of duty or respect; rather, that respect must be a matter of personal choice, not something imposed. Furthermore, that respect must be earned, which corresponds to the modern notion of meritocracy.

4 Family Relations among Three Generations: Duty, Role Playing, and Independence, Part 2*

While changes have occurred in family lifestyle as a result of adaptation to the requirements of employment in the Canadian economy, considerable 'social insularity' continues to prevail in the Sikh community in the sense that traditional values persist. This social insularity has repercussions for Canadian-born members of the third generation since they have been raised both in traditional homes and in a modern society. The parents (first and second generations) have attempted to raise their children (third generation) according to the traditional customs they have brought with them from the Punjab. This has serious implications, since these children are also socialized into modern society through the education system.

Attitudes toward child rearing and human development express what kind of society a person comes from. Traditional and modern societies have their own distinctive orientations toward people and human development. In traditional societies, individuals are oriented toward the collectivity – the family or clan. Within the collectivity, roles are diffuse and status is ascriptive,[1] and children are raised to fulfil their familial roles. In contrast, a modern, developed society is oriented toward the individual, values personal choice, and accords status on the basis of personal achievement. Children undergo the processes of self-differentiation from others (especially from their parents) and of ego-identity formation – processes that foster the realization of their full potential. Ego-identity formation is a popular theme in the West but is distinctly absent in traditional cultures. For children who are being

---

* This chapter is co-authored with Jaswinder Singh Sandhu, who is a graduate student in Counselling Psychology at the University of British Columbia.

raised by immigrant parents with a traditional orientation, yet who must increasingly interact with mainstream society and its modern orientation, the issue of personal identity becomes especially complex.

In this chapter I focus on the traditional and modern understandings of child rearing and human development in order to shed light on the tensions between the generations. The traditional and modern understandings of human development will, in turn, help show how a traditional group adapts to and integrates with its modern host society. This chapter has three parts. The first provides background on the understanding of human development according to Sikh scripture, the *Guru Granth Sahib*.[2] The second analyses the three generations of the Sikh community and identifies the main issues relating to child rearing and human development as they arose during interviews and through participant observation. The final part analyses intergenerational tensions from the perspective of the second and third generations and points to various elements from the Western milieu that have influenced the younger generation and spawned change within the community.

Human Development According to Sikh Scripture

Human development is described by several of the Sikh gurus in the *Guru Granth Sahib*. These descriptions demonstrate the Sikh theological understanding of the person; they also shed light on Sikh attitudes toward child rearing and the stages of life in the context of salvation from both the 'ego' and the cycle of rebirth (*sansar*).

Constituents of People

The *Guru Granth Sahib* teaches that the constituent elements of a person are the soul (*atma*), consciousness (*surti*), action (*karam*), the mind (*antahkaran*), and the body (*sarir*). The soul (*atma*) is at the core of the human being and is regarded as being one with the Supreme Universal Soul (*param-atma*), which is both manifest and transcendental. The other four elements of a person – *surti, karam, antahkaran,* and *sarir* – are the successive layers that envelop the *atma*. The layer closest to the *atma* is *surti*, which is intangible and is affected by *karam*. The three layers farthest from the *atma* – *karam, antahkaran,* and *sarir* – are believed to be perceivable by the *surti*.[3]

The Sikh understanding of the evolution of these layers enveloping the *atma* can be correlated to human development. *Karam* – the second-closest layer to the *atma* – takes three forms: mental action (*mansakh*), verbal action (*vasakh*), and physical action (*sarirak*). Every thought, word, or movement makes an impression on *surti*. These impressions are similar to the Western concept of behavioural habits that become stronger over time. Righteous behavioural habits have positive consequences; less righteous behavioural habits have negative consequences and are self-defeating. *Antahkaran* – the third layer from the *atma* – has four constituent elements: perception (*manas*), intellect (*buddhi*), memory (*cit*), and ego or the sense of being separate from others (*ahankar*). The layer farthest from the *atma* is the *sarir*.[4]

Ego Development

The Sikh scripture outlines two paths of human development: the path of ego reasoning (*manmat marg*) and the path of the spiritual (*gurmat marg*).[5] The first of these is pursued by everyone and can be equated with the Western conception of human development according to life stages. The *manmat marg* is described in the *Guru Granth Sahib* as having four quarters or phases: infancy, childhood/adolescence, adulthood, and old age.[6] These four phases are incorporated into the present analysis of human development and of the three generations.

During the infancy phase, the mind is not conscious of the *atma*. The infant's mind is oriented toward his or her survival needs, which are met initially through the mother's milk. As the infant is nourished with milk, he or she slowly begins to recognize the mother, father, siblings, and other family members as 'other.' The infant develops the sense that 'I am.' However, because the mother and father are so close, the infant remains connected to the parents through a collectivity orientation.

The child learns that he or she belongs to the parents. The parents regard the child as 'their' possession. The child thus begins to develop a sense of pride about belonging to a particular family and caste. As the child develops further, he or she explores the physical world and begins to experience sensual pleasures (visual beauty, musical sounds, tasty foods, fragrances, and sex). There is the possibility of indulgence in sensual pleasures during this phase. The need for sexual pleasure is described as one facet of the full-blooded young person, who is driven by poor judgment. It is believed that young people possess little wisdom and limited ability to concentrate because they are too preoccupied with the desire to experience the sensual pleasures. Even when they fast, visit holy places, or perform acts of piety, these acts are regarded as meaningless because the mind is not totally absorbed in these activities. During this phase it is rare for a young person to travel the path of spiritual wisdom (*gurmat marg*), because the mind has not been trained to focus inward; rather, it is fixed on external experiences.

In adulthood, people are occupied with fulfilling household responsibilities and roles. Adults perform the duties that are prescribed according to their particular familial roles, such as child, sibling, spouse, and parent. Duty (*dharam*) is performed with the intention of acquiring honour (*izzat*) in society. During early adulthood it is the householder's duty to accumulate wealth and acquire honour. However, at late adulthood there is a shift in thinking, so that material riches are no longer experienced as fulfilling. This shift in thinking is related to facing one's own mortality; as the body grows old and material wealth is no longer seen as fulfilling, people must face the wrongs they have perpetrated in the past. Misdeeds lead to feelings of guilt and remorse.

During old age, people are not fit to work, they are incapable of sensory pleasure, and they are approaching death. As in late adulthood, the body and mind are filled with one's *karam* – that is, the mental consequences of one's actions. The accumulation of negative actions leads to the mind being bound by guilt. Goodness and continence cultivated throughout life lead to peace of mind as death approaches. At the time of death, the soul either is liberated (*mukti*) or continues in the cycle of rebirth until it attains liberation in a subsequent life.

Spiritual Development

The second path of human development – *gurmat marg* – involves the attainment of spiritual wisdom and, ultimately, liberation.[7] The *gurmat marg* is the ideal religious path for householders striving to escape the cycle of rebirth (*sansar*), and it is adopted in conjunction with the path of personal development (*manmat marg*). There are five realms (*khand*) that one must move through in order to attain ultimate spiritual wisdom: righteousness (*dharam*), knowledge (*gian*), effort (*saram*), grace (*karam*), and truth (*sach*). Truth is the ultimate realization and experience that the *atma* is at the core of one's being. As this realization unfolds, the *atma* is liberated (*mukti*) from the cycle of birth and death, as it merges with the Supreme Universal Soul (*param-atma*). There is no longer the sense of the 'I' being separate from the 'other'; rather, there is the experience of unity with the all-pervasive Universal Soul. Few people take this spiritual path. The path of the ego (*manmat marg*) represents the basic Sikh theological understanding of human development.

The *Guru Granth Sahib* outlines the broad schema of human development; the *Sikh Rahit Maryada* (Sikh Code of Conduct) sets down specific prescriptions for Sikhs. It requires that Sikhs abide by the four rites of passage (*samskar*). The four ceremonies associated with these rites of passage are the key events in a Sikh's life. They are (1) the naming ceremony performed in the *gurdwara*, where a person randomly opens the *Guru Granth Sahib* and the first letter of the alphabet on the left-hand page becomes the first letter of the child's name; (2) 'baptism,' the receiving of holy water (*amrit*, literally 'nectar') as a mark of belonging to the Khalsa ('the pure' or 'the elect'); (3) the marriage ceremony; and (4) the death rite.[8]

The scriptural references to human development, especially ego development, are made in the broader context of the pursuit of salvation, but they also serve as an excellent description of the culture of family relations as it exists in the Sikh community. The following analysis below makes use of the scriptural references and relates them to each of the three generations of the Sikh community in Canada.

The First Generation and Its Authoritarian Approach

The first generation functions according to the traditional Punjabi values of duty and respect, though economic adaptation has changed the lifestyle of households. The first generation experiences a loss of economic control in Canada but continues to expect respect from other family members by virtue of its seniority. Likewise, the first generation has brought with it from the Punjab the traditional approaches to child rearing and personal development. For the first generation, child rearing consists of meeting the physiological and safety needs of the children and of instilling in them the traditional values of *dharam* and *izzat*; this involves an authoritarian approach to parenting. This approach is punitive and restrictive, with parents placing firm limits and controls on their children. Verbal exchange is often limited.

Traditional Attitude toward Child Rearing

In traditional society, the joint family is economically interdependent. The goal is to fulfil the needs, at the physiological and safety levels, of those who belong to the 'collective ego' or group. Parental love is expressed through the fulfilment of parental responsibilities, that is, by providing the necessities for survival in accordance with the values of *dharam* and *izzat* in the context of the collectivity. As described in the *Guru Granth Sahib*, the mother nourishes the totally dependent infant with milk.[9] The parents provide for the physiological needs (hunger, thirst, hygiene) and safety needs (protection from pain or danger) of the child.

Physiological and safety needs, and the traditional collective sense of belonging are the focus of the first generation. However, this generation rarely meets the two highest stages of Maslow's hierarchy of needs – esteem (the need to be a contributor to society) and self-actualization (the need to reach one's full potential).[10] Interestingly, the physiological and safety needs, and the traditional collective sense of belonging to a family, a clan, and a religion, correspond with the concrete and close-to-life-situation thought forms associated with the first generation's orality mode of thinking. By extension, the modern sense of belonging and the two higher levels of needs in Maslow's hierarchy – which are generally not attended to in traditional society (which focuses on the survival of the collectivity) – correspond to the analytics mode of thinking, which emphasizes abstraction and self-orientation.

The role of parents in traditional society is to provide for the physiological and safety needs of the children and to raise them so that they know and can fulfil their duties as they enter the householder (*grhasthi*) stage of life. The women are taught how to cook, clean, sew and care for their family members; the men are trained in a trade so that they can provide for the family. An eighty-year-old Sikh woman offered a humorous response regarding the traditional focus on rearing women, when she was asked about her level of education.

> *How much education did you receive?*
> I went to school. It was in the home [laughs]. Mother taught caring for the house to the kids. We learned how to cook, make clothing and the value of respect for the elders. We would sit down and the relatives came over and [mother] taught us to say the proper names. There was no school in the village. (Kaur 1.14, trans.)

Clearly, the first-generation women were raised according to tradition so that they would be able to fulfil their 'daughterly duties' in their childhood home and, even more, their 'wifely duties' after marriage. There was no decision to be made: *all* girls were raised to perform their household duties in the service of the collectivity. Similarly, men were raised to fulfil their duty to work on the farm or in a trade – usually the same trade as the father's – to provide for the household. The choice of work was often limited, especially if one was living in a village. Traditionally, one's trade was according to one's birth, with the trade being passed down by the respective elders (Singh 1.5, 1.9). However, some men did attend school to pursue other careers – most often to join the Indian army or take a government job (Singh 1.1, 1.6, 1.15).

In traditional Punjab, infants and young children are extended considerable attention and freedom, with the parents providing for their physiological and safety needs. Young children are indulged, but as they grow older they are subjected to many restrictions and are expected to meet the responsibilities placed on them. It is the general Indian practice to allow very young children to do what they want and then, as they grow older, to limit their freedom so that they learn to fulfil their duties to the collectivity. Controls are imposed on the children as they become adolescents and young adults in order to ensure that they contribute to the collectivity and behave according to cultural norms, such as obeying the commands of elders and not mixing at all with the opposite sex.

In contrast to all this, the Western pattern of child rearing, emphasizes self-orientation. It attends to the needs of the young, and tends to discipline children early in life regarding right and wrong. As children grow older, they are granted more and more freedom. These contrasting approaches to child rearing can raise serious problems among immigrant families in which children are raised traditionally. Young children are indulged according to tradition, yet at the time of adolescence controls are put upon them just at the time when the mainstream culture is beginning to grant adolescents greater freedom and personal choice.

During the youth phase, according to the *Guru Granth Sahib*, young people explore the external world and indulge in sensual pleasures.[11] In order to control young people's exploration of sensual pleasures, parents place restrictions and controls on their children during early adolescence. Also during this time, parents and grandparents guide their children so that they will know how to fulfil familial duties, especially for the married stage of life. Many grandparents of the first generation see themselves and the parents (i.e., their children) as crucial 'coaches' for the grandchildren. Traditionally, Sikh women have been less educated and less exposed to the world beyond the home than men; but at the same time, they have been the most responsible for raising the children, and thus have been the 'authorities' on child rearing. For instance, first-generation females have a lot more to say about child rearing than the males do (Kaur 1.8; 1.4; 1.3), and they emphasize their belief in the need for elders to guide children regarding the right way of living: 'Who is going to advise them [the children]? They have to learn the way children should behave ... When parents teach their children that these are their grandparents and they should respect them, then they learn. The best way is not to criticize the children. It is the duty of their grandparents also to teach their children to go on this path or that path' (Kaur 1.8, trans.). Even though the women have had more influence on child rearing, men also see themselves as their children's coaches. Indeed, 'coaching' reflects the authoritarian molding of children so that they will behave according to the traditional norms of *dharam* and *izzat*. A seventy-seven-year-old Sikh man had this to say about the role of grandparents and child rearing: 'I support the extended family ... A nuclear family suffers when both parents work and inexperienced babysitters watch children. The grandparents who are most experienced in life in the family, are put in isolation, which ruins their life. The children watch too much TV, parents are exhausted when they return from work, have to prepare meals and are tired ... Contrary to this, the extended family has privileges. They have the most experienced babysitters and coaches in the family to coach the younger generation' (Singh 1.1).

The first generation views the Western notion of individualism and self-orientation as a problem in rearing children. The first generation is unable to see the positive aspects of self-orientation. According to them, independence and individualism have a negative impact on the family. Sikhs of the first generation dislike the fact that the children are not responding to their orders (*hukam*) out of a sense of duty or respect. A seventy-one–year-old Sikh man stated that the family is deteriorating because of the notions of independence and individual rights:

Families are going down and it is not that far away for them to be washed away. People now say it is 'my own body,' you have nothing to do with me. The kids don't listen to anybody. They learn at school that 'you are your own boss.' But they forget about taking responsibility. Two to three cases respect elders but most of the kids do not. Often they respect if they want to get a lot out of you. Otherwise, they do not listen ... In India, the elders are at the top of everything and everything is in their name. Here, nothing is in their name. The elders also need to change their mind not to interfere in their kids' affairs. (Singh 1.15)

Because the children (third generation) are not responding to *hukam*, the first generation does not know how to deal with them; the first generation experiences a loss of respect from, and control over, their grandchildren (third generation).

The authoritarian approach, under which children are expected to follow the commands of superiors according to the traditional values of *dharam* and *izzat*, is losing ground in Canada's Sikh community. Members of the first generation as grandparents are exposed to Canadian child rearing practices – for the most part through their grandchildren – but it is really the second generation that directly and profoundly experiences, with their Canadian-born children, the dilemma of traditional child rearing in a modern setting.

In sum, the first generation emphasizes raising children according to the traditional values of duty and respect, but it understands these values only in concrete terms and in the context of a collectivity orientation. The first generation is unable to comprehend the notion of duty and respect in the context of the processes of self-differentiation and self-orientation that are associated with modern society.

The Second Generation and the Conflict in Its Traditional Approach

Like the first generation, the second generation remains rooted in tradition. For example, it is preoccupied with accumulating wealth during the householder stage (as dictated by tradition and referred to in the *Guru Granth Sahib*). However, wage employment and the experience of economic independence in Canada have allowed the second generation to distance itself somewhat from the collectivity. The second generation's partial (i.e., economic) adaptation to Canadian society has transformed the value of duty and respect; this is evident in the way in which it demands respect from its Canadian-born children on account of how hard it has worked to establish the modified extended family in Canada. Regardless of the lifestyle change and redefinition of values, the second generation continues to rear its children according to tradition. Even so, there is evidence that the second generation's approach to child rearing is changing as a consequence of its economic independence from elders, its growing fear of a loss of control over children, and its fear of children going off track.

Traditional Child Rearing in a Modern Milieu

The second generation has adapted to the Canadian lifestyle but has not adopted the host society's corresponding understanding of the processes of self-differentiation and self-actualization. Rather, the second generation continues to raise children in an authoritarian manner: young children are indulged with privilege and freedom; then, as they get older, their freedom is limited by the parents' expectations[12] that their children will fulfil their duties to the collectivity, and also by the controls placed on the children to ensure that adolescents and young adults will behave according to prescribed cultural norms (such as no mixing with the opposite sex).

The traditional, authoritarian approach to child development seeks to have children conform to the norms of duty within the context of the collectivity; in contrast, in modern society the approach is oriented toward the person, and children are considered to be undergoing a process of individuation. Under this latter approach, young people develop a sense of individuality and the capacity for 'connectedness.' For the purposes of this study, a sense of individuality can be defined as including (1) self-assertion (the ability to have and to communicate a point of view), and (2) a sense of separateness (the ability to perceive and to communicate how one is different from others). The capacity for connectedness is taken to encompass (1) mutual respect and sensitivity toward others, and (2) an openness to others.[13] Thus, the modern approach to child rearing is a differentiated one, in that parents encourage children to develop according to their individual abilities.

Many second-generation parents intellectually acknowledge the difficulties their children face in relation to living in a traditional home and yet learning the values of a different culture at school. Some of them even recognize that they must adjust their ways to Canadian society. Even so, it is difficult for them to adapt because their traditional values are so ingrained. A Sikh man of fifty told me that he still fears for his daughter's safety as if he were in the Punjab: 'Traditionally, one has daughters at home until they get married. I am aware that some women can't pursue their careers here as much because they are not allowed to leave the city before marriage. We have to realize that we are not in Punjabi villages. Here, there is [fear of] rape even among the whites ... but rape is the big fear in the Punjab. We parents still have this fear. We need to learn that daughters can learn to take care of themselves more here. It is hard because the fear is still in us' (Singh 2.14).

Here, the father is expressing difficulty in adjusting to the different social and cultural situation in Canada with regard to his duty to protect his daughter. It is hard for such parents to adapt to the social and cultural ways of Canadian society; one can only imagine how difficult they find it to comprehend, let alone attend to, the emotional needs of children relating to self-orientation and independence.

As it encounters consumerism and a higher standard of living, the second generation in Canada has generally translated providing 'all that one can' for the children into simply the giving of material goods, such as good clothes, a big house, and a luxury car. As described in the *Guru Granth Sahib*, the adulthood phase is marked by the desire to possess wealth for *izzat* in the community.[14] According to the second generation, this honour from material goods is 'all that one can do' for the children. Second-generation parents have the capacity to satisfy the physiological and safety needs of their children; it does not necessarily follow that they are familiar with the higher levels of human needs (esteem and self-actualization) and thus able to move toward them. Many second-generation parents provide the basic needs that are familiar to them from their traditional Punjabi background – needs that are articulated and comprehended in concrete and close-to-life-situation thought forms which correspond to the literacy mode of thinking. Important to note here is that the individual sense of belonging and the last two stages of Maslow's hierarchy of needs – esteem and self-actualization[15] – correspond to the abstract thinking and self-orientation associated with analytics. Thus, the last two stages of Maslow's hierarchy tend to be absent in the second generation's literacy mode of thinking. Perhaps the second generation's lack of emotional attention (for a self-orientation) to third-generation children is a result of the second generation not being accustomed to providing it, or perhaps that generation simply does not have enough time to provide it. Which ever the case, the problem with child rearing in the Sikh community is most prominently voiced as a lack of 'communication.' A forty-seven-year-old Sikh woman discussed this problem:

Every family has to communicate with the kids. I think in the ten houses on my street, the parents do not communicate with their kids. Parents are like birds from a cage. When they left India they thought they were freed to a place of good fortune ... The kids are not trained because parents don't have the time. The children are left on their own. Parents give them the money, car, credit card, and so on. Parents need to spend time with their kids. Both parents are working, going to parties, and then are tired when they return home from work. Kids, as a result, go with the flow. (Kaur 2.18)

When parents are busy working, they are able to provide the children with food, clothing, and shelter, but they are not around to communicate with or attend to their children's emotional needs. Regardless, second-generation parents feel that their hard work is, in fact, taken for granted. A frequent comment made by second-generation interviewees regarding their children is that they do not realize how hard their parents have had to work (Singh 2.4, 2.5; Kaur 2.6, 2.13, 2.18, 2.19). Indeed, several stated that the children simply take it for granted – for example, this forty-eight-year-old Sikh woman: 'I feel they [my kids] don't realize how hard parents work and how hard it is to be in the world. They take things for granted. We worked hard to build something. They take it easy' (Kaur 2.6).

The second generation believes that their children have it easy – or at least easier than they had it. It was the parents, after all, who took on the task of establishing the family in Canada. Second-generation parents cater to the physiological and safety needs of their children, but they do not at the same time encourage the children to explore the world outside of their role in the collectivity of the household. Note the response of a forty-eight-year-old Sikh woman: 'Kids are dependent on parents, and they want them to give the house to them [kids]. In Canada, parents have money and are independent ... The typical parents indulge and spoil their son, and make him go against his wife' (Kaur 2.19). Third-generation children, especially sons, are provided with a comfortable lifestyle by economically independent parents, who see this as a means of keeping sons within the household (under the control of the parents) and thereby acquiring *izzat* in the community.

The authoritarian approach to child rearing – especially during the adolescent and early adulthood phases – is not working in Canada in the way that the second generation remembers it did in the Punjab. A change is occurring in the capacity of second-generation parents to discipline children, who are often simply asked to follow the orders (*hukam*) of the elders in the collectivity. According to the second generation, the cultural barrier is a result of Western notions of individualism and independence. Those of the second generation, like those of the first, express a dislike of the modern propensity to 'centralize' the individual. Note the response made by a Sikh man of fifty-six-years: 'The culture wants individuality, independence, and is selfish. Everyone is working here where there is no time. It is totally different from village life. I believe that there is more family conflict here because there is more personality/individual conflict here. I believe that things are changing with other communities, not just Sikh, and that it is happening all over the world. Western values are all over and are affecting the family' (Singh 2.1).

The second generation often expresses frustration at not being able to understand its children, especially during their high school and college years. Importantly, the very concept of teenage years – often viewed as a time of rebellion against parents, during which children undergo the processes of self-differentiation and ego formation – is a modern one that is altogether absent from the traditional mentality. For example, the *Guru Granth Sahib* discusses childhood and adolescence as part of the same developmental phase rather that as two separate phases.[16] Indeed, the developmental phase of identity formation does not hold in Indian culture, nor does the adolescent stage.[17]

Recently enacted child protection laws make it difficult for parents in Canada to discipline their children. These laws are seen by second-generation Sikhs as having completely undermined the traditional Punjabi approach to child rearing by which the old have always exercised control over the young. Parents no longer have the social support of collective controls as their children reach adolescence and early adulthood: 'Nowadays the children want freedom. Before, we had to comply with rules, now there is the rule that a parent is not allowed to hit the kid. Fear is gone from the younger generation.' (Kaur 2.18). Fundamentally, the tension between the second and third generations is related to the opposition between the traditional Indian value of duty and the Canadian emphasis on rights.

The clash between traditional notions of duty (or responsibility) and equal rights for individuals is a real problem and concern for parents (even for non-Sikh ones). But in the case of second-generation parents, there is an added cultural dimension in that they have brought with them to Canada their traditional value system and practices, from which arise specific cultural barriers. One such cultural barrier is that because the traditional (and second-generation) approach to child rearing is to establish collective controls only later on in the child's life, a contradiction arises in disciplining children in a modern context. The pattern in modern culture is that children are taught right from wrong during their formative years, so that they have internalized it by the time they gain independence in young adulthood. The Western approach is to give children freedom as they reach early adulthood; by then they have acquired self-orientation and internalized self-control. A modern society does not provide the collectivity's external control over people, such as exists in a village. (In its place, however, is the legal system, see chapter 6).

Furthermore, second-generation parents believe that by maintaining economic control – by providing material abundance to the children as part of their 'altered' traditional authoritarian approach to child rearing – they are ensuring that their children will do their part for the family in maintaining *izzat*, a value which requires the children to remain in the home. Thus, the third-generation children have not had the guidance or emotional space to fully develop a self-orientation with internalized controls; yet at the same time they have to function in an environment where external controls and authoritarian approaches cannot work effectively.

Instead of embracing the modern approach to child rearing – which includes attending to the emotional needs of the children as they develop within a modern milieu that is oriented toward the individual – second-generation parents adhere to the tradition of respect and authority, a tradition rooted in economic control and seniority. When they themselves were children, members of the second generation feared the traditional authority of their parents and grandparents; now, as parents, they fear the loss of control over their own children.

Fear of Loss of Control

Second-generation parents continue to provide for the basic material needs of their children in accordance with tradition; in Canada, in fact, they have increased their provision of such needs, fearing that their children will leave the collectivity and escape parental control. Under the *Guru Granth Sahib*, parents regard the child as 'their' possession who will bring honour to the family.[18] The fear that children will leave home is very strong among parents because their doing so would break with family tradition and bring dishonour to the family. Indeed, for many second-generation parents, the highest value is *izzat*.

Second-generation parents' fear of losing control over their children in the context of their collectivity orientation is often expressed as concern that their children will become 'Westernized,' which is defined to include dating, partying, travelling, and/or living without the company of family elders. A corollary of this fear is that children who begin engaging in Western social activities run the risk of going off track into alcohol and drug abuse. The pervasiveness of this fear was expressed by a forty-two-year-old Sikh woman: 'Important to me is whether kids are on the right track. I feel okay if they are on the right track with job and not on drugs. If in drugs then I feel very bad. I am very worried about drugs and want to know my children's friends' (Kaur 2.13).

A consequence of the second generation's fear of its children going off track is that the parents place many restrictions on their children. Many of the second generation acknowledge that it is not good to pressure the children 'too much,' because doing so can have repercussions (for example, the children will leave home). Even so, parents place many restrictions on their children, especially the daughters (see 'Experience of the Double Standard,' below). The children, of course, see this as overprotectiveness. Note the response of a Sikh woman of forty-nine: 'I do not have much problem with the kids. But they say [that] if I put too many restrictions on them I am 'overprotecting' them. I know that the Indian kids are overprotected' (Kaur 2.12).

Another Sikh woman had a son who, although not *amritdhari*, cut his hair as a form of rebellion so that he would not miss out on the social scene. The son's act of cutting his hair was a dilemma for the mother and for the family as a whole, yet she nevertheless stated: 'I have a *gurdwara* at home. I am *amritdhari*. I raise [the] kids with religion, but [the] children are not *amritdhari*. I don't believe in pressuring kids although [I] would like to see them religious' (Kaur 2.19).

Many parents who are baptized (*amritdhari*) fear that their baptized children will discard the five *kakars* and live according to a more secular lifestyle, which they also perceive as going off track. In particular, they fear a secular lifestyle will inevitably lead to involvement with drugs (see 'The Making of a GGB,' below).

Even though second-generation parents fear that their children will go off track, there is only limited communication between parents and children. This situation worsens the parent child dynamic, especially because of the increase in the emotional needs of the children that is typically associated with modernity. Consider the response of a Sikh woman who teaches at a Punjabi school: 'Kids are afraid of religion taking away the fun of partying and drinking. Kids don't have the desire to learn because they are exposed to fun things. Parents are also not taking responsibility. Many kids are sent to [...] School for religious teaching and then parents feel they don't have to do anything about it.

There is a lack of communication. Parents don't talk openly with kids. Kids are not feeling proud of who they are' (Kaur 2.16).

Although the understanding of 'feeling proud of who they are' may be subjective and variously defined, the above quotation does point to a crucial issue regarding child rearing and the lack of communication between the second and third generations. The communication barrier between the second and third generations is recognized by the third generation as a cultural one.

In sum, the second generation's traditional mentality remains largely intact. Although the second generation has experienced the effects of economic independence within the family household, it has not accepted the corresponding modern values of egalitarianism and self-orientation and therefore does not raise its children in accordance with those values. Even as the second generation continues to raise its children according to tradition, there is some change in its authoritarian approach, related mainly to the fear of loss of control over the children. Second-generation parents are providing more material goods to meet the physiological and safety needs of their children in order to maintain control over the household in an environment marked by economic independence. Yet they seem for the most part unable to satisfy the emotional requirements for children's personal development – a task more suited to the analytics mode of thinking.

The Third Generation and Its Double Life

Having been influenced by their modern environment, members of the third generation *seek mutual respect* on the basis that they are human individuals with their own ideas, opinions, and feelings. Even while their modern environment influences them, third-generation Canadian-born Sikh children experience, through parental expectations, the pressure to conform to traditional norms. This gives rise to contradictory normative pressures. Contrary to the traditional norms of personal development, third-generation children require more emotional attention in their personal development; this is often expressed in terms of the need for enhanced and more frequent communication between parents and children.

Confronted by the tension between modern society and traditional, uncommunicative parents, third-generation children often cope by living a double life. An extreme example of the consequences of communication breakdown *vis-à-vis* the third generation relates to children who go off track within the community, especially with regard to the phenomenon of the Giani Gone Bad (GGB). This phenomenon provides significant insights into the gap between the second and third generations of Canada's Sikh community with respect to child rearing and personal development.

Pressure of Parental Expectations

Having been raised by second-generation parents according to the Indian traditions of *dharam* and *izzat*, children of the third generation experience the 'pressure' or 'expectation' to live according to the traditional preferences of the parents in order to bring honour to the family. Second-generation parents expect their children to be fit for married life by their early twenties. Many members of the third generation perceive that their personal talents or preferences are not acknowledged, let alone considered, when career choices are being made. Some children are encouraged to 'hurry up' with, or not receive, postsecondary education in order to earn money (by taking a short college program or working on a parents' farm or driving a truck bought by the family). Some children from working-class families are not encouraged to pursue post secondary education; others are pressured to acquire a university education for a career that is both prestigious and well-paying.

In the case of third-generation Sikh males, there is pressure to pursue certain careers for reasons of higher income and status. An example of this is the response given by a nineteen-year-old Sikh man about choosing a career:

> There is pressure to pursue prestigious careers like law, medicine, or engineering. There is also the pressure to study quickly so that you get a job as soon as you can earn money. The pressure is about earning money. Parents think mostly of economics, which has been the main reason for coming and the burden when they came. My father is waiting for me to get a job so that he can retire, even though he has a lot of money. Me and my friends talk about wanting to enjoy ourselves with outdoor activities or travelling before we get married and have a lot of responsibilities with a job, kids, and so on. I feel the pressures to settle down are too strong, not allowing us time to enjoy and develop. Some don't care or have a thought about it, but some want to experience more before taking on responsibilities. [On the other hand,] unlike the white Canadians, I have the security of staying at home. (Singh 3.10)

This quotation refers to the pressure to pursue specific careers and to get jobs quickly; it also demonstrates the desire on the part of the third generation to explore and experience life before marrying and settling down.

Third-generation men also experience considerable pressure as 'sons' to remain home even after marriage in order to care for their parents in old age. This custom is of primary importance for the parents, since it brings great honour to the family. An illustration of this was provided by a Sikh man of twenty-seven: 'My father wants me to live with him; he feels disgraced that his sons are not living under his roof. My father does not support me with what I want to do. Punjabi parents don't pay attention to whether you are good or bad as much as they do to their concern of whether you are living with them' (Singh 3.14).

A great deal of pressure is placed on third-generation Sikh women to marry a suitable partner while they are in their early twenties. Many Canadian-born Sikh women belonging to the third generation are made to feel like failures if they are not married by twenty-five. Parents fear that their daughters may get into romantic relationships with men before marriage. If a daughter were ever to get into such a relationship, it would be a great disgrace for both her and the family. So it is imperative for traditional second-generation parents to marry their girls early.

The focus on marriage has left several women feeling that there is a double standard: they are not allowed to develop to their full career potential. A Sikh woman of twenty-four commented: 'There is a double standard with expectations between boys and girls. Even though I do not drink, I do not like the idea that boys get away with it more than girls. A lot of emphasis is related to girl's sexuality and keeping her virginity for marriage. This is not fair because I may want to do things that are not related to sex. Things are to begin after marriage only. In childhood, father is responsible, then the husband. I do not want to get married now. I want to focus on developing my career' (Kaur 3.2).

Experience of the Double Standard

As discussed in the previous section on the second generation, women are under greater pressure to conform to traditional norms: meeting household responsibilities, serving others in the parental household, marrying young, not socializing the way Punjabi males and other non-

Punjabi females do. With regard to gender role socialization, Talbani and Hasanali had found that the traditional gender roles were maintained among South Asian adolescent females through gender segregation, control over girls' social activities, and arranged marriage.[19] Similarly, during the present study I found that many third-generation Sikh females feel that they are subject to a double standard: their brothers have no household responsibilities, face less pressure to marry, and enjoy more freedom to go out of the home (Kaur 3.2, 3.9, 3.18, 3.23, 3.25, 3.27, 3.32, 3.35).

Many third-generation women are pressured to quickly earn a post-secondary certificate or diploma so as to be employable 'sooner rather than later.' This makes women more marriageable, since they will be able to bring an income into the household; furthermore, a short diploma program means that education will not interfere with women marrying in their early twenties. Too much education for girls is frowned upon, since it is perceived as delaying their marriage.

Third-generation men generally enjoy more flexibility regarding how soon they get married (since they have careers to pursue) and also regarding the social activities in which they engage. In contrast, third-generation women are often raised according to the traditional notion that marriage is the beginning of one's life – that life only begins after marriage. It is no surprise that they object to this notion. A twenty-three-year-old Sikh woman said that girls should be raised to pursue more than just marriage: 'I don't think it is good to keep raising girls believing that marriage is the central, and only thing, to life – they should be encouraged to pursue studies, career. There is a big issue for women in that the husband expects her to live with the in-laws. Many men are not even aware of the issue for females. I am pretty much against the issue of living with one's in-laws. It made sense in farming culture but here it does not' (Kaur 3.23). Parents are concerned about their children being prepared for marriage. Also they pressure their children, especially their daughters, to conform to traditional norms of behaviour, particularly with regard to engaging in 'Western' social activities.

Interestingly, not only the women but some men of the third generation believe that Sikh women are not being allowed to reach their full potential (Singh 3.14, 3.24; Kaur 3.2, 3.9, 3.18, 3.22, 3. 23, 3.25, 3.27, 3.32). They attribute this in part to the pressure women face to marry early in adult life. One Sikh woman of twenty-two remarked: 'A lot of Sikh women are not allowed to go away to study, [thus] hindering their chances of pursuing a career. The emphasis is to marry and not to leave parents until then. The women have to marry young before they get 'ideas' from school. The elders feel that it is a threat for women to study [and that] the women need to be molded by their in-laws ... I have agreed to marry during my studies if I meet the right guy. A real fear or concern of the girls is about the ability to pursue one's career once they are married' (Kaur 3.9).

By tradition, women are not allowed to live on their own away from their parents before they have married into another household. The young woman just cited was going to move to another Canadian city for her studies; however, she explained, her parents were allowing her to do so only because her brother was already living in the same city. Otherwise, she believed, her parents would not have allowed it. The issue of not being able to live on one's own is of particular importance to many third-generation women (Kaur 3.2, 3.7, 3.18, 3.19, 3.23, 3.27, 3.32), especially as it relates to career pursuits. A twenty-three year old Sikh woman believed that her pursuit of a career was being hindered by the ultimate concern of her parents – marriage: 'Girls' careers are affected because it is a big issue for girls to leave the city. It is a huge deal to not live with parents until marriage. Girls are not reaching their goals' (Kaur 3.23).

Interestingly, this concern about the careers of younger women was felt even by an eighty-year-old Sikh woman, who herself had had no choice about receiving an education, since in her village girls did not go to school: 'The home will always be there, but the time to learn is not always going to be there ... To let the opportunity go is to let the fruit rot. When it is ripe, you have to take advantage of it. The parents have ruined her life by not letting her go to school. A parent is doing a disservice to a child by making her think that life is only about marriage. Without going to school, the girl does not develop [the requisite] qualities, and without those qualities the girl becomes a slave to her in-laws. This is what I have seen in my life' (Kaur 1.14, trans.).

According to this first-generation Sikh woman, it is important for girls to develop at school the necessary qualities for life. School is where they build character, and where they learn to stand up for themselves and to be economically independent (even as they simultaneously practise traditional customs, such as staying at home before marriage and respecting and serving the elders).

Double Life and Role Playing

Some scholars, such as Kamaljit Sidhu, contend that the younger generations do not see the host culture and their own ethnic culture as in conflict and that they are successfully integrating the two.[20] In an attempt to construct a model for adolescent development and identity formation among Sikhs, Sidhu focuses on the traditional Punjabi-Sikh ideal, and contrasts it with 'going off track.' But instead of analysing the pertinent issues faced by young Sikhs regarding development and the problems that arise from their going off track, her study asks questions of adolescent Sikhs about internalizing their culture's religion and spirituality. The drawback to this approach is that most adolescents do not understand religion and spirituality (unless religious 'awareness' refers exclusively to external practices, such as the bearing of the five *kakars*). Guru Ram Das himself warns that young people's comprehension of religion and *gurmat* is limited.[21] The present study found that as a result of parents' pressure to conform to traditional norms, children ended up living double lives and playing roles.

It is common in Western society for teenagers to hide some of their involvements from their parents. That said, the third generation's practice of leading a double life is a special coping mechanism for dealing with the pressure to conform to parental expectations of staying true to Punjabi or Sikh tradition on the one hand, and on the other hand the peer pressure it faces at school and in society at large. Many of the third generation, having been raised in Canada, want to participate in the social activities to which they are exposed, but live in fear of how their parents will react. Thus, to cope with the tension, many of them lead double lives, and hide from their outside life. A nineteen-year-old Sikh woman discussed this: 'Many have a double life. My parents, for Punjabi parents, are lenient, but even so I hide the fact that I have a boyfriend. I think I can tell them in two years ... I still keep things from them. I lie about what I am doing, like going to bars, drinking, smoking. Many of my friends lead double lives and hide the things they are doing – dating, drinking, smoking, clubbing, and going to parties' (Kaur 3.7).

Many third-generation women play the role of the 'dutiful' daughter while inside the home – dressing modestly, not wearing makeup, having a modest hairstyle, and so on. But when they leave the house, they change their clothes in the bathrooms of colleges, universities, even shopping malls. A twenty-seven-year-old Sikh man observed: 'Many women live a double life. They leave their house with their hair in a bun and then go to college and change their clothes and let their hair down.' (Singh 3.14).

A Sikh man who had engaged in rebellious-defiant behaviour discussed the double life that the third generation lives: 'Kids grow up and go to the *gurdwara* but see cars, clothes, education handed over to them. Kids get everything – mother gives love through things. Kids are living a double life ... Changing clothes at school is little, there are bigger things [they are] hiding – going to nightclubs. It is comfort zone for the kids and difficult to get out. Hard to get out of that [material comfort]. Parents and kids say it is "like India"' (Singh 3.37).

As noted earlier, some third-generation children may be afraid of losing the comforts their parents provide; others may be afraid to stand up for themselves. In either case, children – both men and women – play roles in order to maintain good ties with their parents for the sake of the smooth functioning of the modified extended family, even while seeking at the same time a more Western social life, which they hide. The former behaviour is governed by the custom of *izzat*, which results in the tendency to hide problems within the family to save face; the latter behaviour is governed by self-orientation, which requires communication for 'personal' development. Leading a double life and playing the role of the 'dutiful' child is a coping mechanism used by the third generation to deal with the tension between traditional expectations (in the home) and Western culture (in the schools and society). This practice has psychological repercussions, such as emotional distress. As communication between children and parents breaks down, alienation grows.

According to modern psychologists like Erik Erikson, adolescent psychological development involves building ego-identity and proceeding through the individuation process.[22] Third-generation Sikh children are being encouraged to maintain the traditional values of the family within a collectivity orientation even while they are living and functioning in a modern environment that is oriented to the individual. The double life as a coping mechanism arises from the dense communication barrier that exists between many second-generation parents and their third-generation children. This barrier rises early in the lives of Sikh children. As a result, many are unable to discuss pertinent issues with their parents.

Communication Barriers

Communication barriers are the main source of tension between the second and third generations. Because the general tendency among the third generation is toward the analytics mode of thinking, that generation is better able to comprehend abstract notions and issues at the psychological level. Thus, it is better able to precisely articulate its needs regarding communication with the second generation.

The most pertinent communication barrier experienced by the third generation relates to issues beyond the concerns of daily living. Parents in the traditional Sikh community do not discuss many things with their children as individuals beyond matters of daily living and the norm of *izzat*. A third-generation Sikh male observed:

> There is no communication with the younger generation. It may differ in degree in different houses. If you do what a father does not like, you will get hit. Once I saw a car accident, and had to give information to the police. My father saw the accident site, the police, and me. He just hit me. He did not ask what happened before hitting me. He asked me after hitting me, 'What happened?' I said, 'Why does it matter? You have already hit me.' One has to do what the parent says. He did not say sorry. Nothing is discussed. The issue of emotions or trust does not exist between parent and child. After a struggle ... I feel I have cultivated trust with my parents, but they still tell me what to do at home' (Singh 3.38).

Many parents take an authoritarian approach to child rearing and discipline their children without communicating with them as individuals with self-orientation – a concept that is foreign to the traditional mind. Parents have limited communication with their children – beyond concrete issues of daily life – and they are also distrustful. The third generation had a great deal to tell me about trust not being an integral aspect of parent child relations in Sikh families. Several third-generation members told me that parents don't even have a concept of what trust is, in the context of parent and child:

> Adults keep control rather than trust. There is always the external keeping an eye on kids. I tried discussing this with my parents but they defend themselves to death. Father controls the house and he does not believe that girls can leave the house before marriage. It has been a long struggle for me, even more for my older sister who had to start breaking the barriers. Trust is not their way of thinking. It is co-existence in the home, everyone has to do their role. When I was young I had natural trust in my parents in depending on them, but then in grade five or so it disappeared,

when they were probing me about talking with boys. Kids rebel or [they are] not strong enough to speak against it. Kids can change it with their family. But mostly a lot of them do not because they are weak to speak about it. (Kaur 3.23)

Likewise, another Sikh woman commented on the issue of trust:

My *dadiji* [father's mother] believes girls should not go anywhere on their own. There is no trust with my father. Trust is something parents don't understand. The issue of trust is foreign to them. The emphasis is on role fulfilment. I feel my mother trusts me, except when she is pressured by my father to inquire about my whereabouts. (Kaur 3.27)

Another consequence of parents' traditional methods of rearing children is that the children are not given the emotional attention or support they require for personal development. Parents discipline children without deliberately guiding them to reach their full potential as individuals. The lack of attention to the psycho-social needs of third-generation children was most clearly expressed by a Sikh woman, when she spoke of a friend who committed suicide even after her friends had warned the girl's parents that she might: 'I had a friend who committed suicide one year after having had an arranged marriage at the age of nineteen years. Her husband came from India and was very possessive, not allowing her to be sociable with others, wear makeup. Her friends tried to talk with her parents and family, but people had the attitude that you put up with it – old-school mentality. She hanged herself in her shop with a letter. Her parents came out and asked what had happened. I was very angry because the problem was discussed by the family only when it was too late. (Kaur 3.18)

The lack of communication between parents and children results in the neglect of emotional issues in personal development. Many of the third generation are not encouraged in their psycho-social development. Parents' concerns are dictated by tradition, with the emphasis on looking good for family *izzat*. Since the tradition of *izzat* dictates what is right or wrong for second-generation parents, the notion of helping their children internalizing values so as to develop independent decision-making (self-assertion) is absent from parent/child relationships. A third-generation Sikh mother of two children discussed the consequences for the younger generation of being raised in the traditional way in Canada:

I want to raise my kids with values knowing right from wrong ... Women do not have the ability to make decisions; they are wishy-washy. Then, when away from home and out of the control of parents, they go to the other extreme, for example, drinking ... I went to [...] with fifteen girls – it was an eye opener: Some did not return for the night. When they returned late the next morning they came back with guilt and played virgin. One was married. They went out with strangers ... The ones who stayed home shunned the girls who returned the next day – playing the role of mother and martyr. The girls do not have a sense of boundaries. They just go to the extreme when they are away from parents. This is not freedom! I have a cousin and her parents trust her. She is not a slut because she has a sense of her parents' trust. She is 'good' because there is trust and she won't get into trouble. There is really not much trust in families. Then there are no boundaries for the kids when they get away and the girls become very promiscuous. (Kaur 3.25)

Many of the interviewees stated that they were not against traditional values, such as caring for elders; rather, care and respect are things that should come from the heart. They should not be about the honour of the family or the demands of role-playing (Singh 3.14, 3.16, 3. 24; Kaur 3.7, 3.18, 3.20, 3.25. 3. 27): 'I don't think reverence [caring for elders] is really being practised. Rather, kids keep the parents for help like babysitting. They don't really feel a big responsibility for parents. The feeling of caring for elders should be internalized. There are only a few [who do that]. Most people don't really internalize the true values' (Kaur 3.20).

Those of the third generation seek respect as individuals. They want to be able to develop as individuals with feelings, with independent ideas, with the capacity to make decisions. But too often there is limited communication between parent and child, so that such development is not encouraged. At times, a consequence of communication breakdown is that children go off track, especially in the case of the GGBs ('Gianis Gone Bad').

The Making of a 'Giani Gone Bad'

Giani literally means 'the one who possesses knowledge,' and refers to a Sikh priest or scholar. In the mid-1990s in Vancouver, increasing numbers of baptized Sikh youth (mainly males) were discarding the five *kakars* and living a more secular lifestyle. These youths were not priests or scholars, but they jokingly referred to themselves as GGBs.

These Canadian-born Sikhs had chosen to become 'secular' as a reaction against being raised according to strict tradition while situated in a modern environment. The GGBs were rebelling against their orthodox Sikh upbringing; many of them even got involved in drug-related activities. The process of the making of a Giani Gone Bad (GGB) provides insights into the gap between the second and third generations of the Sikh community in Canada with regard to child rearing and personal development.

Sikh 'unorthodoxy' is not a new phenomenon. It can be traced back to the colonial era in the Punjab, when the Sikhs came into contact with Western science and thought. This exposure led many young Sikhs to question their traditional system of values and beliefs.[23]

The encounter with Western values caused many young Sikhs to loosen their emotional ties to Sikh values and customs (such as bearing the five *kakars*) because they did not correspond to more modern ones (such as the value of reason and the scientific method) and to the secular lifestyle they desire. These educated youth evolved toward secularism, in a four-stage process: (1) they came to doubt their traditional religious values; (2) they spent less time participating in religious ceremonies and more time being entertained by the radio and movies; (3) they manipulated or trimmed their facial hair; and, lastly, (4) they shaved and cut their hair. Exposure to the modern, secular world view through education had a broad impact on the Sikh youth; that said, the crudest indicator of unorthodoxy related to the manipulation or trimming of facial hair. Initially, men used facial hair-fixers, nets, and other kit to make the facial hair look more 'boyish' or handsome; some also trimmed the beard and moustache. The culture generally turns a blind eye to the manipulation and trimming of facial hair; the complete shaving of facial hair immediately marks a Sikh man as an apostate.[24]

During the early period of Sikh immigration to Canada (the early 1900s), many young Sikhs moved toward secularism. Before immigrating, most of them had been growing their hair since birth and had worn turbans. Unlike some of the educated young Sikhs in the Punjab who questioned their traditional beliefs, Sikhs in Canada cut their hair mainly in order to find employment in a racially intolerant society. Employers preferred clean-shaven workers. Also, Sikh men found it difficult to maintain full-grown hair while working outdoors in British Columbia. For example, Sikh men working on the railways or in logging and mining camps did not have the facilities and the hot sun to wash and dry their long hair.

Furthermore, turbaned Sikhs often suffered racial slurs and violence. Many young Sikhs who wore turbans to school often returned home with their turban in their hands and their hair down after been bullied at school. Thus, many Sikh youth cut their hair in order to integrate more easily into mainstream society. Unlike young Sikhs during colonial rule in India, when unorthodoxy was influenced by Western thought, the Sikh youth during the early immigration to Canada opted for secularism in order to overcome employment restrictions and/or racism.

At first blush, one could argue that secularism arose among early Sikh immigrants because life in Canada led to contact with Western science and thought. In reality, these Sikhs did not go to school, as did their fellow Sikhs in India. Many early Sikh immigrants, on arrival in Canada, began working in sawmills, in part because their families needed money and in part because the language barrier was a major obstacle to obtaining education. Essentially, early Sikh immigrants were labourers and lacked the opportunity to enter the education system. Generally, their access to education was as limited in Canada as it was in rural Punjab.

Only in the 1960s and 1970s did Sikhs begin entering postsecondary institutions. Having done so, they encountered and embraced some of the values of Western scientific thought. The resulting drift toward secularism parallels the earlier drift that took place in British and post-British India. For example, in the late 1970s one Canadian Sikh youth went to university in Michigan to complete an engineering degree. According to his father, as he integrated himself into Western society he lost his 'grain' of Eastern integrity – that is, he became like the Western youth and shaved his beard and cut his hair.[25] Like the educated Sikh youth in India, many Canadian Sikh youth have taken on the Western secular lifestyle after interacting with, and adapting to, Western schools.

Today's third generation is attracted to secularism for different reasons than were the earlier Sikh immigrants to Canada. Unlike the early immigrants, who became unorthodox as a response to poor living conditions and discrimination, third-generation Canadian-born Sikhs are rejecting orthodoxy in order to enter more easily the Western (i.e., secular) lifestyle. At the same time, ironically, these third-generation Sikhs are showing considerable interest in the teachings of Sikhism. Many GGBs openly declare that they would like to learn more about Sikhism and that they want to follow a religious path when they get older.

What, then, drives some Sikhs to become GBBs? In part, GGBs are a product of the clash between the traditional and modern approaches to child rearing and development. GGBs have baptized parents, and most of them were baptized and received the five *kakars* while still in elementary school. Their parents have the mode of thinking associated with orality or literacy, and take a collective approach to life in which religion is mainly ritualistic and symbolic in character. Thus, second-generation parents tend to focus mainly on their third-generation children maintaining the religious symbols (i.e., *kakars*) and performing the religious rituals (i.e., going to the *gurdwara*). (The role of religion among the three generations is discussed in more detail in chapter 5.) Second-generation parents emphasize the external dimensions of the religion rather than the internal ones – such as the religious or spiritual values taught in the *Guru Granth Sahib*. This approach is rooted in their desire to acquire *izzat* in the community. As one third-generation Sikh man put it:

A lot of parents force it [religion, orthodoxy, externals of the religion] on their kids because they have to keep up their reputation. Forcing religion on the kids backfires in every family. Parents need to know how to introduce religion to the kids in a proper way, that is, give enough freedom, teach the kids right from wrong and then bring religion into the picture instead of teaching religion and then the kids can't explore. It gets the kids into trouble and haunts them mentally. It depends on how the kids are brought up and how close the kids are – if parents have respect for the kids, then the kids will have respect for the parents. (Singh 3.26)

The parents desire family honour, and this leads them to force the externals of their religion on their children and to do so in a collective, authoritarian manner. The children of second-generation parents who are baptized (*amritdhari*) often experience greater expectations. They are pressured to conform to Sikh religious orthodoxy; as a result, during their adolescent and early adult years, they face tension between trying to please their parents and wanting to have fun with friends (partying and drinking). Thus, children raised in orthodox families often experience tension and anxiety, especially as they enter adolescence.

It is usually not until puberty that Sikh children actually realize that they are different from others. Despite their orthodox appearance, Sikh children participate in the same childhood activities as their Canadian counterparts. For example, baptized Sikh children participate in sports, birthday parties, theme parks, and the like. However, during adolescence the social activities change to dating and partying, in which Sikh children – and even more so, baptized Sikh children – are not allowed to take part. The peer pressure to participate in adolescent social activities like these fosters feelings of alienation from mainstream society and from their own community. As discussed earlier, many third-generation children cope by leading a double life.

The feeling of being different from others is further strengthened among baptized Sikhs because they have to bear the five *kakars*, especially *kesh* 'covered hair,' which they are not supposed to cut or trim. In adolescent social circles, the five *kakars* and the religious rituals are not seen as 'cool.' It is important to note also that baptized children feel unaccepted even by those Sikh youth who do not maintain the five *kakars*. Essentially, they feel like a 'minority within a minority.' A 20-year-old Sikh man who was raised by baptized parents, and who continues to bear the five *kakars*, commented: 'If you go out with friends, booze and smoking is the norm. Because I don't drink or smoke, people bug me. But I am strong. I can stick up for myself. But it sucks when Punjabi girls look at guys with turbans as not cool to date' (Singh 3.39). The peer pressure to follow fashion trends and to participate in adolescent social activities leads to feelings of anxiety and alienation, not only from mainstream society but also from their own Punjabi community.

As baptized children experience anxiety and alienation from being unable to gain acceptance from peers, they consider integrating themselves into mainstream society so that they can experience the prevailing adolescent social lifestyle: '[The] kids are caged up. So fears get big when they grow up. Parents want to mold their kids ... The goals are set up for you. The parents plan life for kids. Younger generation is doing their things behind their backs – smoking and drinking. [There is] too much confusion for kids to handle – confusion between home, school and society. They don't get guidance at home. The younger generation cope with alcohol – escape from the situation' (Singh 3.37).

Baptized children want to engage in social activities such as parties, but they feel guilt and remorse and are afraid of their parents. To cope with these feelings, they try to combine the traditional baptized and secular lifestyles by wearing rap-style bandanas rather than turbans and by slowly trimming their facial hair into the form of sideburns and goatees.

GGBs strongly identify – as do other Sikh youth – with the American rap culture because of its status as a minority group phenomenon and because of the themes of rebellion and discrimination in rap lyrics.

Their identification with American rap culture sometimes leads them to embrace other aspects of it, such as engaging in drug activities: 'Most brown guys aren't scared of the police. They have a bad attitude. They don't have any responsibility. Parents give them a lot of money because they are rich. Parents are working all the time [not paying attention to kids]. The majority of drug dealers, [who were involved in] shooting, [whom I] knew, have died ... Young guys want to follow the rap culture – they identify with the lifestyle of drugs, money, guns, and women' (Singh 3.34).

Needless to add, many non-Punjabi parents fear the very aspects of rap culture that the rebellious Sikh youth identify with, such as the desire for a lot of 'quick' money, expensive clothes, cars, and women.

The *Guru Granth Sahib* recognizes that it is rare for youth to travel the path of spiritual wisdom (*gurmat marg*), because the mind during adolescence is fixated on external sensual experiences.[26] Even so, Sikh parents react with hostility when their children move away from orthodoxy, and they disapprove of their children taking on a more sec-ular lifestyle. The inability of parents to apply the Sikh theological view of human development to their children's development is rooted in their orality or literacy orientation, which almost ensures that the *external* dimensions of religion are pursued, and that little effort is made to instil in children the deeper religious values taught in the *Guru Granth Sahib*. At this point, tensions build between parents and children: the parents do not explore or discuss their children's feelings, but rather strengthen their authoritarian controls over them in an effort to uphold family *izzat*: 'The main value is shame: 'Don't shame me in front of other people.' Parents take care of kids because they want them to be something for pride – marriage–house–family. They don't encourage kids to be themselves' (Singh 3.34).

As parents enforce controls over the child, the child begins to feel deprived, and out of frustration begins to indulge in maladaptive behaviors such as truancy, drinking, taking drugs, and breaking the law. When these maladaptive behaviours generate hostility at home, the child rebels by renouncing the five *kakars*. A twenty-seven-year-old Sikh male explained the process of Sikh youth going off track: 'Com-munication is very important. Had none with my dad. Once [parents] lose touch with their kids, it is bad. I ran away from home two times. Once you rebel, there is severe punishment. It creates a pattern. Kids then get involved with drug activities' (Singh 3.37).

It is important to note that drug and alcohol abuse and gun posses-

sion are among the more extreme reactions against religious orthodoxy. Not all dissent and rebellion results in GGB-style behaviour. The
secularism that is a consequence of the tension children experience
with authoritarian traditional parents in a modern milieu is just the
extreme end of a continuum that ranges from conformity to rebellion.

Tensions between the Punjabi Household and Western Society

In some studies it has been contended that the younger generations do
not see the host culture and their own ethnic culture as in conflict and
that they are successfully integrating the two.[27] It seems, however, that
there is only a limited basis for this conclusion, which cannot be generalized to the broader Sikh or South Asian community. Nor are the
crude indicators employed for measuring integration – such as natu-
ralization and the wearing of Western clothing for work and the like –
truly reflective of integration.[28]

The aforementioned studies have attempted to show that the
younger generation is succeeding in integrating its ethnic culture with
the host culture; other studies show how that generation, living within
a multicultural society, is in fact 'caught' or 'sandwiched' between two
cultures.[29] Similarly, the present study has uncovered that there are
serious tensions between the younger and older generations – tensions
that underscore the difficulty of integrating the two cultures. Only by
analysing the relations and interactions between the three generations
can one actually discern that tensions indeed exist and that they are,
for the most part, rooted in the transition from tradition to modernity.
As discussed earlier, the main source of tension between the third generation and the first and second generations is that although Canadian-
born Sikh children are raised to conform to traditional mores (collectivity orientation, value of honour) by parents who have adopted the
'techniques' of the West,[30] the children struggle with the fact that in
order to work, these techniques require adoption of the corresponding
system of 'values' (self-orientation, personal choice, and success by
merit).

In economic terms, the second generation has generally adapted
well to Canada, but it has not yet absorbed the Western way of thinking, in such a way that members of the community can achieve their
potential as individuals in a society that emphasizes individualism.
Note the response by a twenty-four-year-old Sikh man: 'The community has done some good: moved forward in business, [material] life,

[Sikhs] have gained power – they are economically advanced. The community should adapt a little to Western thinking. They focus on minor points ... In ten years, more Punjabis should be adapted to a more Western way of thinking. There should be an increase [of well-adapted individuals] in the next generation because they are raised here and should realize the potential that they have. They can be very successful' (Singh 3.26).

Having arrived in Canada from a traditional setting, the Sikh community has not followed the child-rearing approach necessary for self-individuation. So it has been unable to meet the more abstract emotional and communication needs of its third-generation children in a milieu that is oriented toward the individual. A Sikh community- services worker commented: 'Our generation for the first fifteen years was busy earning money to survive and give the children a better life. We had no time to reflect about cultural values. We wanted to provide a good life for our kids and have them get a good education. However, there is a problem in the community. The children are missing attention' (social service 1).

The requirement to encourage children to develop self-orientation and to internalize the inner boundaries of right and wrong contradicts the traditional norms of collectivity orientation, which are based on social control in the form of *izzat*. Sikh children are not encouraged to develop self-orientation; instead, they are raised to follow the wishes of their parents.

Young Sikhs also experience a conflict between their Punjabi household and their Western environment. The third-generation children often have a strong desire for independence, but many of them also fear the economic and social (family and community) losses that would result from opposition. For most third-generation Sikhs, the result is a tendency to live a double life on a continuum ranging from living in frustration, so that there is outward conformity to parental pressures, to living off track in extreme rebellion. A Sikh male of twenty explained this: 'There are only a few who go to the youth groups and they are considered 'geeks' by others. The religious families raise the kids as geeks, but there are [also] kids from those families who get involved with shit. Some live in fear and do what their parents want them to do. Then others go off track with drugs' (Singh 3.34).

Some third-generation Sikhs buckle under the pressure to follow their parents' expectations, and may or may not live a double life; others rebel and at worst go off track. Note the comment of a Sikh male of twenty-seven: 'Balance is not that common. Ones who don't go into drinking and follow parents' plan are nerdy. They go to university to be a doctor, lawyer but when forty years old ... they are still a baby inside. They are not dealing with the situation either. They are living in [through] their parents' (Singh 3.37).

It is apparent that young Sikhs must strive for a balance between traditional notions of duty and the modern value of personal choice and independence. Several third-generation interviewees emphasized the need for a balance between conforming to parents' wishes and doing what one wants. This balance is not easily achieved, but some have struggled to make a success of it. One interviewee noted: 'The youth have to fight with their parents but with a balance. I fought with my father about what I wanted to do, but I did well at school, which showed my parents that I was good. Change is slow. ... I focused on having a balance as a young high school kid: study, sport (basketball, my parents never signed me up in any sports, it was always through school teams), and parties' (Singh. 3.38).

Two other factors are a source of tension in immigrant families: (1) the children are raised to be oriented toward the collectivity under the external control of honour, so they lack both the ability to assert themselves and a healthy sense of separateness; and (2) at the time of adolescence, when controls are traditionally placed on the children, they encounter considerable confusion because they are situated in a milieu where children as they enter adolescence and early adulthood are actually granted *more* freedom and personal choice.

An additional source of tension is that second-generation parents are rooted in tradition with a strong orientation toward the collectivity; as a result, they are often unable to serve as models for their third-generation children in terms of functioning smoothly in mainstream society. This is especially true for girls, who have difficulty modelling themselves after their mothers. Indeed, the third generation's move toward a self-orientation and desire for personal development is itself a source of tension between the second and third generations.

The Younger Generation and Psychodrama

The above discussion points to the problems that exist between the first, second, and third generations in the Sikh community. To date, the Sikh community in Canada has been reluctant to discuss openly such issues as the implications of authoritarian parenting for Canadian-born

children.[31] However, some third-generation members have made concerted efforts to shed light on the negative impact that traditional,
authoritarian parenting has on Canadian-born Sikh children. The third
generation has resorted to enacting 'psychodramas' – comical skits –
the theme of which is intergenerational tension, and the purpose of
which is to raise that issue in the community.

Psychodrama is a psychotherapeutic method that allows clients to
articulate pertinent issues in individual, family, or group settings.[32] A
simple instruction for psychodrama that reflects the underlying concept
is 'Don't tell us, show us.' There are five basic elements in psychodrama:
(1) the director (therapist), (2) the protagonist (client), (3) the auxiliary
(supporting side), (4) the designated area for the performance (stage),
and (5) the audience. The protagonist and auxiliary act out their frustra-
tions and concerns onstage, where the audience can see them.

Although psychodrama is a Western therapeutic intervention, its
technique of enacting (rather than discussing) has a record for being
effective in the Sikh community. This apparently derives from the fact
that the audience of the third generation's skits consists largely of parents and grandparents, whose mode of thinking is that of orality or literacy. Also, the skits seem popular among the older generations of the
Sikh community because they follow the tradition of Punjabi gidda
singing and dancing.

The Punjabi tradition of singing and dancing about issues close to
the life situation is called *gidda*. In village Punjab, women occasionally
get together and, instead of talking about their problems in a group,
sing and dance about their life situations or about the problems typically faced by women (as mother-in-law, daughter-in-law, wife). In
gidda, women form a circle and clap to a beat while one or two take the
lead in singing metaphorically or implicitly about their relationship
with their husband, mother-in-law, children, and other family members. As the lead vocalist sings and the other women clap, several
other women dance in a circle, acting out the contents of the song. For
example, the singer may sing about how the mother-in-law oppresses
the daughter-in-law while one woman acts out the wicked mother-in-
law and another acts out the overworked and unhappy daughter-in-
law. *Gidda* songs with family themes are not usually performed in
open forums; instead, they are performed within a particular support
group. In contrast, festive *gidda* singing and dancing (with appropriate themes) is regularly performed at festivals and during wedding
ceremonies.

Like Punjabi traditional *gidda* singing and dancing, the third generation's skits address problems in the home. These skits depict the implications of following traditional (i.e., authoritarian) parenting styles in a
Western milieu. The skits are performed in open forums at cultural
shows at colleges and universities. Some skits have been shown on a
multicultural television program called 'Punjabi Vibes.'[33] One of the
goals of 'Punjabi Vibes' is to bring issues to the fore without directly
discussing them within the community; this follows the underlying
concept of psychodrama. Note the explanation of one of the main goals
of 'Punjabi Vibes,' offered by one of its co-founders: 'One of the goals
is ... to communicate issues indirectly so it has an impact on the community.[34] We bring up issues in a comical way. You can't say things
directly, people get defensive/protective and don't listen. When you
do it in a comical way, they are more likely going to be affected by it'
(media 1).

The comical skits have become very popular among the youth, especially because they bring to the fore issues they have experienced personally – for example, having a Punjabi background and traditional
parenting while growing up in Canada. One of the skits is '*Desi* Family
Ties' (*desi* literally means indigenous and refers to Indian or Punjabi) –
a revamping of the 1980s sitcom 'Family Ties.' '*Desi* Family Ties'
depicts the implications of the authoritarian parenting style. For example, a Canadian-born girl is talking on the phone with a boyfriend, but
changes the topic of conversation when her traditional father enters
the room, to give the impression that she is actually talking to a girl-
friend. An episode like this sheds light on the double life many third-
generation children lead, having been reared by parents with a traditional parenting style.

Traditional Punjabi *gidda* singing and dancing and the third generation's comical skits are not performed deliberately as therapeutic inter-
ventions. That said, *gidda* songs and comical skits at least acknowledge
issues that are not otherwise openly discussed either in the family or in
the community.

Conclusion

In view of the above, two conclusions can be drawn regarding family
relations among the three generations of Sikhs in Canada: (1) While
ego development as outlined in the Sikh scripture (*Guru Granth Sahib*)
is descriptive of the relations within traditional Punjabi families,

attachment to one's family honour (*izzat*) is viewed by the third generation as an obstacle to self-realization. *Izzat* continues to be the main source of tension between the three generations of the Sikh community in Vancouver, as the third generation seeks aid in the individuation process. (2) The different communicative patterns pertaining to each of the three generations of the Sikh community is a source of tension within families.

The modern requirement of encouraging children toward self-individuation undermines the traditional norms of collectivity orientation. Consequently, there is clash between the traditional and modern approaches to child rearing. The first generation raises children with concrete thought forms and with values (*dharam* and *izzat*) rooted in tradition. To ensure conformity with the traditional norms of behaviour, it takes an authoritarian approach. This approach, which focuses on parents fulfilling the physiological and safety needs of the children, does not acknowledge individual self-orientation.

The third generation requires the satisfaction of emotional needs as an aid to the individuation process; it also requires the internalization of the boundaries of right and wrong. These requirements contradict the traditional norms of personality development (collectivity orientation), which depend on the social control that is inherent in *izzat*. Not surprisingly, third-generation Sikhs encounter tensions as a consequence. It would seem that psychodrama, as it is used in skits at cultural shows and on TV programs like 'Punjabi Vibes,' is one effective mechanism to resolve these tensions.

Meanwhile, the second generation is continuing Punjabi traditions while distancing itself somewhat from the collectivity. There has been some attenuation of its authoritarian approach, related mainly to the fear of loss of control over children and their going off track. The second generation as it experiences economic independence, is overindulging its children by offering material comforts in order to ensure that they conform to tradition so as to maintain family honour. However, although second-generation parents provide for their children's physiological and safety needs (often in excess), they seem generally unable to satisfy their more intangible emotional and communication needs.

5 Religion among the Three Generations: Oral Transmission of Customs, Reading about the Sikh Tradition, and Inquiry into Sikhism

Religion is the foundation of traditional societies. The family in traditional societies provides its members with prescribed roles and ascriptive status; religion sets the norms of behaviour for the collectivity of the family and for the community as a whole. In fact, a wide range of normative structures of behaviour, from the social domain (means of social control) to the spiritual (means to salvation), are imparted by religious traditions. For its part, the traditional mentality views religion and the wide range of ethical and social norms as an integrated whole. In contrast, modern societies distinguish between religious, ethical, and legal norms, and religion is oriented in such a way that there is individual choice concerning religion and one's relationship with God.

Like the other great world religions, Sikhism is rooted in traditional society. Although the Sikh scripture (*Guru Granth Sahib*) is universalistic in its teachings, Sikhism has for the most part been followed by the regional linguistic-cultural group known as the Punjabis. Because their religious identity is rooted in traditional society, parts of the Sikh community after they leave the Punjab continue to approach religion as encompassing the earlier broad range of normative structures of behaviour. The Sikhs in Western Canada, as a fragment of the community outside its 'homeland,' are facing pressure to adjust to the tensions between modernity and their traditional religious world view.

Several recent studies on the Sikh diaspora have examined the Sikh quest for an independent religious state and the growing importance of religion in the group identity of the Sikhs.[1] It seems, however, that we must approach the three generations of the Sikh community in Canada from the premise that their encounter with modernity is affecting their personal experience of religion. (The communal aspect of religion is discussed in chapter 6.) The transformative impact of modernity on the traditional mode of thinking is driving a different approach to, and comprehension of, religion and religious practice. In turn, the traditional and modern approaches to religion have become a source of tension between generations.

In this chapter I focus on the role of religion and religious practice, including the role of the *Guru Granth Sahib* (scripture) and the *gurdwara* (temple), in the lives of the three generations. An exploration of continuity and change regarding what members of the three generations seek from religion reveals different attitudinal patterns – patterns that correspond to the distinctive generational modes of thinking and that reflect the impact that modernity is having on the role of religion.

This chapter has three parts. In the first I discuss the historical development of Sikhism, including Sikh beliefs and practices. In the second I analyse the religious beliefs and practices of the three generations of the Sikh community in Vancouver, including their conceptions of what constitutes a Sikh. In the last I discuss the tensions between the three generations regarding religious practice. The analysis in the second part points to both continuity and change in the practice of Sikhism, especially with regard to the differences between Punjabi culture and Sikh religion. The intergenerational tensions discussed in the third part provide insights into a group whose religious identity, although rooted in traditional society, is now facing the challenge of modernity.

Development of the Sikh Religion

Sikhism is often referred to as a syncretistic religion, because it draws on both Hinduism and Islam.[2] Although it has both Hindu and Islamic elements, we should be cautious about referring to Sikhism as syncretistic. Sikhism grew out of Indian soil and shares a number of features with Hinduism, most notably its world view of *sansar*, the religious concept that unifies all Indian religions. At the same time, Sikhism shares a number of features with Islam in that it denounces icon worship and emphasizes a personal God, albeit without attributes (*nirgun*). Although the Sikh tradition bears some resemblances to Hinduism and Islam, it has developed its own unique beliefs and practices, which mark it as distinct.[3]

Lineage of the Ten Sikh Gurus

The founder of Sikhism, Guru Nanak (1469–1539) was the first of the ten human Sikh gurus. As a reaction against the religious and social

practices of fifteenth-century India, such as icon worship and ritual-
ism, Guru Nanak and other poet-saints (*bhagats*, such as Kabir and
Ravidas) taught two principles: all external forms of religion must be
rejected, and the divine name (*nam*) must be recited for the sake of
spiritual attainment. Guru Nanak taught that this inner devotion to
nam is open to all, irrespective of gender or caste. His theological and
social stance on equality opposed the orthodox Hindu belief that salvation is open only to men of the three higher classes – *brahmin, kshatriya,*
and *vaishya*. The Sikh gurus also denounced practices they perceived
as unjust to women (i.e., child marriage, *sati*[4] and the prohibition of
widow remarriage). However, the tradition of *stridharam* (including
the duty of the wife to serve her husband) has continued among Punjabi adherents to Sikhism.[5]

Before Guru Nanak died, he appointed Guru Angad (1504–52) as his
successor. Because the Sikh community was growing so rapidly, Guru
Angad opened more religious centres and made copies of Nanak's
hymns for distribution. He created the script of *Gurmukhi* (literally,
'from the mouth of the Guru'). *Gurmukhi* was later used to write the *Sri
Adi Granth* (later referred to as the *Guru Granth Sahib*), and from that
time on was used by Sikhs for writing in Punjabi. The third guru, Guru
Amar Das (1479–1574), established new ritual and devotional practices. For example, the ceremonies for births and deaths were to be performed with hymns written by the Sikh gurus. Guru Amar Das had a
tank built at Govindval and established it as a pilgrimage place or
tirath (*tirtha* in Sanskrit) for Sikhs. He also compiled a collection of
hymns, including several hymns of *bhagats* such as Kabir and Ravidas.
Because the community was growing so rapidly, Guru Amar Das was
unable to guide all followers of Sikhism. Consequently, he established
parishes (*manjis*), and appointed people to spread the teachings of the
Nanak panth (the path of Nanak) and to collect offerings made to the
centres of worship.

Guru Ram Das (1534–81), the fourth guru, founded a town around
the religious tank built by Guru Amar Das. This town, called Cak Ram
Das, was to become the centre of Sikhism. The fifth guru, Arjan Dev
(1563–1606), built the *Harimandir* ('the house of God')[6] at Cak Ram Das.
After the temple was completed, the town was renamed Amritsar, 'the
pool of nectar.' This was the first Sikh community that could be clearly
distinguished from Hindu ones. Guru Arjan Dev began building other
towns with Sikh temples and tanks (Taran Taran, Kartarpur). He also
compiled the sacred writings of the Sikhs into a unified text, the *Adi*

Granth (later called the *Guru Granth Sahib*). In a hymn, Guru Arjan Dev described the *Adi Granth* (or *Guru Granth Sahib*) as a vessel where 'you will find three things – truth, contentment and contemplation; in this too, the nectar that is the Name of the Master supports all' (*Guru Granth Sahib*, 1429).

Guru Arjan Dev continued to grow the Sikh community, which attracted followers with its calls for equality and the equal distribution of resources. When he refused to pay the Mughals a tax of 200,000 rupees, he was executed.[7] The martyrdom of Guru Arjan Dev under the rule of the emperor Jehangir marked the beginning of a long history of political conflict between Sikhs and the Mughal Empire.[8] By this point, the Sikhs were being perceived as a threat to the Mughal dynasty.

Guru Arjan Dev's successor, Guru Hargobind (1595–1644), conceptualized the need to combine 'spiritual' and 'worldly' concerns – *piri–miri*. This was a reaction to internal disputes within the Sikh community over succession in the guru lineage as well as to the external struggle against Mughal rule and oppression. Many Sikhs belonged to the *khatri* and *arora* castes, often described as trading castes; perhaps originally they were of the *kshatriya* (warrior) class. Many of the *jat* caste – predominantly farmers – also converted to Sikhism. *Jats*, like many other lower castes, were drawn to Sikhism by its strong emphasis on social equality and its concomitant promise of social mobility. The *jats* had long experience with protecting their agricultural lands against invasion, and were easily persuaded by Guru Hargobind to take up arms to protect Sikhism from Mughal oppression.[9] There were two succeeding gurus: Guru Har Rai (1630–61), who maintained the *piri–miri* aspects of Sikhism, and Guru Har Krishan (1656–64), who died of smallpox at the age of nine.

Guru Teg Bahadur (1622–75), the ninth guru, is revered as a martyr. Because he defended the right of Hindus to practise their religion, he was publicly beheaded in Delhi by Mughal officials. Following this, his son, Guru Gobind Singh (1666-1708), became the last human guru of the Sikh lineage. In response to Mughal aggression and in the quest for social justice, Guru Gobind Singh crystallized the concept of *piri–miri* as integral to the Sikh religious organization by establishing the Order of the Khalsa ('the pure' or 'the elect'). Initiation into the Khalsa order is marked by the receiving of sacred water (*amrit sanchar*). Members are required to wear five symbols to mark their Sikh identity: *kesh* – 'covered hair,' *kachcha* – 'shorts for underwear,' *kara* – 'steel bangle,' *kirpan* – 'steel dagger,' and *kanga* – 'comb').

God was now called *sarab-loh* – 'all-Steel' – and according to Guru
Gobind Singh was to be worshipped in the form of a sword: the sword
as the symbol of the inner battle with the ego and the external battle, as
a last resort, for social justice against the (Mughal) enemies. Guru
Gobind Singh, who became popularly known as a 'Saint-Soldier,' pro-
claimed that he was to be the last human guru of the Sikh lineage.
Having proclaimed this, he bestowed the status of the Word of the
Guru on the *Guru Granth Sahib*.

The Universal Teachings of the Sikh Gurus

The Sikh world view posits the cycle of birth, death, and rebirth (*sansar*) and sets the goal of religion as to liberate its followers from this
cycle (*mukti*) so that they merge with the Ultimate.[10] The simple recitation of the divine name (*nam*) is the means to this goal. The introduc-
tory verse of Guru Nanak's *Japji-sahib* – the *Mool-mantar* ('root
mantra')[11] – is regarded as the foundation of Sikh theology. The *mool-
mantar* provides the Sikh theological understanding of the nature of
the Ultimate and humankind; that is, *Ek Onkar* is eternal, creator and
saviour, and is to be realized by humans in order for them to escape
from the cycle of rebirth:

> One Onkar, the cosmological existence manifest in all,
> is the truth,
> [Ek Onkar] is creator,
> is without fear, without enmity,
> has a timeless form,
> is beyond the cycle of rebirth, self-existing,
> and is realized by the grace of the Guru. (*Guru Granth Sahib*, 1)

The *mool-mantar* provides the Sikh understanding of the Ultimate; it
is also regarded as grace (*parsad*). The mere recitation of the *mool-mantar* is the means to the goal of liberation as set out by Guru Nanak and
his successor gurus.

A central theme that follows from the Sikh world view of the universal creator is the universality of humankind, the religious ideal that all
humans are equal and ultimately the same. Guru Gobind Singh, and
many *bhagats* and gurus, wrote about the oneness of humankind:

> Some are Hindus, others are Muslims,

some are Rafjis, Imam and Sufis,
but all races [humanity] should be recognized as one. (*Dasam Granth*,
'Akaal Ustat' 15.85, 1078)[12]

The line 'but all races [humanity] should be recognized as one'[13] is
one of the most popular lines about universal humankind among the
Sikhs, and they repeat it often in public lectures and temple sermons.
According to Sikh teaching, God has many names; of these, the favourite among the Sikhs is the Infinite Light that dispels darkness (*waheguru*). The goal is not to identify with God; rather, it is to abandon
one's ego through the recitation of *nam* – the symbol representing the
eternal spirit of creation – so that one becomes aware of the true nature
of reality (beyond the physical world). The third guru, Guru Amar
Das, explained that *nam* was to be recited as the means to escape the
illusion (*maya*) of the physical world and to attain the Guru (God):

Through the Divine Will [*hukam*],
the infant is born,
and the family nourishes it with love.
As the infant enters the world,
the consciousness breaks away from the Soul,
and desires begin to erupt as *maya* starts its rule.
Such is the nature of *maya* that the Absolute Being is forgotten,
attachment to others occurs,
and worldly love flourishes.
Nanak says: those, who are connected [with *nam*],
through the Guru's grace,
attain [*Ek Onkar*] while living in *maya*. (*Guru Granth Sahib*, 921)

Through the recitation of *nam*, a Sikh is to attain detachment from
illusion but connectedness with the Guru while living in this world as
a householder within *maya*. Although *nam* and prayers can be recited
at home, many Sikhs prefer to gather at the *gurdwara*.

Gurdwara ('The Door to the Guru') and Sikh Religious Practice

Gurdwara, which literally means 'the door to the Guru,' refers to the
place in which a devotee meets the 'Guru' – the *Guru Ganth Sahib*. A
Sikh temple has features that distinguish it from Hindu temples. For
example, instead of one entrance (as in a Hindu temple, which tradi-

tionally has not been open to lower castes and untouchables), there are four, signifying that the temple is open to all. The concept of the Sikh temple as 'open to all' is most clearly expressed and realized in the custom of *langar*. *Langar* literally means 'community dining hall,' and refers to the offering of food to all who come to the *gurdwara*. The practice among Sikhs is to eat in the *langar* (dining hall) before or after saying prayers in the prayer hall. The food offerred in the *langar* is regarded as a gift from, or the grace of, God.

The Sikh custom of *langar* was revolutionary because not only was it open to all, but everyone was to eat together. The 'open to all' dining hall shattered Hindu caste barriers by breaking with the orthodox Hindu customs of religious and social purity (by tradition, Brahmins do not eat with the lower castes because it is considered polluting). Not only are the caste barriers broken through communal eating, but those who want to perform acts of service (*seva*) may involve themselves in the preparation of the food, regardless of gender, age, and caste.

In the early 1920s there arose a *gurdwara* reform movement, during the course of which icons that had been placed in the *gurdwaras* were removed in order to rid Sikhism of the last remnants of the Hindu religion. It is noteworthy, however, that even today the Sikhs' ritual treatment of the book (scripture) parallels Hindu rituals for the presiding icon of a temple – for example, the rituals of dressing up the scripture or icon and of putting the scripture or icon to sleep. The Hindus have consecrated icons in home shrines (permanently or temporarily) for devotion; similarly, some Sikhs keep the *Guru Granth Sahib* at home (permanently or temporarily) for daily prayers and reading – either *sadharan path* ('intermittent reading') or *akhand path* ('continuous reading').

As part of the Sikh reform movement, the Shiromani Gurdwara Parbandhak Committee (established in 1925 by the Sikh electorate to administer the principal gurdwaras) issued the *Sikh Rahit Maryada* (Sikh Code of Conduct) in order to distinguish Sikh Punjabis from other Punjabis.[14] Besides outlining the three fundamental religious rules and four rites of passage for a Sikh (described in chapter 3), the *Sikh Rahit Maryada* provides the following definition of a Sikh:

Any human being who faithfully believes in
(i)   One Immortal Being,
(ii) Ten Gurus, from Guru Nanak Dev to Guru Gobind Singh,
(iii) The *Guru Granth Sahib*,

(iv) the utterances and teachings of the ten Gurus, and

(v) the baptism bequeathed by the tenth Guru and who does not owe allegiance to any other religion,

is a Sikh.

The *Sikh Rahit Maryada* includes prescriptions for the Sikh daily prayers, for the rituals that should be performed in the *gurdwara*, and for the reading of the scripture (*Guru Granth Sahib*). Moreover, it prescribes the behavioural norms expected of 'baptized' Sikhs (*amritdharis*, those who have taken *amrit*),[15] who are required to bear the five *kakars* instituted by Guru Gobind Singh, to eat a vegetarian diet, to abstain from smoking, and to marry an *amritdhari* Sikh. In laying down the code of conduct for an *amritdhari* or Khalsa Sikh, the *Sikh Rahit Maryada*, in effect, differentiates the practices of 'baptized' Sikhs (*amritdharis*) from those of Hindus and Muslims.

It is important to note that although the focus of the *Sikh Rahit Maryada* is the baptized (*amritdhari*) Sikh, by tradition Sikhism has also recognized Sikhs who are not baptized: These Sikhs ('learners'), who follow the principal requirement of wearing covered uncut hair (*kesh*) along with the other *kakars*, are referred to as *keshdharis*. The Sikhs who do not follow this chief requirement but who do believe in the spiritual teachings of the gurus are called *sahajdharis* (slow adopters). There are also many Hindus – especially from the Punjab – who revere the human Sikh gurus as *sants* and who prostrate before the Sikh scripture even while continuing with their Hindu religious practices.[16]

Finally, there are, today, non-Punjabi followers of the Sikh religion, who are referred to as 'Gora' (white) Sikhs.[17] Most Gora Sikhs are affiliated with the 3HO – Happy, Healthy, and Holy Organization. The 3HO emerged during the 1970s under the leadership of Harbhajan Singh Puri (Yogi Bhajan) on the west coast of North America. At present, the 3HO is based in New Mexico. For the most part, the Gora Sikh community functions separately from the Punjabi Sikh community. Although Gora Sikhs have a high regard for the universal teachings of the *Guru Granth Sahib*, they also regard as equally authoritative the teachings of Yogi Bhajan, especially his unique emphasis on *kundalini* yoga. A nineteen-year-old Gora Sikh man, who had been raised in a Gora Sikh family, commented: 'There is a particular focus on the specific teachings of Yogi Bhajan and the practice of yoga' (Gora Sikh 3.1). According to Willard Oxtoby, this emphasis on yoga and the teachings of Yogi Bhajan is perceived as 'too Hindu' by the Punjabi

Sikhs who highlight the 'distinction between Hindus and Sikhs.'[18] Many members of the three generations agree that Yogi Bhajan's movement is 'too Hindu'; some among the second and third generations also see the 3HO as having a 'hippy' or 'new age' orientation that misrepresents the Sikh religion, since it digresses from the actual teachings of the Sikh gurus.

The First Generation and Oral Transmission of Customs

The first generation approaches religion as a set of normative structures that touch on all aspects of human behaviour and life. Religious tradition is understood as laying down norms for the whole of life, from the social domain to the spiritual. The oral mentality sees knowledge as largely inherited; it follows that elders are the best source of knowledge ('wisdom'). A correlative of this position is that the orally transmitted (cultural or religious) beliefs *are accepted at face value*. These religious beliefs and customs are expressed in a concrete manner and are most commonly articulated through the telling of stories and the show of respect and devotion for sacred space. Those who belong to the orality mode of thinking are more comfortable with the telling of stories of religious people (including hagiographies) than with discussions of theology that move beyond the attributes of the Ultimate.

The first generation is having to adapt to a new environment. In doing so it is experiencing changes in lifestyle, and this is having an effect on religious practice. They are generally unable to comprehend or accept modern society's abstract, self-oriented approach to religion. As a consequence, the first generation experiences tension with the third generation with respect to changing values.

Orality and the Transmission of Customs

According to the traditional mentality, one is born a Sikh; that is, religion is inherited at birth and is not a matter of choice. Many members of the first generation, who consider themselves Sikh or 'Jat-Sikh,' have limited access to the scripture since they are illiterate. Whatever they know has been passed down orally to them. They are able to recite the prayers and narrate the stories about the gurus. They may recite the daily prayers by rote (more common among women than men), but that does not necessarily mean that they understand the teachings contained in the scripture in the modern sense of comprehension. Several interviewees of the first generation who had the literacy mode of thinking pointed out that many Sikhs actually do not know the teachings of the gurus. One interviewee, a seventy-one-year-old man, explained that many people who are called or referred to as Sikh are so only by birth, not by choice or awareness of the religion: 'It is difficult to make uneducated people see things differently ... They are Sikhs because they are born in a Sikh family' (Singh 1.15). Likewise, *hukam* is understood as following orders set in stone rather than as an underlying governing principle that can be applied in various circumstances.

The first generation expresses its devotion or religiosity through a face-value acceptance of and respect toward sacred space and sacred speech. First, its members are aware of sacred space and of how one gives respect to that which is sacred. They show this awareness by prostrating themselves before the scripture and by making salutations before a picture of a guru or *sant*. Second, they recite prayers or the *waheguru* (Sikh mantra). The power resides in the very recitation of the mantra or in the sacred words of the gurus (*gurbani*). Classical devotional Sikh hymns are meditative tools for connecting with the Guru (the Absolute). The sacred words of the gurus are set to classical music (*rags; ragas* in Sanskrit) so that they can evoke a distinctive spiritual aura that affects the heart and enables the devotee to experience the nectar (*amrit*) of the Guru. Note the words of Guru Arjan Dev:

> Connect with the melody of the hymns
> [through which] the *nad* ['the sound current'] of *Ek Onkar* resounds!
> Such a devotee lives alone in the One,
> reflects on the glory of the One,
> and merges with the One. (*Guru Granth Sahib*, 885)

The Sikh understanding of *nad* is that it is eternal as well as the essence of the Guru as it resonates within the hymns. Thus, experiencing the Guru is facilitated through the practice of chanting Sikh hymns.[19]

Finally, devotion is expressed by narrating religious stories or accounts about the gurus and martyrs, referred to as 'sacred biographies' (which belong to the traditional pan-Indian genre of hagiography). These stories are a mixture of fact and legend about historical figures, and include miracles and supernatural births. 'Sacred biographies' reflect religious or societal concerns and are not strictly speaking historical accounts. Rather, their purpose is to transmit kernels of abstract truth. Hagiographies are suitable for the orality mode of thinking, in the sense that they convey a supernatural message in concrete terms.

Many members of the first generation – especially those who are illiterate – believe in what they are told. For them, the *gurdwara* rituals, the rote recitation of prayers, and the telling of stories about the gurus are the only means to know the religion. Likewise, the first generation has learned to revere and offer devotion to the *Guru Granth Sahib* and to the pictures of the gurus solely by virtue of their sacred status – that is, without questioning why they are sacred. These items are simply sacred, and thus devotional respect is due to them. There is an absence of concern about and reflection on the nature of the sacred; there is also a lack of inquiry – a feature of orality – into the theology expounded by the gurus.

Because the first generation is from a traditional society, it approaches its religious tradition as encompassing all aspects of human behaviour. Religious beliefs and social customs are viewed as an integrated whole. This is most interestingly reflected in the fact that the spectrum of religious practice among the first generation is narrow. Whether they are baptized or not, and whether they associate themselves or not with the more recent political categories of 'moderates' or 'fundamentalists,' members of the first generation seem similar because they adhere to the traditional approach to religion. Even when they are not baptized, they still live according to many of the inherited traditional norms. This is especially the case with women. First-generation women will pray daily and not eat meat or drink alcohol, whether they are baptized or not. Most first-generation members, even when not baptized, are *keshdhari*: Sikhs who wear the *kesh*, 'uncut hair.' The orality mode of thinking and the traditional approach to Sikhism as it exists among first-generation Sikhs is reflected in the comment of a seventy-year-old man associated with a 'moderate temple': 'People have built their personal houses out of the donations [to the *gurdwaras*] ... I did bad things too, I smoked, drank, and cut my hair. I have grown my hair because the *gurdwara* likes you to have a turban on when serving food. [They should] remember me as having good *karam* and have good thoughts of me' (Singh 1.5, trans.).

The above quotation explains good *karam* in terms of whether or not one drinks, smokes, and cuts one's hair. Although Sikhism encompasses all norms relating to human life, the generation belonging to the orality mode expresses these norms in concrete terms close to its life situation.

Consistent with a traditional mentality, the first generation treats religion as inseparable from culture; thus it is likely to treat customs such as arranged marriage as part of religion. The first generation often speaks of religion interchangeably with culture (Singh 1.1, 1.2, 1.5, 1.6, 1.7, 1.9, 1.12, 1.15, 1.16; Kaur 1.4, 1.8, 1.10, 1.11, 1.13, 1.14). A seventy-seven-year-old Sikh man, in commenting on the differences between Hinduism and Sikhism, referred to religion as encompassing culture as well: 'Culturally, Hinduism and Sikhism are the same except Sikhs pray with the *Guru Granth Sahib* and Hindus with the Vedas. Religiously, there is no caste in Sikhism, only at marriage is caste a concern, whereas for Hindus it is for religious areas of life. Sikhism is for the brotherhood of mankind and the fatherhood of the Almighty' (Singh 1.1).

As the first generation encounters modernity in Canada, it faces the painful requirement to adapt.

Perspective on Change

The first generation, being mostly illiterate, has limited access to the Sikh scripture and is limited as well by the orality mode of thinking; even so, its members do note the change in religious practice that has occurred within the Sikh community in Canada. They observe that Western values have influenced how Sikhism is practised, that the traditional respect for sacred space is changing. A Sikh woman of eighty attributed the change in religious practice in Canada to the change in lifestyle and values:

> In India, people practise religion with devotion. When there is Akhand Path, the first priority of the family giving it is to bring the scripture and [to see that] the ones reading it are well fed and clothed and given respect. Only then do we worry about our own family members. In Canada, people don't care about the devotion and only care about socializing with families and the focus is not on the reading of the *Guru Granth Sahib* and the person who is doing it. The *gurdwara* is becoming social. We will speed up Akhand Path because families say they are too busy and have to leave by 12:00. They get the *granthi* to read faster.' (Kaur 1.14, trans.)

The first generation recognizes that the Western lifestyle has influenced how Sikhism is practiced; also, they often comment cynically on *gurdwara* politics. They believe that the environment in the *gurdwaras* is different from their memory of *gurdwaras* in the Punjab. This is evident in the comment of an eighty-year-old Sikh woman, who is religiously orthodox and politically moderate: 'Here [in Vancouver], it [the *gurdwara*] has become corrupt because of politics and money ... *Gurdwaras* have lost their religion. I only go to the *gurdwara* if I am invited to a wedding or some special worship, otherwise I have my own *gurdwara* at home, where there is the *Guru Granth Sahib*' (Kaur 1.4).

Disillusionment over the *gurdwaras* is pervasive among the first generation. This was obvious in the interviews, even when the actual topic of discussion was some other aspect of the religion. A seventy-six-year-old Sikh woman, while talking about a hospital that was being built in India in memory of her deceased son, felt compelled to comment negatively about the *gurdwaras*: 'It is in God's hands. We built a hospital [in India] in his memory ... They [poor patients] get eye operations and they are treated free and are served for seven days ... My son's hospital is the *gurdwara* where somebody gets life. In the *gurdwaras* [here] the people collect money and fight. We [through the hospital] are giving life' (Kaur 1.8, trans.).

Many in the first generation are dissatisfied about the politics in the *gurdwaras* and the lack of interest shown by the *gurdwaras* in the elderly. Even so, the *gurdwaras* are one of the few places where elders – especially those who have migrated to Canada more recently – can gather to socialize: 'Some families do not have the time for the elderly ... The elderly feel bad and then go to the *gurdwara* and talk with the other elderly and feel a bit of a community' (Kaur 1.13, trans.).

Change is most obvious, however, in the tensions between the first and third generations.

Tensions with the Third Generation

As in many other areas, tensions have developed between the first and third generations over the practice of religion. The first generation experiences a gap between its traditional approach to religion and the more modern approach of the third generation. It finds that the third generation does not always practise the Sikh religion and seems to have moved away from it. The first generation attributes this change to the influence of Western culture. An eighty-six-year-old Sikh man commented: 'They [youth] are stronger here in Canadian culture, dating; path of youth here is into smoking, drugs. We need to persuade youth about the teachings of the *Guru Granth Sahib*. We need to be organized' (Singh 1.16).

Moreover, the first generation is uncomfortable with the third gener-ation's tendency to question traditional beliefs and customs – for example, they wonder why one should not cut one's hair. A seventy-one-year-old Sikh man commented: 'The young generation questions without logic and is not sensible. One has to follow faith blindly. They are always asking 'Why?' and want an answer' (Singh 1.15).

The first generation sees a distinct lack of interest on the part of the third generation in practising Sikhism. One important factor, in its view, is that parents make little effort to teach their children about Sikh religion; this in turn is related to the nature of existence in Canadian society. Members of the first generation feel that the younger genera-tion must make an effort to learn about it. One Sikh woman of eighty years noted: 'The kids don't know about the religion because parents are busy at work; and the grandparents don't have the energy to teach because they are busy caring for them. No real effort is made for kids to learn ... If kids really want to learn, they have to go out and find it, like the kids who want to party go out and find it ... They need the Guru's blessing' (Kaur 1.14, trans.). In other words, if the third genera-tion is capable of functioning in the modern host society, then it also is capable of learning about its own religion.

Another factor in the third generation's lack of interest in the religion is believed to be the fact that the teachings and prayers in the *gurdwara* are in Punjabi and thus difficult for them to understand. However, the really crucial factor seems to be that grandparents are simply unable to answer young people's questions. Indeed, in this respect, young people may actually have an advantage because they can read books on the gurus or English translations of the scripture.

Among the first generation, illiteracy is quite common, and as a result, Sikh elders have had to learn about their religion mainly through oral transmission. In this regard, the second generation is in a somewhat better position, since it can read the scripture and the his-tory of the Sikh gurus and the tradition. This does not, however, allevi-ate the tensions between the first and third generations.

The Second Generation and Reading about the Tradition

Traditional practices are often redefined in the process of transition from traditional society to modern society. The second generation demonstrates some distancing from the family as a collectivity. Also, some second-generation Sikhs have chosen to become baptized after having been raised by unbaptized parents, even as other family members remain secular. Although the second generation maintains the traditional values of the religious tradition according to *hukam* (order), there is some change in its approach to religion. It does not view religion as bearing on all behaviour, with religion and culture constituting an integrated whole. However, the second generation has not yet accepted the modern approach to and understanding of religion. The limited nature of the change in the second generation's attitudes toward religion is most evident in the context of the tensions between the second and third generations.

Redefinition of Religious Practice

The second generation has learned about the Sikh religion largely through oral transmission from parents and grandparents in the Punjab. Like the first generation, it has learned that religious beliefs and customs should be accepted at face value based on the traditional value of *hukam*. It basically accepts the practices that have been handed down through the ages, but without necessarily knowing or caring about the reasons underlying those practices. Many members of the second generation have been raised as Sikhs by illiterate first-generation parents, so their knowledge of the actual teachings of the scripture is fairly limited. As a consequence, many of them tend to believe, mistakenly, that the orally transmitted Sikh beliefs and customs are based on scripture – on the *Guru Granth Sahib*. A baptized Sikh man of fifty-four commented: 'Majority of peoples is with a farming background – living in the fields. They are not that educated, they are the 'working class' peoples. They go to the *gurdwaras*, bow their head, eat food, meet people. They go to *gurdwara* for special functions ... Sikhs don't know about it; they do not understand the *Guru Granth Sahib* ... The Sikh people are traditional, the ritual type and do not have a research mind' (Singh 2.11).

A Sikh woman agreed, noting that most Sikhs do not know the teachings of the *Guru Granth Sahib*, and simply practise the customs and rituals handed down through the generations: 'People say they are religious, but do not practise. Many people do things just as ritual. People need to believe 100 percent in the *Guru Granth Sahib*' (Kaur 2.16).

The traditional religious values and practices have been carried over from the Punjab by the first generation, and they remain quite pervasive among the second generation. Even so, one can discern some changes in religious practice. In adapting to the modern economy, the second generation has changed its lifestyle, and this has included adjusting its religious practices. In order to adjust to a racially intolerant environment and to integrate themselves into the economy (i.e., find work), many Sikhs discarded external symbols and stopped practising the religion (Singh 2.2, 2.3, 2.4, 2.5, 2.8, 2.9, 2.10, 2.11, 2.14, 2.22, along with many fathers of the third generation). Also, some of them – for example, the parents of two third-generation Sikh women and one third-generation Sikh man – became involved with the Christian church as a means of 'integration' because they thought it was 'the modern thing to do' (Kaur 3.18, 3.25; Singh 3.16). Furthermore, with its structured lifestyle in modern society, the second generation experiences a lack of time, with the result that many go to the *gurdwara* only for social events (as opposed to attending *gurdwaras* regularly for prayer and worship).

In his study of Hindus in Canada, Harold Coward found that although religious identity is growing in importance among them, they 'live as a minority group in a secular, materialistic culture and so the contextual reinforcement of family practice, experienced in India, is simply absent in Canada.'[20] The basic reason for the lack of contextual reinforcement is, as some complained, that there is 'not enough time to memorize the religious texts.'[21] Because the Hindu and Sikh cultures are similar in so many respects, we can take this finding to apply to Canada's Sikh community as well. For example, Sikhism, like Hinduism, has early-morning meditation as a part of its daily practice; in Canada, however, not many Sikhs have time for this because of the lifestyle change. Actually, it is not so much the lack of time so such as – because of the more structured pattern of life in modern society – the lack of time *at specific times of the day*. Also, for some Sikhs in Canada, religious practice has a lower priority. In any case, it is worth noting that only a few elite members of the traditional society have actually studied and memorized the religious texts. Most Sikhs have learned only the daily prayers and the practice of respecting sacred 'spaces' such as the scripture and the picture of a guru.

That said, differences do exist between the first and second generations with regard to how religion is approached and understood. For the first generation (orality), as noted earlier, religious tradition provides the normative structures that bear on all aspects of human life, which are viewed as an integrated whole; religion governs life in its entirety. For these Sikhs, religion and culture constitute a single entity.

This integratedness that is so characteristic of the first generation begins to break down with the second generation. The first generation, even though situated in Canada, has little interaction with modern society and functions mainly within a social network removed from that society. In contrast, the second generation interacts with Canadian society, even if primarily in the economic realm. It is also preoccupied with making money and establishing the modified extended family. Ironically, participation in the Canadian economy frees up more leisure time for this generation – time that it can devote to religious activities, such as arranged *akhand paths* (scriptural readings), which often take the form of social occasions. For the second generation, life is more differentiated. There may not be time on a daily basis to engage in religious activities (e.g., attending the *gurdwara*), yet the structured 'weekend' leisure time makes it possible to arrange religious/cultural functions. A forty-six-year-old Sikh woman commented: '[In the Punjab] we did not have time to go to the *gurdwara*. Everyone had to work hard on the farm. The women always have a lot of responsibility in the home. It begins at sunrise and finishes at sunset. Here, we have more time to do [*akhand*] *paths* and go to the *gurdwaras* for functions. We are able to read about the religion here too' (Kaur 2.19).

The first and second generations share the same basic beliefs and practices; furthermore, both generations acquired these beliefs largely through oral transmission. The second generation insists that its children retain the Sikh religion. However, its limited knowledge of that religion becomes evident when it has to deal with the third generation. By and large, cultural practices such as caste, arranged marriage, children's obedience, and *izzat* constitute the basic content of what the second generation perceives to be religion. That generation tends to identify Punjabi culture as its religion, and it applies authoritarian controls to ensure that the third generation conforms to it. Note the comment of a forty-nine-year-old Sikh man who, having been clean-shaven for many years, became *amritdhari* in 1998: 'The parents need to be more educated about the tradition and religion because they are two different things. Parents need to be able to answer the kids' questions. People think religion is tradition – like the caste system and superstitions – yet these are contradictory to the scripture. There is a lack of education, especially among the women. The women need to be more educated because they are the ones who pass a lot to the kids' (Singh 2.14).

Compared to the first generation, the second is more complex in both religious and social terms. The second generation is more diverse in its ways of practising religion. Some become clean-shaven, others get baptized; some call themselves moderates, others are referred to as fundamentalists (see chapter 6). Those who call themselves 'moderates' consider cutting their hair and discarding the *kakars* as essentially 'modern.' Note the response of a twenty-six-year-old Sikh man: 'My father cut his hair upon arrival to find a job. It was considered "modern." He was told by my relatives [to do this] ... Up to the age of eleven, I did not know anything about my religion. I had my hair cut' (Singh 3.24).

Literacy and Reading Sikh History

The second generation has strong residues of oral culture. Many of the second generation were raised by illiterate first-generation parents and learned about their religion through oral transmission but they also acquired the ability to read the scripture and other books on the Sikh tradition. Having this ability, some have sought to learn about their religion. Interestingly, in the very process of reading about the Sikh tradition, these people have come to realize just how limited their knowledge is. A second-generation Sikh woman explained that it was not until recently that she truly learned about the religion:

> I have been *amritdhari* for one-and-a-half years. My sister taught me about living like an *amritdhari*. I go to *gurdwara* to do the rituals. Most people go to do rituals, ask for what they want, get *prasad*, and go home. One has to be in a devotional atmosphere to learn the Sikh religion, where stories will be told to the children. Most homes do not have people telling kids stories about the Sikh gurus. Most families tell the cultural folktales only. There are no preachers explaining *gurbani* [scripture], they are not educated. Most people in the village are uneducated. About 5 per cent are educated in the village. Living with my sister gave me a devotional atmosphere ... My sister tells the kids stories about the Sikh gurus. I learned from friends and *kirtan* [hymn-singing]. (Kaur 2.20)

It is interesting to note that only through studying the scripture herself did this woman realize that most of what had been handed down to her by the elders was folktales and ritual customs rather than the actual teachings of the gurus.

It is important to note that although the second generation has access to the scripture through reading, history is the most popular form of reading. Indeed, reading is often confined to Sikh history and politics. Although these subjects can be very conceptual, they are still accessible to those who have the literacy mode of thinking, which focuses on empirical and concrete ideas or 'facts.' The interest in and comprehension of Sikh history thus reflects the second generation's literacy mode of thinking; that is, history is a fit subject for the thought form that remains concrete and close to life situations. In fact, some among the second generation who are well versed in Punjabi still find the *Guru Granth Sahib* and sermons in the *gurdwaras* difficult to comprehend. This difficulty in comprehending the scripture and *gurdwara* sermons is rooted in the fact that Sikh theology may be too abstract for the literacy mode of thinking.

Some distancing from the collectivity orientation is evident in the biographical accounts of interviewees from the second generation. Personal choice or personal experience has led several of them to pursue religion. For example, one forty-nine-year-old Sikh man spoke of his religious experiences during his young adulthood, which eventually pointed him toward the path of a baptized Sikh (*amritdhari*): 'I came to Canada with hair cut and beard shaven. However, in 1972 I had several experiences of being drawn to my guru (*bapuji*) and became more religious. I started to be vegetarian, stopped drinking like I did with my mill co-workers. I pray early in the morning at three a.m.' (Singh 2.9).

Another example is that of a Sikh man of fifty, who became more religious when he was seeking meaning in life at a time when he had moved to Vancouver's Lower Mainland, where there was a Sikh community with which to engage:

> When I left [a town on Vancouver Island] and settled in [Vancouver's Lower Mainland], I started to be interested in Sikhism. In my forties, I started to search for the meaning of life. It is the time people see others die and have to face getting old and their mortality. I studied the religion for seven or eight years ... I went to the *gurdwara* and attended the religious functions to learn and found I needed to go further. I was asking myself – What is the *Guru Granth Sahib*? What is in it? I found a mentor to teach me more about the practice of Sikhism and the essence of spirituality. I took *amrit* two years ago. (Singh 2.14)

This individual is providing a personal account of his religious life; he also is showing how he studied the religion through reading in order to learn about it.

While there is some exercise of personal choice among the second generation, it often occurs in the context of a collectivity orientation. For instance, the most common reason given by second-generation Sikhs for beginning to study their religion was Operation Bluestar. In discussing the changes that occurred within the Sikh community, a Gora Sikh stated that Operation Bluestar served as a catalyst for many Sikhs to turn to traditional Sikh religious practice: 'The 1984 Operation Bluestar was a wake-up call for the community. People realized that their *dharam* is precious. It brought the community together and made people realize that identity is really important. People realized that one does not have to give up religious *dharam* to assimilate in Canada' (Kaur 2.15).

References to Operation Bluestar as the catalyst for embracing the Sikh religion were frequent (e.g., Singh 2.10, 2.11, 2.14, 2.22; Kaur 2.16, 2.19). One Sikh woman spoke of the change in her husband: 'I was born in India and came to Canada in a marriage. I married a Canadian-born Sikh who became *amritdhari* after Operation Bluestar [because the event] made him curious about his religion. He was clean-shaven before. He taught himself Punjabi and studied the religion on his own' (Kaur 2.16).

The capacity to learn about the religion by reading the scripture and history books is evidenced in the above quotation. Although many second-generation Sikhs study their religion, much of their discussion of spirituality remains at the concrete or literal level, and revolves around concrete ideas and practices as described in the *Sikh Rahit Maryada* and history books, rather than the scripture itself.

Some members of the second generation offered personal accounts of the role of religion in their lives. Many commented on the state of Sikh religion as they see it, especially with regard to the problem of educating young, Canadian-born Sikhs. A Sikh man of fifty-four emphasized the need for intergenerational dialogue: 'Parents just want children to listen and follow what they say. There need to be leaders and role models for the younger generation. There also should be intergenerational dialogue. People are lost: kids are from parents who are mentally living in Punjab and physically living in Canada' (Singh 2.11).

This statement highlights the fact that the Sikh community is still attached to Punjabi tradition and thus the Punjabi approach to religious instruction; it also reflects the gap and resulting tension between the older and younger generations. This is most evident in the communication barriers between the second and third generations.

Communication Barriers with the Third Generation

Although the second generation is able to read the scripture and history as well as stories about the Sikh tradition, comprehension remains at the literal level. The second generation's traditional approach to and literal comprehension of religion creates the possibility of tension with the third generation, which tends towards the analytics mode of thinking. The second generation experiences communication and cultural barriers with the third generation based on its different mode of thinking as well as its attitude and approach to religion. The communication barrier with the third generation as experienced by the second generation relates to the perceived 'rude' nature of young Sikhs' analytics mode of thinking, which involves questioning Sikh religion and traditions. Note the response of a Sikh man of fifty-four: 'Children don't go to the *gurdwara* because they don't understand Punjabi, the *giani* ['priest']. The kids don't like the preacher telling stories, which are not logical. The kids are educated here. They will not accept the illogical stories. The kids like to ask questions and get answers. The *gurdwara* does not have a modern approach. Preachers are not highly respected and [they are not] intellectuals. The traditional things are carried out in the *gurdwara*. The younger generation should learn through Internet or scholars, where they can ask questions' (Singh 2.11).

Many of the second generation express regret that the older generation generally did not have access to the religion. The third generation, in fact, because it can read, enjoys more access to the religion than either the first or the second. A baptized Sikh woman of forty-eight told me: 'The *gurdwaras* need to change a little for the youth. They are becoming like a business, not a family/relationship. *Gurbani* needs to be explained to the younger generation ... Children should study about their religion, they are all educated and able to do it on their own, unlike us who did not know how to read' (Kaur 2.18).

Tension between the second and third generations arises from the tendency of the second generation to interpret literally the Sikh tradition (hagiographical and historical events); in contrast, the third generation wants to understand the conceptual teachings of the scripture.

Related to the communication barrier are cultural barriers in the approach to teaching the religion. The older generations want to maintain the tradition of hierarchical relationships whereby the older generations give orders (*hukam*) to the younger generation and the younger generation unquestioningly obeys: 'The *Guru Granth Sahib* helps in living daily life and to rise above daily life. Most [Punjabis] are not wise [about the teachings] and wait until something bad happens which forces them to see the need for change. The wise are open to change. Punjabi culture gives more control over kids. People use religion to keep control rather than grow. Ego is the weakness. Everyone wants to be king in the home. We have made Sikhi [Sikh tradition] like ownership – holding it' (Singh 2.11).

The desire for control over children, together with inability to reach out to young people, is the key issue in the transmission of the Sikh tradition today. There is tension between the older and younger generations as a result of communication and cultural barriers. The third generation does not enjoy the sense of fulfilment that elders experience simply by following the traditional customs and rituals that have been transmitted orally. The second generation generally acknowledges that there is tension between it and the third generation, but its traditional mentality makes it difficult for it to accept the fact that its children can choose, or not, to seek a personal relationship with God (instead of accepting the customs at face value).

The Third Generation and Inquiry into Sikhism

An important distinguishing feature of modernity is that knowledge is regarded as progressive and as resulting from inquiry. The third generation, like the second generation, may be able to read Sikh religious history; however, its tendency toward inquiry is considered highly disrespectful by the first and second generations with their traditional mentality.

The children of immigrants (third generation) have been raised in the modern host country of Canada, and this generates tensions between the traditional values they learn at home and the modern values and practices they learn at school or absorb from the society at large. As a result, the modern values of personal choice, self-orientation, and success by merit conflict with the traditional values of respect and duty. There is no doubt that this conflict in values has an impact on the third generation's changing approach toward religion and is causing confusion between culture and religion, alienation from inquiry into Sikhism, and the desire for religion to be a personal choice.

Confusion between Culture and Religion

For the third generation, the *gurdwara* has been the central place in learning about Sikh religion. The third generation's most common form of exposure to Sikhism is going to the *gurdwara* with the family on social occasions – for example, weddings, or religious events such as Guru Nanak's birthday or Baisakhi.[22] Most of the interviewees for the present study acknowledged that they had been exposed to their religion by going to the *gurdwara* as children. However, most of them also described going to the *gurdwara* as a social activity rather than a time for prayer or for learning about the religion. Note the response of a twenty-one-year-old Sikh man: 'I was not exposed to religion at all. I went to *gurdwara* for weddings but never got religious instruction ... I never talked about religion with my grandmother' (Singh 3.6). Note also the comment of a twenty-seven-year-old Sikh man: 'I had very minimal religious training when I was growing up. I did not hear stories from my parents, and my grandparents were not around much. I went to the *gurdwara* with my family several times a month, but it was more of a social event than spiritual. It was a place where my mother would meet Punjabi friends – it was a social club' (Singh 3.14). The focus on social occasions and religious festivities has meant that many among the third generation do not have a foundation in the teachings of the Sikh religion.

The *gurdwara* has been the most important place for learning about the religion; that said, many from the third generation also learned about Sikh religion and history through traditional storytelling. The stories belonging to the traditional pan-Indian genre of hagiography ('sacred biographies') reflect religious or societal concerns and are not strictly speaking historical accounts. Thus, hagiographies are a useful way to transmit conceptual thought for the orality mode of thinking but can seem 'illogical' to the analytics mode of thinking, which favours critical inquiry and scientific exploration.

Some third-generation interviewees told me they were exposed to the religion through stories told by their grandparents (Singh 3.4, 3.33; Kaur 3.7, 3.8, 3.27), but most said they were not (Singh 3.1, 3.3, 3.4, 3.14; Kaur 3.2, 3.9, 3.25). And those who heard the stories as children found that although the stories had some worth as traditional accounts of the gurus, they were not really informative in the sense of answering questions about the religion – questions for which they still have no answer. A nineteen-year-old women told me that for her, the stories were superficial: 'The stories I heard from *gurdwara* or family [when I was growing up] were superficial, lacking depth, which I am seeking ... For my parents, religion was the last priority but I wish and feel it should be more' (Kaur 3.7).

The three generations differ in their attitudes toward hagiography. They also differ in their understandings of the relationship between religion and culture. It was striking that many third-generation Sikhs were uncertain about what differentiates religion from culture. As a consequence, many young Sikhs who were born in Canada, who are just beginning to develop their analytics mode of thinking, speak of culture as religion (Singh 3.4, 3.5, 3.10, 3.37). For instance, several interviewees thought that arranged marriages and caste affiliation (even to the extent of identification with specific geographic and cultural regions such as Malwa, Majha, and Doaba) constituted their religion; at the same time, they showed no awareness of the actual religious teachings of the scripture. When asked about religious beliefs, these individuals seemed bewildered and did not know what to say. A Sikh woman of thirty realized that she had been raised in 'confusion' about religion and culture:

> When I was a child, I see now that I confused religion with customs. Because I associated the customs with religion, I had a negative feeling towards Sikhism – not allowed to go out, wearing Punjabi suit in the home, cooking and cleaning in the home for my brothers ... I was corrected several times when a *rumal* [handkerchief] was not properly covering my head and my back was facing the *Guru Granth Sahib* ... I was not taught about what is in the *Guru Granth Sahib*. I feel ripped off when I realize that I could have had a good religion from the *Guru Granth Sahib* when I was growing up. (Kaur 3.25)

Religion and culture are confused because of the second generation's approach to imparting religion to the third generation and also because of modernity's impact on how individuals approach religion.

Third-generation Sikhs who have developed the analytics mode of thinking ask questions about their religion; it was these individuals who were best able to articulate to me the confusion between culture and religion among Canadian-born youth (as well as the second generation) (Singh 3.14, 3.15, 3.16, 3.17, 3.21, 3.24, 3.26, 3.28, 3.30, 3.38; Kaur 3.7, 3.9, 3.18, 3.23, 3.25, 3.27, 3.31, 3.32). Take, for example, the statement of a twenty-year-old Sikh woman: 'There is confusion between the theology and customs of Sikhism/Punjab. There is equality [of human life] in terms of the theology. However, because of this confusion people, both males and females, turn away from the religion. The issues of equality in terms of culture and custom need to change and will over time ... Parents came in the 1970s and have had enough time to realize that they have to be aware of the identity and cultural issues existing in Canada' (Kaur 3.8).

For the most part, those who had developed the analytics mode of thinking were able to articulate their frustration that Punjabi customs are being passed down from their parents as religion when, in fact, *these customs are often in direct contradiction with the scriptural teachings.* Most often, it was the position of women and the role of caste that third-generation members pointed to as contradicting the scripture. A twenty-three-year-old Sikh woman expressed profound frustration at this:

> *Kismat* is not abuse. Guys do not put up with shit because of *kismat.* [Women] should fight abuse because they are in the right. *Guru Granth Sahib* is greater than cultural norms. What is understood as *kismat* is culturally defined. I am born in a religion, which states [establishes] equality [between men and women, between caste and caste] ... Grade 8 kids are interested if they can relate to you. The difference between religion and culture needs to be made clear [to them]. Discuss male and female equality, issue of caste. Kids are antireligious until they hear that [there is a difference between culture and religion]. Kids are confused because their parents present religion as culture mixed with religion. They have problems with the way the older people present it. (Kaur 3.27)

Those members of the third generation, who possess a highly developed self-awareness and a analytics mode of thinking, are clearly able to separate religion fom culture. As a consequence, they are able to highlight many pertinent issues that arise out of the differentiation. Women, especially, reproach the confusion as a hindrance to their efforts to achieve social equality in the face of the Sikh community's cultural norms. A twenty-three-year-old Sikh woman noted: 'There is confusion in the community, both young and old, regarding religion and culture; while they interact they are not the same. Culture deals with the day-to-day affairs whereas religion is an addition. The problems are not with the religion, they are with the culture. If the cultural problems are helped, then one would be free to practise the religion' (Kaur 3.23).

Alienation from Inquiry into Sikhism

Some of the third generation were taught about the Sikh religion as children; most, however, have found that religion is not a priority for their parents or for the community. Their parents are too busy adapting themselves to Canada's economy; that, or their parents and the community lack the knowledge, the interest, or the inclination to teach them about the religion. Many third-generation interviewees contrasted this situation with that of the Christian community; several of them noted that Sikh parents and/or the Sikh community do not 'think of educating like the Christians do' (Singh 3.6, 3.14, 3.19, 3.37; Kaur 3.19, 3.25, 3.27). Several third-generation interviewees – albeit not most – motivated by their own curiosity, had tried to learn more about the Sikh religion. Most often, their inquiries into Sikh tenets had been stimulated by the reading of English translations of the scripture, or particular hymns or history books (e.g., Singh 3.1, 3.3, 3.14, 3.16, 3.24, 3.33, 3.34; Kaur 3.7, 3.9, 3.18, 3.19, 3.27): 'I went for all the positive points in the *Guru Granth Sahib*. One of the biggest influences for me was a book my dad brought home for me – *Nitnem-banis* translated by Harbans Singh Doabia – the translations of Sikh prayers' (Singh 3.24). Similarly, a twenty-four-year-old Sikh man said: 'I love reading, especially history, but it is a hobby. I have read a lot about Sikh history and culture' (Singh 3.3).

Self-study is viewed by young Canadian-born Sikhs as a necessity if they are to learn about the religion. Yet, inquiry is often perceived as 'disrespectful' by those with the traditional mentality that is associated with the orality or literacy modes of thinking, since for these people, religious beliefs and practices are to be taken at face value. Several third-generation interviewees recognized that young Sikhs had to educate themselves about their religion, but they also maintained that there are not enough resources available for that purpose, such as books in English. Furthermore, parents and the *gurdwaras* have not developed any modern approaches to teaching Sikh religion.

Some of the third generation have been teaching themselves about their religion; unfortunately, most have only a rudimentary knowledge of the Sikh tradition, such as rote knowledge of some of the daily prayers, some familiarity with rituals surrounding the *gurdwara*, and a limited awareness of two or three gurus (usually Guru Nanak and Guru Gobind Singh). Generally speaking, the third generation is ignorant about the Sikh belief system, the actual teachings of the Sikh scripture, and the meaning of the prayers. Similarly, Gurinder Singh Mann has noted that American-born Sikhs lack awareness of the Sikh tradition; he attributes this in part to the failure of the *gurdwaras*.[23] This present study, however, finds that the third generation's lack of awareness of the tradition is not entirely the fault of *gurdwara* leaders and second-generation parents; in considerable part it is caused by language and communication barriers.

The third generation on the whole experiences language and communication barriers with the older generations. Importantly, it often runs into a language barrier in the *gurdwaras*: scriptural Punjabi is different from Punjabi as it is spoken by many of the third generation; furthermore, it is more difficult to understand. Most third-generation interviewees noted that even though they know Punjabi, they were unable to follow the Punjabi used in the *gurdwaras*. Consider the response of twenty-seven-year-old Sikh man: 'I was not interested in religion much and could not understand what the preachers said. Even though I spoke Punjabi, it was difficult to follow the *Guru Granth Sahib* Punjabi and the teachings' (Singh 3.14). Similarly, a Sikh man of twenty-eight stated: 'In my childhood, I remember that I just sat in the *gurdwara* without learning anything. I understood very little because they did not explain the words [*bani*]. My parents emphasized learning Punjabi and that I should learn the *bani*' (Singh 3.13).

Most third-generation Sikhs said they found it difficult to follow the Punjabi in the *gurdwaras*; however, two of them (Singh 3.11; Kaur 3.20), who were born in India and spent their formative years there, told me that they did not have a problem in following the scriptural teachings in the *gurdwara*. One of them, a twenty-year-old woman who had migrated to Canada six years earlier, told me: 'I have no problem understanding *gurbani* having been brought up in India. However, I can understand how the youth born here would have trouble following the teachings at the gurdwara here. I think there should be some English translation' (Kaur 3.20).

A number of third-generation Sikhs have asked for English in the *gurdwaras*. This suggestion is frowned upon by many of the first and second generations, who regard understanding the scripture in Punjabi as the only 'right' way. Note the response of a twenty-four-year-old Sikh man: 'When you ask for the *gurdwara* to provide a service in English, they answer that you should learn Punjabi. A lot of children speak Punjabi but are unable to understand *Guru Granth Sahib* Punjabi. Besides language, there is a lot of difficulty getting literature about Sikhism in the libraries, even in the *gurdwara* libraries. *Gurdwaras* are geared toward the older generation or new immigrants – there is very little interest in the youth' (Singh 3.15).

There is also a language barrier with respect to the English translations of scripture and prayers. Most of these translations have been made by those whose mother tongue is Punjabi; this means that the English translations are highly literal and do not necessarily convey the 'essence' or meaning of the religious teachings in the modern English idiom. Translations are more effective when they are made to the translator's first language. It would be better if English translations of Sikh scripture were made by someone whose first language is English.

Some communication barriers are rooted in the gap between tradition and modernity. Take, for instance, the approach to learning. Modern education encourages critical thinking. In contrast, the older generations of Sikhs have simply learned the prayers and sayings from their parents by rote, without really understanding what they mean: 'Older generations heard the stories and were in the environment to absorb the religion. This has been perhaps taken for granted. The stories were heard and remembered. Education in Punjab is by rote. Education is different here, and there has to be a way to reach out to the younger generation because they are not in the same environment, nor do they learn the same way' (Singh 3.5).

Similarly, a twenty-four-year-old Sikh man stated that the reasons for practising the customs are not passed down: 'The parents know the basics only, which they learned from their parents – they mostly just know the rituals and do not even understand the reason for following the rituals ... The *gurdwara* will always be there. The older and younger people will go to the *gurdwara* because of the customs, but the next generation won't know why [they are going or what they are doing]. Everybody does what everyone else is doing, but most people go without knowing why' (Singh 3.26).

These comments from third-generation Sikhs are significant in that they express concern over not knowing the reasons why one follows particular customs at the *gurdwaras*. The older generations do not express the same concern. The first and second generations follow the customs in the *gurdwara* because that is what has been passed down through the ages. In contrast, Canadian-born third-generation Sikhs have been educated in Canada, so they think more critically and tend to want to know why things are the way they are. This desire to know inevitably results in many questions. Note the predicament of a twenty-three-year-old Sikh woman: 'Religious teaching and upbringing was fine until I started to question and be inquisitive about things. My father did not mind questions which he could answer, but any questions which asked "why" about things got the response "Don't ask why. [It is] because I said so." If he could explain he would love to, but if I said something does not make sense then he would not like it' (Kaur 3.27).

The desire to learn about – and, it follows, raise questions about – the religion generates tension between the older and younger generations. Most third-generation Sikhs find it difficult to question the elders about traditions because of (1) the negative reaction of the older generations to the very act of questioning, (2) the inability of the older generations to answer the questions, and/or (3) the 'rehearsed' answers, which are not suited to the analytics mode of thinking. There is a gap between the traditional mentality and the analytical mentality. Take the response of a twenty-eight-year-old Sikh man: 'My mother would not be able to answer my questions because she [herself] never asked – she just carried on the tradition. My parents don't know the answers to many questions the young ask because they just accepted it as it is' (Singh 3.13).

Many third-generation Sikhs don't even bother to ask because they have found that they are not allowed to question religious beliefs and practices. A twenty-seven-year-old Sikh man stated: 'The youth don't feel comfortable approaching older people because they give rehearsed answers and don't really answer the questions' (Singh 3.24). Likewise, note the comments made by a twenty-year-old Sikh man, who describes his family as very religious and who expects him to take baptism in the future: 'There is a gap between the older generation and the young in terms of being able to answer one's questions like, "Why not cut hair?" I don't ask the older generation because they will just say "It is the way." One can't expect them to answer' (Singh 3.10). Yet another interviewee told me: 'I asked my parents simple questions. You can ask "How?" but you can't ask "Why?" I feel more comfortable asking friends rather than *gianis*' (Singh 3.26).

For Canadian-born Sikh men the questions often pertain to the keeping of the hair or more general aspects of the scripture and customs. For women the most common concern revolves around the scriptural ideal of equality between the sexes as against the position women actually have in the community. One Sikh woman told me that although she tried to inquire about it, her questions were not answered: 'I ask questions particularly regarding women's issues, which upsets people because they say that it is questioning the tradition. I asked about women's issues at [...] temple and was given the [Sikh] *Rahit Maryada* and told it says women and men are equal. One has to look at and distinguish women in the context of theology and [in the context of] customs. People often are uncomfortable with my questions about women and the Khalsa. There is a gap between the earlier way of approaching tradition and the way of learning and thinking things through' (Kaur 3.9).

The second generation's approach to imparting religion makes it more difficult for the third generation to follow Sikhism. When young Sikhs ask questions about the religion, they are seen as disrespectful, and the traditional mind can easily interpret disrespect as rejection. The older generations, because they perceive questioning as disrespectful, tend to discourage the third generation from inquiring into the nature of things, including religion. Yet surely in order to encourage third-generation Sikhs to take to the religion, exploration must be allowed and supported, especially since that is the modern approach to religion.

The older generations misinterpret the questions or independent ideas of the third generation, because people of a traditional mindset have always accepted the words of their elders, because elders must be respected for their accumulated knowledge. Note the experience of a twenty-four-year-old Sikh woman: 'It is hard for me to have my parents try to see my point of view without seeing it as a negation of their beliefs. There should be room for choices. However, for them there is only one way to do things, one way of seeing things. They feel I am not right if I do not pray twice a day' (Kaur 3.2).

There is also tension between the first/second and third generations with respect to the changing approach to religion – an inevitable development when a religious tradition encounters modernity.

Desire for Personal Choice

In the traditional approach to religion, the collectivity accepts what has been passed down through the generations. In contrast, the modern approach is based on personal choice, because modernity is oriented to the individual. This difference between the traditional and modern approaches is evident in the changing attitude toward religion among the third generation. Young Sikhs are moving away from inherited religion and acting on their desire for personal choice in religious belief and commitment. The categories of 'moderates' and 'fundamentalists' are of great importance to the second generation. Such religious/political categories are much less important to the third generation, who are more concerned about the role of religion in their individual lives. A broad range of opinions exists among them. Some see religion as central to their lives and as defining who they are (Singh 3.4, 3.5, 3.14); others see it as important (Singh 3.13, 3.26; Kaur 3.2, 3.8); still others see it as not very significant (Kaur 3.25, 3.27). Finally, some feel that religion should be more important to them than it actually is (Singh 3.11, 3.26; Kaur 3.7, 3.19, 3.22).

Thoroughly unlike the first and second generations, the third generation feels that religion should be a matter of personal choice. In contrast to Sidhu's study, which focused on adolescents who were internalizing the traditional Punjabi-Sikh ideals of religion and spirituality,[24] the present study finds that the parental pressure placed on children to conform to 'concrete' traditional norms results in double lives and role playing, and that in fact young Sikhs desire to exercise personal choice in religious matters. Many third-generation Sikhs perceive the commitment to follow a religion or religious orthodoxy as a personal one. Several interviewees stated that baptism should take place at a young age (e.g., Singh 3.4, 3.36; Kaur 3.34, and especially Kaur 3.8, who 'did it because of my parents and school'), but most third-generation *amritdharis* (Singh 3.5, 3.14, 3,24; Kaur 3.9, 3.31) and most third-generation non-*amritdharis* with *amritdhari* parents (Singh 3.10, 3.13, 3.15, 3.16, 3.30; Kaur 3.2), told me that the taking of *amrit* should be undertaken only when the person is mature enough to understand both the religion and the commitment involved. An *amritdhari* of twenty-seven, who made an independent decision regarding baptism, told of his experience: 'It was only when I was eighteen years old that I turned to religion for fulfilment. I remember being with a party crowd, and it was when I was in a club with a lot of smoking, drinking, and sex going on that I was inspired to be more religious. I borrowed two books on Sikhism from the local library ... My father is clean-shaven. I was baptized in April 1992 out of personal choice' (Singh 3.14).

Another *amritdhari* believed beginning in Grade 9 that religion should be based on a personal choice and cannot be forced on children: 'I find it is a personal thing: the interest in finding out more about one's background, questioning about the tradition. The desire to learn and know more was a personal thing. It is an individual choice and it is the responsibility of the individual to learn. There has to be more responsibility in learning about one's tradition ... Can't force kids to learn about religion and history' (Singh 3.4).

For third-generation Sikhs who are not *amritdharis* and who do not have *amritdhari* parents, the issue of personal choice regarding baptism is not a major concern. However, several did speak out against the 'forcing of religion' on children.

As seen in chapter 4, the move away from Sikh orthodoxy during the 1990s was related to parent/adolescent relations and to psychosocial developments rather than to religion. Interestingly, the three Sikh men I interviewed who had engaged in rebellious-defiant behaviour – including involvement in drugs – have all continued to maintain an interest in religion. But, according to them, there was a lack of education about religion and a lack of space for personal choice. One of these men commented: 'I was forced into being an *amritdhari*. I was pressured by my parents. Since I was born I never cut my hair. I started to shave my beard at around seventeen years old ... You can't feed a kid when he is not hungry. I believe I will take *amrit* when I feel ready. My mom and *dadiji* pressured me ... When I have my own kids, it will be their choice. I won't force keeping their hair or baptism on them' (Singh 3.30).

Another distinguishing feature of third-generation Sikhs is their desire to comprehend or grasp the essence of the religion, beyond its concrete forms. They are exploring the spiritual aspects of religion and, more often than not, are distancing themselves from religion as an institution. This change in attitude is expressed as a desire to 'interiorize' the essence of the teachings. Consider the response of a Sikh man of thirty, who was 'swept away' by the Khalistani movement after Operation Bluestar, but then pursued his own path: 'People are quick to grab symbols without knowing their essence – they want a quick essence. There is too much emphasis on the external practice without interiorizing the Sikh religion ... I don't think anyone is born a Sikh. The day you are baptized is the day you are Sikh ... True Sikhs are like the Jedi [from *Star Wars*]. Guru is the guide for the Khalsa' (Singh 3.16).

This present study finds that although many third-generation Sikhs tend to distance themselves from Sikh religious institutions, third-generation children whose parents are involved in temple politics – whether as 'moderates' or as 'fundamentalists' – remain oriented to the institutional aspects of the religion. In contrast, many third-generation children whose parents have no immediate involvement with temple politics show less interest in such aspects of the religion. In fact, the children whose families are distant from temple politics are the ones who have either removed themselves from religious practice altogether or are independently inquiring about Sikhism and the Sikh tradition. Some of these individuals say they are 'searching.' For example, a twenty-one-year-old Sikh woman averred: 'I am searching now ... I just want to explore possibilities but this is not always well received by the older generation. I find exploration is not encouraged or liked ... I don't want religion to limit me ... I respect the young who are dedicated of their own accord. I feel you have to see why one is converting. One should choose to take *amrit*. It should not be forced upon you because that has a bad outcome. They [the older generation] only know their religion in authoritative terms. People should be dedicated and responsible when they take *amrit*' (Kaur 3.19).

Some, however, have abandoned the Sikh religion because of the politics associated with it: 'My older sister blames her not going [to the *gurdwara*] on politics, but politics should not prevent her to go to temple. She did not go when there was not a problem of politics. My younger sister [nineteen years old] asks me, "What has God ever done for me?"' (Singh 3.12).

Still others have redefined their own Sikh belief and practice: 'I pray every a.m. and p.m., using the names taken by the gurus. I use Sikh terminology. The *gurdwara* is meant to be the place of purest intent, the House of God. You can go there and worship without getting involved with the politics ... They identify [themselves] with the categories "moderates" and "fundamentalists." I think the whole problems of religion are issues regarding human nature, not God. I will raise my children with the philosophy of a higher being to respect, but everyone needs to find it within themselves in life experience' (Singh 3.33).

There is a strong current of change in approaches to religion: religion is now being perceived as a personal affair that should be based on individual choice. This has been accompanied by an explicit emphasis on the importance of interiorizing the values of the religion or scripture, as opposed to 'blindly' practising its customs and rituals. Note the response of a twenty-eight-year-old Sikh man:

'I think the interiorizing of Sikh beliefs is what is important and should be where you start. Some people put too much importance on the external aspects ... I was baptized when I was a kid. I was too little to be aware of the meaning. I do not think it is good to pressure kids with religion or to baptize them when young because they don't know what it is about. I do not follow the baptized way of life – like praying every morning and night, understanding *gurbani* and applying it to my life. I think if I get baptized again, I need to first attempt to live like that and then get baptized. Why take the step without fulfilling it? (Singh 3.30)

Likewise, a thirty-year-old Sikh woman observed:

What is important is if the person who is practising it is good. There is no right religion. I have no problem with the external aspects of religion – the external aspects of a baptized Sikh – but there has to be the internal part too. The community needs to understand love for humanity, to show love for people. Religion is not just the tangible aspects of religion. (Kaur 3.18)

Clearly, the third generation is moving toward the analytics mode of thinking, which tends toward a self-conscious and self-exploring approach to religion. Its centrepiece is the notion of interiorizing religious values in pursuit of a personal relationship with God through the exercise of personal choice.

Identity: Punjabi Culture and Sikh Religion

Although the Sikh scripture is universalistic, most of those who follow the religion have come from a single regional linguistic-cultural group – the Punjabis. When one observes the Sikh community, one notices that it does not always make a clear distinction between Punjabi identity and Sikh identity. As a consequence, there has been much debate over Punjabi-Sikh identity. The relationship between Punjabi culture and Sikhism is a function of how the Sikh community evolved in its early stages. During the early nineteenth century, according to Harjot Singh Oberoi, the boundaries between the Punjabi Sikhs, Hindus, and Muslims were 'blurred.' Not until the formation of the Singh Sabha (1880) did a distinct Sikh identity begin to crystallize.[25] Because Sikhism grew out of Punjabi soil, it was inevitably a bearer of Punjabi culture, which it shared with the much more numerous Punjabi Hindus and Punjabi Muslims. But it also grew out of a struggle against Muslim rule, and in the course of that struggle found common cause with Punjabi Hindus. Under British rule after 1849, there were new stirrings within the community to emphasize its separate identity. The British were eager to encourage this in order to thwart what they saw as rising nationalism under Hindu leadership. From the last quarter of the nineteenth century there was a gathering movement, which strengthened over time, to distinguish the Sikhs from the Hindus.

The issue of a distinct Sikh identity has reverberated in the Sikh diaspora, especially since Operation Bluestar (1984), which served as a catalyst for some Sikhs to seriously reassert their distinct identity. However, which elements in the community are Punjabi rather than Sikh – in other words, which are cultural rather than religious – remains a contentious issue. Several scholars of the Sikh diaspora have discussed the complex relationship between Punjabi culture and Sikh religion in the diaspora. For example, Owen Cole has asked, 'Is it necessary to be or become a Punjabi or to become or be a Sikh?'[26] Norman Buchignani has suggested three approaches to the study of the Sikh diaspora: (1) Sikhs as an ethnic-based cultural community, (2) Sikhs as a minority group, and (3) Sikh religion and culture.[27] And Verne A. Dusenbery asserts that it is 'not always clear-cut whether or not to talk about the Punjabi or Sikh diaspora.'[28] If we apply the literal meaning of the term *diaspora*, it would seem that the Sikh community cannot technically be considered an ethnic diaspora because the Sikhs came to the West of their own accord seeking a better standard of living. The term can be extended to refer to those Sikhs who are seeking a homeland, but such an extension would certainly not include the entire community.[29]

When one looks at the Sikh community in Canada, it is clear that most of its members are Punjabi and thus share many customs and practices with Punjabi Hindus. However, even though there are similarities in culture and language, it is the Sikh religion that distinguishes the community from other Indo-Canadians. It is the religious affiliation with Sikhism that binds the community together. Even when there are strong differences, Sikhism serves as the cord tying the Sikhs to their community. The present study finds that dispite this common identity, each generation of the three being studied has a different view of the relationship between Punjabi culture and Sikh religion.

The first generation calls itself Sikh; its members approach religion and culture as an integrated whole. Its members refer to themselves as Sikh, whether they are orthodox or not. The second generation calls itself Sikh or Jat-Sikh but often takes traditional customs to mean religion; its members and some members of the third generation confuse cultural norms with religion (e.g., *izzat* and arranged marriages) and tend to identify themselves as 'Jat-Sikh' and to talk about a 'Sikh culture.' In contrast, the third generation is internally differentiated. Some of its members call themselves Punjabis, others Sikh, still others both Punjabi Sikh. These people confuse Sikh religion with Punjabi culture and may identify with either. And, even though a given member may be strongly inclined to claim one identity over the other, the underlying understanding is always that Punjabi is synonymous with Sikh.

It is important to note here that in Vancouver, many third-generation Canadian-born Sikhs refer to themselves as Punjabi. However, after some probing, I found that many young Sikhs who referred to themselves as Punjabi used that term interchangeably with Sikh, with the understanding that the two are synonymous. There is an ironic reversal of ethnic identification here: 'Hindoo' was the name used by Canadians to refer to all Sikhs, Hindus, and Muslims in the early years of Indian immigration to Canada,[30] whereas nowadays Punjabi has come to be used by Sikhs to refer to themselves alone, even though there are also Hindu and Muslim Punjabis in Canada. Note the reaction of a eighteen-year-old Gora Sikh man who socializes with Punjabi Sikhs: 'But they [Punjabi-Sikhs] think a Sikh is a Punjabi, and told me that I could not be a Sikh because I am not Punjabi' (Gora Sikh 3.1). Interestingly, the Canadian-born third-generation Sikhs who initially identified themselves as Punjabi were often heavily involved in the Punjabi folk dance (*bhangra*) scene. Moreover, the youth who are baptized (*amritdhari*), and who were deeply involved in the *gurdwara* scene, often initially identify themselves as Sikh.

Conclusion

An examination of continuity and change in religious attitudes among the three generations reveals that attitudes correspond to the distinctive generational modes of thinking, and also reflect the impact of modernity on religion's role in society. The traditional understanding of religion is that it provides normative structures bearing on all aspects of human behaviour, which are viewed as an integrated whole. However, as the predominantly traditional Sikh community encounters modernity in Canada, religion tends to become differentiated from social customs.

Invariably, the tensions that have arisen between generations are related to the interaction between tradition and modernity. The first generation is for the most part illiterate, and it expresses its religiosity through the collective and unquestioning practice of religious customs that have been passed down through oral transmission. In contrast, the third generation has been educated (at least up to high school) in a modern milieu, and this has generated a self-conscious approach to religion that includes the questioning of practices within Sikhism, the conceptual expression of religious notions, the desire for personal choice, and an emphasis on a personal relationship with God. Meanwhile, the second generation follows traditional customs and tends to regard its culture as its religion. Intergenerational tensions in Canada's Sikh community arise from the fact that the Canadian-born children – who are influenced by the ideals of self-differentiation and expanded personal choice that go with belonging to the modern mode of thinking and cultural ethos – are expected to practise their religion as it is traditionally practised, and to do so without questioning it.

We now move from the tensions in the matter of religious practice experienced among the three generations in the Sikh community at the personal level (discussed in this chapter), to the tensions present at the community level with respect to (1) the community's relationship to the Canadian society, (2) the impact on the community as it encounters diversity, and (3) the consequences for the community as it functions in the context of a Western cosmopolitan environment that is also oriented toward multiculturalism.

6 Community Honour among Three Generations: Social Control, Cultural Preservation, and Ethnic Insularity, Part 1

Like many other immigrants, most Sikhs came to Canada solely for a better economic life. Although the original motive was economic, the act of migration to a different society has inevitably generated profound social and psychological changes within the Sikh community. I have already analysed these changes at the personal level in relation to family structure, child rearing, and religious practices. Now it is time to consider the socio-political development of the ethnic community as a whole, especially from the perspective of the three generations. The Sikh community can be viewed as a single religio-ethnic group in its interactions with modern Canadian society – a society that has embraced the social value of universalism and the political culture of democracy and whose federal government is committed to multiculturalism.

The three generations of the Sikh community manifest distinctive ways of thinking about and looking at the value standards of the community. These ways of thinking are rooted in the larger historical process of societal development. Traditional and modern societies have distinctive patterns of behaviour and value standards, including means of social control. In traditional societies, the community is based on particularistic and diffuse patterns of behaviour (clan mentality and 'fused' social institutions). In contrast, modern societies such as Canada are marked by both universalism and specificity, in the sense that the various social institutions are differentiated (e.g., political, social, legal, religious).[1] These fundamental differences in the two types of society illuminate the process of adaptation and integration of a traditional immigrant group in relation to the modern host country; they also shed light on the development of the Sikh community in Canada.

This chapter has three parts. The first provides background material on the socio-political environment and major events that have influenced the evolution of the Sikh community in British Columbia. The second analyses continuity and change in attitudes toward questions of community honour within the ethnic group among the three generations as the Sikhs confront modernity in an environment outside its homeland (multiculturalism and the role of the media are discussed in chapter 7). The third discusses the tensions among the three generations in relation to their understanding of the Sikh community in Vancouver. To this end, it analyses the dynamics of the relations between the three generations in the light of Canadian society in the late 1990s. Intergenerational tensions are to be expected in a community that was transplanted from traditional village life and that has had to adapt and organize itself in a new environment, which itself has changed over time.

Socio-political Influences on the Development of the Sikh Community in British Columbia

The *gurdwara* has been the religious centre for Sikhs for the past three centuries. It was also the centre for all early 'East Indian' migrants[2] in their struggle to survive in Canada. The *gurdwara* has played a central role in the East Indian community's adaptation to the host country. In turn, the socio-political interaction between the *gurdwara* and Canadian society at large has affected the development of the Sikh community in Canada. The various socio-political influences on the Sikh community's development can be seen in light of five different phases: (1) Sikh immigration under the British Crown (1908–47), (2) the Canadian policy of assimilation (1947–60s), (3) the Canadian policy of multiculturalism (1971–present), (4) the Sikh diaspora and the mobilization for a sovereign state in the Indian subcontinent (1980s–90s), and (5) political relations between the *gurdwara* and the mainstream (1980s–present).

The East Indian Community under the British Crown, 1908–1947

During the early period of their immigration to Canada, the Sikhs varied in their political allegiance. The overwhelming majority of them remained faithful to the British Crown, but a handful fought against it for the independence of India. This split between those Sikhs who

allied themselves with the British and those who fought for Indian
independence is most evident in the historic conflict between Bela
Singh, a spy for the British agent W.C. Hopkinson, and Mewa Singh,
who fought against the British Crown and was eventually convicted of
murdering Hopkinson.[3]

The oldest organization for East Indians in Canada is the Khalsa
Diwan Society, founded in 1906. The society built its first *gurdwara* in
1908 on West 2nd Avenue in Vancouver[4] and was incorporated under
the B.C. Societies Act in 1915. This society was a place not only for religious practice but also for social and political activities. Although
many Sikhs remained loyal to the British Crown, many others were
politically active through a Vancouver *gurdwara*-based organization,
the United Indian League (1908–11), as well as through the San Fran-
cisco–based Ghadar Party (1913–19), which had India's freedom from
British rule as its single-minded goal. The Ghadar Party called on the
East Indians – mostly Sikh – to return to India to fight the British. One
example of its efforts to encourage East Indians to return to India to
help the Ghadar ('mutiny, revolt') movement was the poster 'The
Bugle of the Army of Mutiny' (February 1914), which stated:

> We must return to India and start a revolution.
> Get on a boat and go to your country and
> prepare some men to fight for the mutiny.[5]

East Indian immigrants involved themselves in the struggle against
British rule in India. They also fought against discrimination in Canada. First, in 1909 the congregation at the Vancouver *gurdwara* (Khalsa
Diwan Society) successfully fought the government's proposal that
East Indians relocate themselves to British Honduras; they saw this
proposal as a scheme to expel East Indians from Canada. Next, the
Khalsa Diwan Society and the Hindustan League (1912–14) protested
against the Canadian immigration requirement of 'continuous journey'
from the country of origin, which was intended to prevent East Indians
from entering Canada. The fight against the discrimination embodied
in Canadian immigration law came to a head in the *Komagata Maru*
incident, when on 23 July 1914 a Japanese ship with Indian immigrants
on board was refused the right to dock at Vancouver's Burrard Inlet.

The East Indians who succeeded in immigrating to Canada faced a
number of formal legal restrictions. They could not vote, nor could
they join the military or serve on juries or school boards. They also suf-

fered restricted access to jobs in public works. They also experienced informal restrictions with regard to housing, education, public facilities and services, and labour rights.[6] In order to find employment, many Sikhs cut their hair, shaved their beards, and adopted Western clothing. Some even anglicized their names.

The Canadian Policy of Assimilation, 1947–1960s

Canada changed its immigration laws at the time of India's independence from the British Crown in 1947. As a consequence, Sikhs could now become Canadian citizens with the right to vote. In the wake of these political changes, the Khalsa Diwan Society (1947–present) became concerned about immigration and the practising of Sikhism. Following the trend in the Punjab, where in the 1920s the Ghadar Party had transformed itself into a communist group, a leftist (inter-religious) organization emerged in British Columbia, independent of any *gurdwara*, with an ideology of social activism.[7] The East Indian Canadian Citizens Welfare Association (EICCWA) founded in 1952 and active until 1970, focused on two issues: immigration and racism. The EICCWA was a pan-East Indian organization that lobbied the government on (especially) immigration policies.[8] It urged the government to allow family members to immigrate through the sponsorship system.

Many Sikhs at this time were discarding their external Sikh symbols and embracing the Western, 'modern' lifestyle, in the belief that they had to do so if they were to be accepted by mainstream Canadian society. Tara Singh Bains described the environment of the 1950s and 1960s:

> When some families did settle, starting in the 1920s, the men forced their wives to adopt the Western way of life by wearing skirts. Giving up Punjabi dress and wearing skirts seemed odd to those ladies and caused them grave anguish, but they had no other recourse. When they attended the gurdwara, they could not sit on the floor in the right position without exposing their thighs. The management bought heavy curtain cloth in long pieces up to twenty yards each, and the ladies would sit in rows and pull the cloth over their knees to keep warm in winter and to cover their legs. Sometime during the following year [1968] a few ladies attended the *gurdwara* wearing Punjabi dress ... I asked him [a member of the management committee] what was wrong with women in Punjabi dress, and he answered that these women were the first to come that way and they would not be accepted by the general Canadian society.[9]

It is important to note that although there were always Sikh families who maintained their external religious symbols, they did so with great difficulty. Local Sikh communities made an effort to integrate into mainstream Canadian society; but they also built *gurdwaras* throughout the province, even in isolated small mill towns and fishing ports. During the 1960s and 1970s, the growing Sikh community was striving for upward social mobility, through higher education and business success; for the sake of that mobility, its members felt compelled to take on a modern or 'integrated' lifestyle.

The Canadian Policy of Multiculturalism, 1971–present

The largest influx of East Indian in migrants occurred during the 1970s, especially 1971, when the Liberal government under Pierre Trudeau initiated the policy of multiculturalism. During the early years of official multiculturalism, the focus was on the 'celebration of diversity' and cultural preservation. Although more Sikhs were being permitted to immigrate to Canada, they continued to encounter much hostility and racism in their dealings with mainstream society. Also, during the 1970s, the leftist East-Indian organizations, with their concerns about immigration, racism, and labour rights, gained considerable momentum in the Vancouver area.

Many East Indian leftist banded together to fight racism through the B.C. Organization for Fighting Racism (1975–80), the Indian Peoples' Association of North America (1975–77), and the East Indian Workers Association (1977–90). The last two organizations fought especially against the exploitation of workers. There also emerged the Canadian Farm Workers Union (1980–3), a leftist organization established to combat the exploitation and poor working conditions faced by farm labourers in British Columbia.[10]

In the mid-1970s, while these leftist organizations were at their greatest strength, the Sikh *gurdwara* community became divided, because some of the newer immigrants wished to maintain the traditional customs that they had brought with them from the Punjab. Simultaneously, elections were established for the *gurdwara* executive committees; the first of these was held in 1978, at Vancouver's Khalsa Diwan Society.[11] By this time the sentiment was growing among Sikhs that the Indian government was marginalizing the Sikhs in the Punjab. As one consequence, several organizations were formed with the goal of promoting religious orthodoxy.

The Akhand Kirtani Jatha,[12] an orthodox group of baptized Sikhs, came to prominence in Vancouver in 1970.[13] The clash between Nirankari Sikhs[14] and the broader Sikh community in April 1978 in the Punjab was the catalyst for the Jatha movement to defend Sikh orthodoxy. However, the group soon split into two newer groups: Babbar Khalsa and the Akhand Kirtani Jatha (AKJ). The international Jatha group consisted of a very small core of people in Vancouver, all of them strong supporters of a separate Sikh religious state, independent from India. The Babbar Khalsa, an international organization based in Vancouver, consisted mainly of ex-AKJ members. Its most charismatic member, Talwinder Singh Parmar, was a controversial leader. Although his close associates suspected him of 'working for the Indian Intelligence Service,' he later became a prime suspect in the Air India bombings of 1985.[15]

The Sikh Diaspora and the Mobilization for Statehood, 1984–1990s

During the 1970s, tensions grew over who should control the *gurdwaras* in Vancouver's Sikh community. These tensions were, basically, between earlier and more recent immigrants, between orthodox and unorthodox Sikhs. Then, during the 1980s, a drastic change took place in the community in the aftermath of Operation Bluestar. In reaction to armed separatist activity inside the Golden Temple at Amritsar, the Indian government invaded the temple on 3 June 1984. In response to the invasion, many Sikhs felt victimized and reverted to their traditional Sikh religious practices, which they had earlier neglected in Canada.

Many non-baptized Sikhs felt threatened, and returned to their religion in order to preserve their heritage; in addition some traditional baptized Sikhs began to involve themselves in the Khalistani movement. The popularity of this movement was evidenced in the growth of several organizations in Vancouver, which held as their single-minded goal the establishment of a separate Sikh homeland (Khalistan or 'Land of the Pure'). The following groups involved themselves in anti-Indian government protests: Babbar Khalsa International (1981–2003), the International Sikh Youth Federation (1984–2003), and the World Sikh Organization (1984–present).[16]

The International Sikh Youth Federation (ISYF) focused its attention on the Surrey-Delta *gurdwara*, which as of 1984 was still controlled by pro-Indian Congress and 'comrade' Sikhs. Two years later, in 1986, the Federation took control of this important *gurdwara*. Meanwhile, the oldest and most prestigious *gurdwara* in Canada, the Khalsa Diwan Society on Ross Street in Vancouver (sometimes referred to as the Ross Street Gurdwara), was taken over in 1985 by World Sikh Organization (WSO) activists, who chose its new management committee. Later still, the Khalsa Diwan Society was taken over by the ISYF. The WSO was supported by many Akalis.[17] It was generally perceived as more moderate, the ISYF as more radical and uncompromising in its fight for an independent Sikh state.[18]

Several organizations working for an independent nation-state called Khalistan emerged during the 1980s, but most Sikhs in the community remained detached from them and did not become separatists. During 1984–5, leftist groups held meetings for unity among Indians in Canada, but ISYF supporters regularly disrupted them, resulting in brawls. Several people, however, did speak out publicly against the Khalistani movement and its violence – for example, the leftist leader Hardial S. Bains[19] and pro-Indian Congress leader Ujjal S. Dosanjh, who in 2000 would become premier of British Columbia. For speaking out, Dosanjh was assaulted in February 1985 by a man wielding an iron bar.[20]

During this period, while Canadians were becoming more tolerant of other cultures and religions, two incidents took place that enraged the broader Canadian community. In 1984, some Sikhs celebrated the news that India's Prime Minister Indira Gandhi had been assassinated; and in June 1985, two bombs exploded on Air India Planes. One bomb destroyed the plane above the Irish coast, killing the hundreds on board, and the other exploded while the plane was on the ground at Tokyo's Narita Airport, killing two baggage handlers. As a result of these two incidents, many Canadians began to associate the Sikh community with terrorism, and began to resent Sikhs for 'importing' Punjabi political disputes to Canada. At the same time, many Sikhs resented being judged unfairly because of these events.

Some Canadian MPs grew worried about Sikh organizations and their single-minded, militant efforts to establish an independent state. Most vocal was Canada's external affairs minister, Joe Clark, who in 1987 wrote a letter to seven provincial premiers requesting that they boycott Sikh organizations. This led to heated debate in the House of Commons about Sikh organizations, Canadian national security, and Canada's policy of multiculturalism, which seemed to be supporting multicultural charity organizations that were mobilizing ethnic communities for political agendas.[21]

Meanwhile, the Canadian government had been fine-tuning its multiculturalism policy. The Canadian government adopted the Charter of Rights and Freedoms in 1985; then, in 1986, it enacted the Employment Equity Act to combat discrimination and advance social and economic integration through affirmative action and institutional 'mainstreaming.' This act was also an attempt to enhance intercultural understanding.[22] The term 'Indo-Canadian' came into use during the 1980s as a result of Canada's policy and ideology of multiculturalism. *Indo-Canadian* was now the official term to be used in referring to Canadian citizens whose origins were in India. Although this term is now used by Canadian society generally, people of Indian heritage tend strongly to identify themselves and their community with their regional language group and/or religion (i.e., Hindu, Sikh, Tamilian, Ismaili, and the like).

Mainstream and Gurdwara Political Relations, 1985–Present

Sikhs did not receive the right to vote until 1947; since then however, they have been involving themselves in the Canadian political process at the municipal, provincial, and federal levels. Initial Sikh political involvement had been through the *gurdwaras*, as part of campaigning for equal rights in Canadian society. However, multiculturalism has made appealing to the 'ethnic vote' and mobilizing support from ethnic organizations an important aspect of mainstream political activity. The largest resource of the Sikh community in mainstream politics has been and remains the *gurdwaras*. Both Punjabi[23] and non-Punjabi politicians, whatever their political affiliation, make the *gurdwaras* the focus of their vote-catching in elections.

Political divisions within the Sikh community have at times erupted into disputes over who manages Vancouver's *gurdwaras*. In January 1998 the ISYF was ousted from power in the Surrey-Delta *gurdwara* through a joint effort of (non-baptized) communist and pro-Indian Congress Sikhs as well as baptized Sikhs who opposed the ISYF. In reaction to this, the ISYF raised the issue of using tables and chairs in the community dining halls (*langar*) in the *gurdwaras*. On 20 April 1998 the Akal Takht, the Sikh religious governing body in Amritsar, issued a *hukamnama* (edict) on the *guru-da-langar*. This edict against the use of tables and chairs in community dining halls was not accepted on 29 May 1998 by the temple management at the Surrey – Delta *gurdwara*. The issue surrounding the use of tables and chairs in the temple dining halls turned out to be a successful means for ensuring that followers of the Akal Takht – comprised of new Punjabi immigrants and baptized Sikhs (*amritdharis*) (including those who had been originally involved in the joint effort against the ISYF) – would attend a newly established Surrey *gurdwara*. Opponents of the move saw it as a strategy for channelling *gurdwara* funds for organizational ends or for supporting a separate Khalistan. This issue, which played strongly in the media, hardened community divisions between the 'moderates,' who favoured the use of tables and chairs in the dining halls, and the 'fundamentalists,' who obeyed the edict requiring the use of mats. Many *gurdwaras* on the Vancouver Lower Mainland 'sat out' this conflict – for example, like the Nanak-sar Gurdwara (followers of the Sant Nand Singh[24] lineage tradition), the India Cultural Centre of Canada (Sikhs with an allegiance to Indian nationalism), and the Akali Gurdwara (based on the Akali approach to an autonomous Punjab). These three *gurdwaras* share a feature worth noting: none chooses its executive committee by election.

Each generation of Sikhs reflects a distinct phase of adaptation to Canadian society; that said, this adaptation has been occurring in an environment buffeted by internal and external socio-political change. An analysis of the views of the older and younger generations regarding the role of the community should shed light on how the Sikh community has evolved in Canadian society. So let us turn to this issue.

The First Generation and Social Control

The first generation largely continues with its traditional approach: it sees the religious and cultural dimensions of the community as 'fused' rather than differentiated (as in modern society).[25] As a consequence, the first generation persists with the traditional cultural value of community *izzat* (honour) – a value it has brought with it from the Punjab. Even as they try to adapt to living in a modern society, first-generation Sikhs continue to operate according to kinship loyalties ('particularism') and take a diffuse approach to social institutions. They continue to maintain their traditional notion of community *izzat* as a means of social control, and they continue to view the *gurdwara* as the centre of community life.

Community Honour (Izzat) as a Means of Social Control

The first generation has brought with it from the Punjab the traditional clan and particularistic mentality, as well as the value of community honour. Particularism is very strong among the older generations in

Canada. Kinship relations provide a social network for them, and have also been an important asset in facilitating Sikh immigration to Canada through the sponsorship system.

The first generation places much importance on kin group, on the home village or region, and on caste, especially at the time of marriage. Many of the first generation reject the idea of mixed marriage, even when 'mixed' involves a partner from a different region of the Punjab. Take the response of an eighty-year-old Sikh woman: 'I don't agree with interracial marriages because cultures are different. I don't want to see the blood mixing. I felt so bad and disrespected when my grandchildren were marrying white people. I could not stop them' (Kaur 1.14, trans.).

The value of *izzat* at the community level is extremely strong among Sikhs and is expressed through the notion of behaving properly to save face, be it the family's or that of the community. *Izzat* is traditionally understood as the respect one expresses by acting in conformance with traditional mores. There is a strong orientation toward behaving in accordance with what others say or will say. Traditionally, this is how people's behaviour has been controlled. Indeed, maintaining community *izzat* is the governing principle for social behaviour; one attains and maintains *izzat* through one's actions, such as helping others in need. Note the comment made by a Sikh man who possesses the orality mode of thinking: 'We had *izzat* [in the Punjab]. If someone was in trouble, [we would] help them. But now it is not like that ... *Izzat* is nowhere like that now, not here [in Canada], not there [in Punjab], all that matters [now] is money. When I go to the Punjab my son serves me, and also my daughter-in-law, but many [do not]' (Singh 1.9, trans.).

In the same view, dishonour is traditionally defined as lack of respect and improper conduct and thus the inability to save face. First-generation Sikhs continue to hold to this notion. An eighty-year-old Sikh woman commented on the tragic murder of a young woman: '*Izzat* is respect, and that girl did not respect her family. What the family did to the girl [it is alleged that they killed her for marrying a rickshaw driver] is making dirt rotten – it is not *izzat*. How can they say it is *izzat* killing their daughter when now the whole world knows' (Kaur 1.14, trans.). According to this woman, the young girl disrespected her elders by not marrying a man according to her family's wishes. The family believed that killing her upheld *izzat*; in fact, it did not, because the family failed to save face in the community.

First-generation Sikhs still live by the value of community *izzat*, but they often admit that community *izzat* has changed since being transplanted to Canadian society. The second generation mistakenly takes *izzat* to mean status based on one's wealth and material possessions: 'When someone gets off [an airplane] in Canada from India, they forget about *izzat*. [They think], "We are free to do what we want." ... You can't have [real] *izzat* based on the house or money because material possessions can come and go' (Kaur 1.14, trans.). Thus, the first generation understands *izzat* as saving face based on family name and reputation; the second generation understands it as saving face based additionally on the modern value of success through personal effort and the capitalist value of accumulating material possessions.

Among first-generation Sikhs, the pressure not to disclose information about oneself or the family to others within the community remains very strong. The goal is to save face by not being seen or talked about. As a result, problematic issues such as alcoholism and wife abuse are often left unaddressed at the community level. This behaviour extends to exaggerating about good things and hiding or lying about negative aspects relating to the family. To save face, first-generation Sikhs often refuse to look at or speak about dishonourable occasions or actions. Following the orality mode of thinking, the first generation assumes that that which is not seen or spoken of does not exist. For example, there is a tacit understanding that if you don't talk about drugs to children, they will not take drugs, and conversely, that if you mention drugs to children, they *will* take them.

The first generation faces tension with the third generation over questions of *izzat*. The third generation is often perceived by the first as disrespectful when it acts in accordance with Western mores. For example, public displays of romantic affection are perceived as dishonourable for the community, even though such displays are common in Western culture. A Sikh woman of eighty: 'People here do not have *sharam* [sense of shame]. We know about kissing but why do they have to show this in public. We know all that goes on, but keep this in the house. Why does this have to be shown in the public, on TV?' (Kaur 1.4). So there is tension between the first and third generations about community *izzat*. The first generation expresses this tension in concrete terms associated with its orality mode of thinking.

Gurdwaras as the Centre of Village Life

The culture that first-generation Sikhs have brought to Canada is strongly rooted in traditional society and is oriented toward the fusion of all dimensions of community life. There is little differentiation between religious life and social life. For the first generation, religion encompasses a wide range of normative behaviours; it follows that the *gurdwara* as a religious institution has a multifaceted role in the community.

The *gurdwara* reflects the traditional 'fused' approach to society. In its central religious role, it is the 'door to the guru.' At the *gurdwara*, devotees prostrate themselves to the *Guru Granth Sahib* and chant passages from it; they also receive from the *langar* a food offering that is regarded as a gift or grace from God, reflecting the Sikh theological and social stance on equality. At the same time, in village Punjab the *gurdwaras* are places for social work; they are where devotees fulfil the Sikh value of *seva* ('service') – help or contribution to the community. The Sikhs have a tradition of providing community help through donations of food, clothing, and money as well as through service in the *gurdwara*. An eighty-year-old Sikh woman provides an example: 'The *gurdwaras* in Vancouver [Lower Mainland] are not like [those] in the Punjab. In Punjab the *gurdwaras* were the centre of social services, [like for] helping the poor, seniors, youth. The people [here] don't care for the seniors ... The [...] Temple only built the centre but not much is done to help the seniors or youth. Because we are [now] in the *kal yug* [the dark age] – Guru Nanak spoke of this and it is here' (Kaur 1.4).

Through the *gurdwaras*, members serve the needy. They also assist in the maintenance of the temple and contribute to the *langar*. *Gurdwaras* also maintain schools that offer classes to both the youth and adults.

In the Punjab, besides all this, *gurdwaras* provide accommodation to travellers. Because hotels or motels are not often found in traditional agricultural societies, and tea shops are scarce in rural areas, *gurdwaras* have served as stopping places: 'The hospitality of the *gurdwaras*, their free meals and lodging, is more than a symbolic expression of the idea of community as a patrimony shared equally by Sikhs. It also makes the *gurdwaras* the principal system of public accommodation for the rural people of Punjab.'[26] Furthermore the flagpoles that stand next to the *gurdwaras* served as signposts for travellers before roads came to the Punjab.

Finally, the *gurdwaras* have been a place where people gain political status in the community. The history of political involvement in the *gurdwaras* is a long one. During early Sikh history, politics revolved around internal disputes regarding succession in the guru lineage and external battles against Mughal rule in the protection of Hindus and Sikhs. The most frequent comment about religion and the community – mentioned by all first-generation interviewees – was with regard to

gurdwara politics. Although many first-generation Sikhs express dissatisfaction with such politics in Canada, *gurdwaras* remain important to
them. They are where first-generation Sikhs gather to create a social
network or a 'home' based on tradition. For the first generation, *gurdwaras* play an important role in mobilizing the ethnic vote to influence
mainstream politics. It is interesting that first-generation Sikhs tend to
vote (usually with a 'thumb print') according to their clan alliances.

In sum, first-generation Sikhs emphasize the traditional value of
honour, which they understand in very concrete terms and which they
articulate in the context of a collectivity orientation close to their life
situation. They function according to the traditional Punjabi custom of
community honour, they uphold the traditional notion of community
izzat as a means of social control, and they retain a diffuse orientation
toward the *gurdwara* as a central place in their life, even as they experience change in its modern environment.

The Second Generation and Cultural Preservation

The second generation has largely continued with the values of *izzat*,
clan loyalty, and the centrality of the *gurdwara*. Despite all of this,
because of some distancing from the collectivity, Sikhs of the second
generation have, to a certain extent, redefined those values. The continuity of these somewhat redefined traditional values is a source of tension between the second and third generations; it also has affected the
development of the community at large in the context of modernity.

Community Honour and the Preservation of Culture

The traditional Punjabi value of *izzat* and concern about saving face
with regard to the family or community remain quite pervasive in the
second generation's mode of thinking. Second-generation Sikhs are
strongly orientated toward behaving according to what others are
likely to say about them and the collectivity. As noted earlier, this is a
traditional means of social control. An example of the mentality of the
second generation, which is rooted in tradition and yet has experienced some distancing from the collectivity, is this comment: 'In Canada, we have the freedom to change our name. We can change our
name to hide which caste we come from. People don't have to know if
you come from a low caste' (Singh 2.23).

This comment refers only to the matter of choice of name change;
however, it also indicates how strongly behaviour is determined by

one's clan or caste. That is, group *izzat* governs behaviour, and this results in the need to 'hide' one's background. In contrast, the American hero – according to the modern ideal of universalism and achievement – is self-made and has succeeded in rising above a poor or lower-class family background.

Second-generation parents operate from the premise that they must preserve their honour within the community. As with the first generation, they are likely to face enormous pressure not to disclose information about themselves or their family to others in the community. Likewise, they greatly fear that people will malign the family or community. So it is hard for people facing difficult situations in their lives to ask for help even when they must. This is especially true for members of the second generation, who have developed some distance from the collectivity. For example, a forty-nine-year-old Sikh woman faced the challenge of breast cancer: '*Izzat* plays a big factor in the community. When I was diagnosed [with cancer] my mother told me that she was not telling anyone ... I think they don't want others to know because it is a bad thing, perhaps people will think that the kids are not suitable for marriage because there is cancer in the family ... They don't give support or say positive things' (Kaur 2.12).

A community worker in a largely Punjabi neighbourhood believed that education about social and medical problems must be addressed in the light of the Punjabi value of *izzat*:

The community needs to be educated about culture and problems such as drugs and AIDS. The families suffer when this occurs in their homes ... In the culture these are taboo subjects. Tolerance has to be cultivated so that they can learn and be helped by the surrounding resources. These things are kept secret and then the families suffer from not being able to use the support system. Some people need to talk but have no one [to talk to] about their stress. They come crying to me because they don't feel comfortable talking to many people. It is very hard for them holding things in. In one case, a woman had a nervous breakdown and had to go to India for several months because her son went on the wrong path of drugs and so on. It is unhealthy for them to hold these tensions in but they don't have people to talk with. They are concerned about *izzat* and saving face of the family. (social service 1)

Izzat may function smoothly in traditional societies; it is basically incongruent with modern societies, in which there is differentiation among the political, social, legal, and religious areas. It is very difficult to implement *izzat* effectively in a modern society, because enforcing it can run afoul of the law and the broader society, whereas traditionally it has taken precedence over social and legal norms. In a large cosmopolitan society, the ability to ensure social control according to *izzat* breaks down. It is more easily maintained in the smaller towns and villages of the Punjab. Under the impact of modernity, it is breaking down in Indian cities: 'This [change of values] is happening in India as well ... in the big cities with the influence of the West. However, it is happening faster and more here in Canada. In India, there still continues to be social control (especially in small towns and villages). Jullundur city and district are still conservative' (social services 2).

Second-generation Sikhs share the traditional value of maintaining *izzat* within the family and community, but their approach to it has changed somewhat. Honour, no doubt, continues to be determined by the traditional value of ascriptive status. However, since the second generation's encounter with economic independence and business opportunities, *izzat* has come to be increasingly determined by the material goods one is able to afford. Because of the impact of modernity and economic independence, *izzat* is being increasingly determined by achievement rather than solely by ascriptive status: 'There is a lot of competition in the community, like who has a bigger house, and therefore there is a lot of pressure to make a lot of money ... The focus on money has caused a change in values, like lack of respect toward elders' (social service 2).

The preservation of culture – something that was taken for granted in traditional society – is also understood or approached as bringing *izzat*; that is, honour is now also commonly based on whether or not the children are following Punjabi customs in Canada. When their children break away from traditional mores, second-generation parents experience great dishonour and fear that others will talk ill of the family. A forty-three-year-old Sikh woman had her children attending a Punjabi school: 'Parents who send their children to [...] School are not interested in their child's academic development, aspirations, or goals. They send their children there because it is a controlling environment. You see, the parents like [...] School because there is no alcohol, drugs. The traditional values of child discipline from India are preserved there. The quality of teaching is poor but it is the traditional environment that the parents want. They don't want Western values in their homes. For example, they fear their daughters dating or marrying white guys' (Kaur 2.21).

There are two Punjabi customs that second-generation Sikhs experience as crucial for maintaining family honour: the children should marry within the community – and, for some, from the same region in the Punjab – and at the appropriate ages; and the sons should remain in the parental household after marriage. Consider the comment of a Sikh man of fifty: 'There is community pressure that it is honourable if your son still remains with you. Otherwise, people think and gossip as to what was wrong that your child is leaving home' (Singh 2.14). Similarly, note the remarks of a Sikh woman of forty-six: 'Some people show off that their kids are so nice because they are.staying with them, but it is because they want to save money and have *izzat*' (Kaur 2.19).

Izzat has become synonymous with the preservation of traditional culture; it has also become a major source of tension between the second and third generations. A social service worker in the Punjabi community commented:

> Mixed marriages are disapproved in our community but in reality it has to be dealt with because eventually it will happen. We are living in Canada. The problem of Punjabi culture is that we are not that open. This [ethnic insularity] makes it harder for communities to be accepting of children changing and getting integrated here [in Canada]. [Change] is inevitable because we are here for good. People for the most part don't carry the notion of going back to Punjab. They realize this is their home because their children and grandchildren are here. People are selling their land in the Punjab. Eventually we are going to have to deal with the conflict between the two cultures and accept the differences and changes. But quick change is no good, it has to be done with thought, reflection. Quick change results in picking up the wrong things. (social service 1)

The issue of tension between the second and third generations is well articulated by third-generation Sikhs in terms of their experience of ethnic insularity (see below).

Socio-Political Role of the Gurdwara

Second-generation Sikhs are rooted in tradition and have a particularistic and diffuse approach to social institutions; at the same time, they are facing pressure to adapt to modernity, which requires an approach to society based on universalism and specificity. Modern society distinguishes between religious, ethical, and legal norms; traditional societies, in contrast, have 'fused' social standards. The second generation's behaviour, as it adapts to modern society, corresponds more to a 'prismatic' social setup,[27] which is neither the fused traditional pattern nor the fully differentiated modern one but rather something in between.

In Canada there has been a change in the *gurdwaras'* political role in the community. Canadian *gurdwaras* operate according to the traditional value of particularism and diffuseness; however, second-generation temple administrators are now perceived as community leaders in the media and political mainstream, since the temples have become the locus for mobilizing the ethnic vote at the municipal, provincial and federal levels. The prayer halls of the *gurdwaras* are where mainstream politicians come to give campaign speeches. Just as Sikh leaders use the *gurdwaras* for political purposes in India, second-generation Sikhs participate in *gurdwaras* as a means to engage with the Canadian polity. Perhaps it is the traditional political role of the *gurdwara* that makes it so easy for Sikhs to adapt to Canadian politics. That said, there is also a difference in how *gurdwaras* are used for politics in the Punjab and Canada. In the Punjab, political discussions take place at the *gurdwaras* in the dining halls or in the fields surrounding the temples. In contrast, in Canada, political speeches and the like are held in the prayer halls themselves, and this disrupts the sacred space. Note the comment made in an interview by a highly revered Sikh preacher, Giani Sant Singh Maskeen:

> In my thinking, wherever there are prayers, the Guru's word being uttered, and *gurbani* [words of the guru], there should be no politics in that place. Like at Darbar Sahib (prayer hall; Golden Temple at Amritsar) only *kirtan* (hymn-singing) can take place, and no discussion of politics. For politics, the place is the Akal Takht [a building set up by Guru Hargobind across from the *gurdwara* complex for resolving social issues]. Similarly, wherever there's *kirtan* and explanation of *gurbani*, there should be no politics discussed in that place. There should be another place selected for politics. Those who want to speak on politics and discuss the management of the *gurdwara* should create a separate place for such discussions because the vibrations that the *kirtan* produces are ruined by politics.[28]

Second-generation Sikhs involved in Canadian *gurdwara* politics (temple administrators) are able to attain political status and derive economic benefits even while remaining in a familiar Punjabi milieu. Furthermore, the *gurdwara* allows second-generation Sikhs to engage in politics more intensively because there are fewer language, communication, and cultural barriers in that location. This makes the *gurdwara* a valuable political resource for the Sikh community. Second-generation Sikhs on the whole strongly embrace the democratic process even while tending to vote according to their kinship or clan loyalties (rather than according to political platforms or ideologies). The comments of one Sikh MP from a largely Punjabi riding are worth noting in this connection:

> Traditionally, it [the *gurdwara*] is not only a place for religion but also for social issues. They need to get involved with community reform, helping families. They don't have a clear objective. Instead, they get involved with federal, provincial, and municipal politics, which is not their role ... [They should] encourage people to promote cultural organizations; sponsoring culture in a community; but it is not governments' responsibility for maintaining this ... They [Sikhs] are thought of as a united power, thus an ethnic resource, but politicians do not realize how they function. The lobbying of the government is by 'community leaders' who are gurdwara administrators. (political 1)

While the *gurdwara* is the ethnic base for mainstream political involvement by the second generation, the temple administrators have given very little thought to the needs of young Sikhs. The relative neglect of young Canadian-born Sikhs stems from their being seen as having English-language skills and therefore able to function on their own in the larger society. Moreover, Punjabi mores and cultural nuances (i.e., respecting elders, going to the *gurdwara*, maintaining links with the *gurdwara*) are believed to be easily absorbable by young Sikhs through osmosis. The second generation, which predominantly possesses the literacy mode of thinking, takes for granted the learning process with respect to tradition, since its own members at one time went through it in the context of an oral culture.

The present study finds that in fact, the second generation is becoming increasingly concerned about reaching out to the young Sikhs because the 'kids are from parents who are mentally living in the Punjab while physically living in Canada' (Singh 2.5, 2.10, 2.11; Kaur 2.13, 2.17, 2.15, 2.21). At the same time, there is increasing concern that the political divisions in the *gurdwaras* are having a negative impact on the Sikh community, especially the younger generation. One counsellor stated in private: 'In five or ten years there will be a big increase in *gurdwaras*. Religion is going to be more present. The politics affects the children in the religious beliefs but also politics will always be there. I hope that the moderates and extremists eventually see how the division affects the community on the whole' (counselor 3).

Several of the second-generation Sikhs I interviewed suggested that there needs to be a cultural centre with a modern approach for the youth; but they also cautioned that politics can also infiltrate a cultural centre. Meanwhile, third-generation Sikhs tend to doubt the worth of any cultural centre if it is based on the 'clannish' leadership and particularistic approach that the second generation displays in the *gurdwaras*. Younger Sikhs speak of the lack of leadership among the older generations in the sense that everyone wants to be 'king.' It is often considered a part of the Sikh clan mentality that everyone is 'king' or leader; the people of this community tend to resist being perceived as subordinates. Joyce Pettigrew observed that, in the Punjab '[Jat Sikhs] did not regard themselves as subordinate to another person' and that their political culture is factional.[29] Note the comment of a twenty-two-year-old Sikh man about the need of leadership in the community: 'I think what is needed is some sort of organization with strong positive leadership. There are a number of organizations, which do exist, but I don't think they are having the impact they have the potential to have. Really, what is needed is a lot of thankless effort on the part of dedicated individuals to offer some sort of service or organization to which the youth can always turn to for help and direction as far as culture is concerned' (Singh 3.4).

Gurdwaras may well be neglecting young Sikhs; but it must also be noted that they provide places of refuge for new immigrants. Most of the second-generation Sikhs attend the *gurdwara* mainly for social functions such as weddings and religious holidays; the more recent immigrants gather in the *gurdwaras* on a regular basis in order to create a 'home' for themselves in their new host country. The *gurdwara* is the one place in Canada where they can relive the memories of Punjabi village life and be in a familiar environment. As a consequence, many new immigrants come to associate themselves with the 'moderates' or the 'fundamentalists.' The newcomers are often more inclined to go with the 'fundamentalists,' because the latter are more likely to practise the traditional ways that the new immigrants are used to back in the Punjab. However, clan and caste loyalties, rather than theological or ideological orientation, are often the crucial factor in choosing which *gurdwara* to affiliate with. Many new immigrants attend the *gurdwaras* and thus seem to be involved with their politics; in fact, the real

activists in *gurdwara* politics are the members of the executive committees who have been living in Canada since the 1960s and 1970s and
who have established political networks.

The diversity in religious and political affiliations among Sikhs
extends even to families. It is not unusual to find third-generation Sikhs
joking about how some family members are 'moderate' while other
ones are 'fundy.' Note the comment about the categories of 'moderates'
and 'fundamentalists' in Vancouver by a Sikh woman who came to
Canada through an 'arranged' marriage: 'My family [in the Punjab] is
religious and follows the tradition of sitting on the floor in Punjab but I
am not Khalistani ... There are some Khalistanis in my family and some
who are not' (Kaur 2.17). It is also not uncommon for 'fundamentalist'
parents to have secular children.

In summary, the second generation is rooted in tradition and continues to practice the Indian value of community honour. However, the
change in environment has found a redifinition of *izzat*. Second-generation Sikhs are facing considerable pressure to acquire material goods
for status, and are also demanding that their children continue with
Punjabi customs in order to preserve the family's honour. They have
embraced the notion that cultural preservation defines community
honour, but as a whole they have not succeeded in distancing themselves from the collectivity; in broader terms, they have failed to conceptualize the serious difficulties that arise in any attempt to function
according to tradition in a modern context. In contrast, the third generation is able to articulate the underlying negative impact of this situation on the community.

The Third Generation and Ethnic Insularity

Third-generation Sikhs tend toward self-orientation and are able to
articulate theoretical and abstract ideas. The children of immigrants
(i.e., the third generation), having been raised in Canada, tend to interact more with mainstream society; as a consequence, they experience
conflict with the traditional value of *izzat* as a means of control, and
desire to move away from the traditional clan mentality.

Community Honour and Ethnic Insularity

The traditional Punjabi value of *izzat* and the concern over saving the
honour of the collectivity have been carried over from the Punjab by

the first and second generations (grandparents and parents). As a consequence, the third generation has been raised in Canadian homes that operate according to *izzat*. A twenty-three-year-old Sikh woman remarked:

> Everything runs on *izzat*, the community runs on *izzat*. People are always concerned with what others think. People need to stop worrying about what others think, about what others are thinking, worrying about what others are doing, who they are with. They are always comparing, gossip promotes it and the kids start doing the same. No one wants the son or daughter to look bad, parents lie about their children when they are in trouble with the cops, and so on. The parents want to look good and in the end look like they are perfect. It is partly so that they can get a good partner for their kids for marriage. (Kaur 3.23)

Izzat pervades the community. Some third-generation interviewees pointed out that even when their parents speak of being modern and open to Canadian culture, their statements must be taken with caution. Most parents, to some degree, want their children to live according to Punjabi mores because of their concern over what other Sikhs will say. A twenty-two-year-old Sikh woman commented: 'Parents may talk about being open to Canadian culture and people, but it should be taken with some caution as they would still not want it to be with their children. Parents will not talk of the problems they encounter because *izzat* is so strong' (Kaur 3.3).

An example of the personal experience of tension with second-generation parents over saving face for the family is provided by a twenty-three-year-old Sikh woman: 'I am being pressured to get married. My younger sister is living with a white man and was completely ostracized by our father when she was dating him. My dad wants to restore *izzat* ... The biggest concern is *izzat*, what others think. The problem is that the family is always seeking status for *izzat*. They do this through money' (Kaur 3.27).

Likewise, another Sikh woman explained how her sister had been ostracized by the family for dishonouring them: 'I have a sister who was shunned by all the family. Our parents' friends also shunned her because they were following our parents' lead [*izzat*] – they would not go against the parents out of respect ... She was the first girl in the family to go to university and got away with a lot. When she was married to a Punjabi in the U.S.A. it lasted only a few weeks and she returned to home divorced. This was a dishonour to my parents. My father will never change as he will always think he was in the right [i.e., she should have stayed with her husband]' (Kaur 3.25). As this quote suggests, among third-generation women, the issue of *izzat* most often revolves around marriage.

Most third-generation Sikhs view *izzat* as 'hurting' the community, especially because it hinders dealing with the community's problems. One Sikh man, who has engaged in rebellious-defiant behaviour, noted: 'Parents don't care, don't worry about the law; keep hush hush because of *izzat*. *Izzat* is ruining the community ... Parents are rigid – trained all their life in *izzat*. Young generation grown up with this' (Singh 3.34).

Similarly, a Sikh woman of twenty-two years observed: 'The community has to become more open and acknowledge issues and problems rather than act as if they don't exist – like homosexuality, AIDS, women's inequality, and breast cancer. *Izzat* is very strong and part of it but the community does not know how to counter it. Feels that these people are better left alone. Instead, there should be help provided to these people. We are not living in la-la land, so we too have these problems. Issues such as women's issues need to be addressed by the community' (Kaur 3.9).

Likewise, a twenty-two-year-old Sikh woman commented on how her family dealt with a member dying of AIDS: 'A relative in my family had AIDS and died of pneumonia. No one discussed about him being sick until he had died. It was a secret and it remains something not to be talked about' (Kaur 3.3).

Many third-generation Sikhs dislike the traditional value of *izzat* and acknowledge its negative implications for living in a modern society. But they offer very few suggestions for changing it. A few see education as the most important means to overcome it. There is a general belief among third-generation Sikhs that each successive educated generation will address the issues in a more forthright manner and thus weaken the pervasiveness of *izzat*: 'I don't know how to break through it [*izzat*] because it is strong. However, eventually it will weaken as my generation grows up. I believe it is not just *izzat* but also a lack of education. My generation is educated and will address health issues in a more open way. Traditional thought should be incorporated in education, otherwise how are they supposed to know it?' (Kaur 3.8).

Interestingly, while the third generation acknowledges the difficulties that the traditional value of community honour creates for functioning in modern society, it admits to being caught in it itself. This generation states that Canadian-born children carry on the value of *izzat* because it is so strong within the community and because it is the behaviour they are accustomed to. To varying degrees, many third-generation Sikhs seem to follow the practice of community honour, out of choice or familial pressure or because they learned this pattern of behaviour when young. According to a Sikh man of twenty-two, the traditional practice of *izzat* has continued because so many people are unable or unwilling to break away from it: 'Punjabis are ghettoized. All go to school with mostly East Indian kids. Not exposed to different views. The kids become separate from other groups. At university, there is not much interaction with others in classroom ... It forms a world in a limited way and then kids hate it. Everyone in my generation hates the East Indian culture [of *izzat*]. There is an immaturity because of the narrowness of their world view ... They are not experienced in a broader sense [mainstream]' (Singh 3.33).

Many Canadian-born third-generation Sikhs experience ethnic insularity (unless they have moved out or have been ostracized), and refer to it as the 'Punjabi Bubble' (discussed further in chapter 7). The community's clannish mentality also results in divisions. One Sikh man underlined: 'There is clannish mentality. The community keeps getting divided – it should stick together. The younger generation whose parents are involved with *gurdwara* politics is following their footsteps in the *gurdwara*. They need to think with their brain. We [my TV show partner and I] counterbalance each other. I am from Doaba and my parents are for chairs. I don't care about it. [...] is from Malwa and for sitting on the ground. People can't get too clannish with us because we represent two different sides of the community' (media 1). Third-generation Sikhs see the clannish mentality as encouraging ethnic insularity even while dividing the community.

Malaise with the Gurdwaras

The *gurdwara* has traditionally been the centre of community life. However, the politics of the *gurdwaras* is an issue much talked about by the third generation. Some maintain that politics is the reason why they *don't* go to the *gurdwara* (Singh 3.10, 3.15, 3.16, 3.21, 3.26, 3.33, 3.37; Kaur 3.22, 3.24, 3.25, 3.32); others continue going to the *gurdwara* to pray and ignore the politics (Singh 3.11, 3.12, 3.14, 3.34; Kaur 3.7, 3.19, 3.20, 3.23, 3.27). A twenty-year-old Sikh man noted: 'I know a lot of people in my age group who abandoned religion because of the politics: they feel the *gurdwaras* have become corrupt by internal politics; there is no religion, so why bother ... The *gurdwara* tradition is going to decrease because people won't have the religion behind them to draw them to the *gurdwaras*. The younger generation is not going to be interested in going to *gurdwara* in the way the older generation goes' (Singh 3.10).

Whether they attend the *gurdwara* or not, third-generation Sikhs generally experience a malaise with *guardwara* politics. For the first and second generations the *gurdwara* is an important political resource for mobilizing the ethnic vote; that is not the case for the third generation.

Besides which, some third-generation Sikhs associate traditional or orthodox Sikhism with extremism or terrorism. One baptized Sikh woman of twenty-five stated: 'When relaying Sikhi [the Sikh tradition], the *gurdwaras* do so from hard-line views. This turns off a lot of people and widens the gap (between *amritdharis* and non-*amritdharis*). This is the case especially for the younger generation, and now they are not talking about religion at all. There is a stereotype that those wearing turbans are extremists or terrorists' (Kaur 3.31).

Similarly, a nineteen-year-old Sikh woman, whose parents associate themselves with the moderates, commented: 'My parents at first were very proud that I was becoming more religious; however, then they became afraid that I would become a fundamentalist and get baptized. Being religious is equated with being fundamentalist/extremist but it should not be' (Kaur 3.7).

The perceived malaise encountered within the *gurdwaras* is ascribed not only to their politics but also to the prevalence within them of the clan and village mentality. Third-generation Sikhs perceive *guardwaras* as lacking interest in the advancement of the Sikh community in Canadian society:

> The *gurdwara*, rather than making the community propel forward, is moving the community backwards. The gurdwara never brings in young or new blood ... The *gurdwara* has control over the community, so people in position in the *gurdwara* don't want to let go of their power ... I do not interact with the Punjabi community because I find they are 'village like.' The community regresses rather than progresses. The *gurdwaras* are not doing their job here. I do not go to the *gurdwara* because I do not want to hear the politics. The *gurdwara* should speak about religion and distinguish it from customs like women's issues. (Singh 3.21)

Some third-generation Sikhs have drifted away from the *gurdwaras* because of the politics and the clan mentality associated with them; others have turned away from them because of the lack of organization and facilities to truly learn about the religion. A twenty-year-old Sikh woman commented: 'There is a lack of organization in the community. Organization is partially difficult given the political and religious divisions. They are just building *gurdwaras* but what use is this if the younger generation is not aware of the tradition, religion. If they are not given the intangible aspect of culture and religion these *gurdwaras* are going to be empty down the road. They do concrete things, such as building new structures, but lack awareness of the need in being involved with the education of religion' (Kaur 3.8).

Third-generation Sikhs, whether or not they attend the *gurdwara*, do not find that the *gurdwara* fulfils its role either as an agency of social action or as an institution that really teaches the religion. Thus, they conclude that they need to go elsewhere to learn about the religion.

The Canadian Sikh Community as It Develops outside Its Homeland

In his study of the Sikhs in England, Arthur Helweg differentiates between two waves of Sikh immigrants, each with a distinctive mentality. The first wave consisted of Sikhs with a colonial mentality in that they regarded Western culture as superior and therefore to be preferred; the second was comprised of Sikhs who wanted to keep their traditional culture.[30] This finding that the distinctive mentalities among Sikhs abroad are related to successive waves of immigrants is an important one that is not unique to England. However, perhaps it should not be applied strictly to Sikh immigrants elsewhere. In another study that specifically addresses the Sikh diaspora in Canada, Joseph O'Connell notes the increase of 'Khalsa Sikhs,' by which he means baptized Sikhs, as a consequence of the more recent immigration of Sikhs:

> There is always the fundamental distinction between initiated Khalsa Sikhs and non-Khalsa Sikhs, a distinction that has been the focus of serious conflict within some Sikh congregations, especially in British Columbia, where 'new' Punjabi immigrants insisting on Khalsa standards have challenged the accommodations by 'old' Canadian Sikhs to prevailing Canadian customs. At present, those upholding Khalsa norms – whether they constitute a majority or not – are dominant in most gurdwara management and other community affairs, and in the image presented in the Canadian public as to who a Sikh is.[31]

In the present study I have taken the position that there is a long history of variation in political alignments among the Sikhs, which has caused friction among them. In the colonial era, some Sikhs joined Britain's Indian Army at the same time as other Sikhs, such as Shahid Bhagat Singh (1907–31) and Shahid Udham Singh (1899–1940), fought for Indian independence. In the early 1900s in Vancouver, there was a conflict between Bela Singh and Mewa Singh; the former spied for the British in Canada and the latter rebelled against the British Crown. There is no doubt that the strong influx of Sikh immigrants during the 1970s generated friction between the new immigrants, who tended to be more traditional on arrival, and the older Sikhs, who felt a sense of privilege, having been in Canada for a longer time. The resulting tension led to a political struggle over control of the *gurdwaras*, which was exacerbated when elections were introduced to them. But, it is clear that such internal conflict is nothing new among Sikhs; as noted earlier, Sikhs in Vancouver and elsewhere have always varied in their political affiliations.

Furthermore, these differences in political affiliations are often rooted in clan loyalties rather than theological or philosophical disputes. This phenomenon arises from the second generation's literacy mode of thinking. Consistent with that mode, second-generation Sikhs have distanced themselves to some extent from the collectivity and are adapting to modern society. They therefore behave in a manner that falls in between the fused traditional pattern and the fully differentiated modern one (i.e., in a manner more in accordance with the 'prismatic' social setup). There has been some distancing from the collectivity, but not a great deal, since their behaviour is still determined mainly by clan loyalties. Note the comment of a Punjabi educator: 'The people don't really think in terms of theology but more in terms of clan and family alliance. There is village mentality ... I wish that the community would be more unified ... Regardless, people are split by the clan behaviour. This is due to lack of education' (educator 2).

This tendency to clan loyalties has resulted in much political factionalism, which was evident in the early 1980s and continues into the present.[32] It is noteworthy that, as Verne Dusenbury observed, Canadian Sikhs have not succeeded as a distinct ethno-cultural group in lobbying for Sikh interests at the municipal, provincial, and federal levels. For example, they have been ineffective in speaking with a united voice; in joining with other organizations to strengthen their cause; and in explaining past incidents that enraged the broader Canadian community, such as the celebrations by some Sikhs on hearing of the assassination of Indira Gandhi in 1984.[33] The Punjabi Sikhs who have succeeded in the Canadian political process at the provincial and federal levels[34] tend, in fact, to be the ones who minimize their 'Sikhness,' who distance themselves from Sikh concerns, and who identify themselves as 'Indo-Canadian.'[35]

More recently, 'fundamentalism' has become a source of community friction in both the Punjab and the Sikh diaspora. Fundamentalism is a wider phenomenon that goes beyond Sikhism and is seen in the rise of many fundamentalist movements around the world. Many scholars have tried to understand the nature of fundamentalism. Martin Marty and Scott Appleby have examined the rise of fundamentalism in the twentieth century; in their view, modern fundamentalist movements are based on a selective retrieval of doctrines, beliefs, and practices in reaction to a sense of threat to the religious or 'sacred' identity of the believers. These movements are oriented less to a return to the past than to the re-creation of a social and political order that looks to the future, when good and evil will enter an apocalyptic struggle.[36] Similarly, in her thorough study of fundamentalism in Judaism, Christianity, and Islam, Karen Armstrong views it as a phenomenon rooted in (1) the fear of annihilation and desacralization, and (2) an orientation toward the future.[37]

More specifically in relation to the Sikh community, Harjot Oberoi describes Sikh fundamentalism as founded on the belief in a utopia that is God's plan. He contends that Sikh fundamentalism is in fact a millenarian movement. He surveys the socio-political dimensions – primarily the Sikhs' quest for recognition by the Indian government and their loss of land, power, and control – but he does not demonstrate how the 'fundamentalist' beliefs of millenarianism are rooted in Sikh scriptural tradition. Rather, he offers a handful of extracts from speeches by Jarnail Singh Bhindranwale, the leader of the movement for an independent Sikh state, in order to demonstrate how millenarianism characterizes the Sikh tradition.[38] Actually, millenarianism – the belief in a future time of ideal peace and happiness (based on the Christian belief in *Revelation* 20:1–5 about the second coming of Christ, when He will reign on earth) – contradicts the basic Sikh world view and religious goal of escape from the cycle of birth, death, and rebirth (*sansar*).

In the Punjab, the term Sikh fundamentalism is popularly used in reference to Sant Jarnail Singh Bhindranwale (of the Damdami Taksal[39]) and his movement for an independent Sikh state called Khalistan. The movement grew in strength after Operation Bluestar in 1984. That said, the campaign by many Sikhs in the Punjab for special political recognition can be traced back to the time of Indian independence, the partition of the subcontinent, and the creation of Pakistan, which serves as a useful precedent. In his thorough study of Punjabi politics after Indian independence, Baldev Raj Nayar examines the quest by the Akali Dal, the Sikh political party, during the 1950s and early 1960s for a Punjabi-speaking but really Sikh-majority state called Punjabi Suba, through protest movements and parliamentary action.[40] For many Sikhs, the Akali Dal's campaign for special recognition by the Indian government was a failure, despite its remarkable achievement in obtaining the Sikh-majority state in 1966. The autonomy provided by the new state did not, however, satisfy a large number of Sikhs. When the Akali Dal came to political power in the Punjab, it moderated its stance somewhat, though it continued to press for more autonomy.

The success of the Green Revolution in the 1960s and 1970s had a tremendous impact on the Punjab, by widening economic disparities and increasing the numbers of educated – and unemployed – young Sikhs. Many Sikhs began nursing a grievance about being discriminated against by the central Indian government even though the Sikhs were in power in the Punjab. All of this led up to the emergence, in the late 1970s, of an ethnic-national movement[41] for an independent Sikh state under the leadership of Sant Jarnail Singh Bhindranwale. This movement can be understood through the paradigm of antistate terrorism.[42]

In the Sikh diaspora, the term 'fundamentalism' is double-edged: it refers to Sikh organizations such as the ISYF and Babbar Khalsa, which mobilized Sikhs abroad for Khalistan during the 1980s and early 1990s, but it also refers to those orthodox Sikhs who favour sitting on mats in the dining halls (i.e., they follow the Akal Takht). More accurately, the Sikhs who have chosen to follow the Akal Takht and its edict to sit on mats are traditionalists (i.e., they adhere to tradition) or orthodox (i.e., they conform with the established standards of the religion). The first- and second-generation Sikhs, however, have readily taken to using the term 'fundamentalist' to describe these groups, in contrast to the term 'moderate,' which they apply to those who stand apart from or oppose them. It may or may not be appropriate to refer to the followers of the Bhindranwale movement for an independent state as fundamentalists. It would be more accurate to refer to the politically 'moderate' Sikhs who practise the fundamental principles prescribed in Sikh religious scripture and doctrine as 'orthodox.'[43] Some orthodox Sikhs support a separate Khalistan; many do not. In fact, some Sikhs who attend the 'fundamentalist' *gurdwaras* resent being referred to as such because this implies that they are Khalistanis or are associated with political violence. At the same time, some more secular Sikhs sympathize with Bhindranwale's movement because they identify with the ethno-nationalist movement for greater autonomy for the Punjab.

Four Phases in the Sikh Community's Adaptation and Integration

Many scholars have attempted to delineate the processes of ethno-cultural adaptation.[44] Several have differentiated two stages of adaptation: (1) the immigration phase, during which the immigrant community 'settles in' the host country while maintaining its cultural structures and practices; and (2) postimmigration phase, which involves cultural change (variously defined by scholars).[45] Other scholars have identified intergenerational phases: (1) the first (or immigrant) generation and the transplantation phase; (2) the second generation and the rejection phase; and (3) the third generation and the rediscovery phase.[46]

In his study of the Sikh community in England, Helweg delineates four phases in the Sikhs' adaptation process: (1) the premigration phase, during which there is interaction on the basis of inaccurate information (stereotypes) between the host and home communities; (2) the freedom phase, during which males are away from the home country yet closely linked to it, typically by earning money to send back home; (3) the conflict phase, during which there is tension between the traditional lifestyle of the immigrant community and the norms of behaviour of the host society; and (4) the settlement phase, during which immigrant communities become permanent in the host country.[47] These four stages can be taken to apply to the Sikh immigrant community in Vancouver.

The Sikh community in Vancouver, like the one in England, is highly diverse because it includes many waves of migration, and various sectarian and political affiliations. This means that its members are at different stages of adaptation to Canada. Even so, one can delineate various phases in the adaptation process that are particular to the Sikh community in British Columbia. Having conducted intensive field research on the cultural and social aspects of the community, I have arrived at four basic phases that are evident among the three generations of that community:

- *Phase 1, the myth of return:*[48] Sikhs come to Canada to make money in order to buy land in the Punjab, to which they have every intention of returning.
- *Phase 2, reality of staying*: immigrant Sikhs accept that they are not going to return to the Punjab. They either have sold or are planning to sell their land there because their 'children have no link with the land.' Some may, however, continue to keep their house or land in the Punjab so that they can visit their village on holidays.
- *Phase 3, ambivalence on cultural change*: Sikhs in Canada regard Canada as their home and come to view cultural change as inevitable. However, such change is acceptable only 'so long as it is not for my own children.'
- *Phase 4, reality of cultural change*: the children are viewed as being Canadian and cultural change is accepted even for 'my own children.'

The Sikh community in Canada covers the entire spectrum of these phases. However, *most members of that community lie in the second and third phases*. On the basis of interviews, it would seem that the first generation of the Sikh community belongs largely to the first and second phases (although one Sikh, who has been in Canada for more than twenty-five years, is in phase 4). Many Sikhs in this generation came to Canada to make money, and intended to return to the Punjab eventually. Note the comment of a sixty-five-year-old Sikh man: 'I came to Canada in 19 – to make money ... It was a shock for me to work in a sawmill after having a government job in India ... After one month working in the mill I thought I would return with my family after saving money to return. I found it hard to adapt. But after working to save money to return, you end up staying' (Singh 1.17).

Other first-generation Sikhs, however, came to Canada under the sponsorship system to join their families already here, and therefore accept that they are not returning to the Punjab. In either case, the first generation is moving toward selling (Singh 1.16; Kaur 1.4, 1.8, 1.13) its land in the Punjab, since its children are losing their ties to it (Singh 1.17). Besides which, their grandchildren are in Canada. Note the comment of an eighty-six-year-old Sikh woman: 'I thought I would return after four months [on coming to Canada]. I saw my grandchildren dependent on nannies and felt I needed to care for them. I felt pulled toward my kids ... The majority of elders are unhappy. They feel stuck here in Canada but have sold their land in the Punjab. The elders who get pension are better' (Kaur 1.13).

The second generation of the Sikh community seems to belong to the second and third phases. These Sikhs accept that they are not returning to the Punjab and have either sold or are planning to sell their land there because the 'children have no link with the land.' This segment of the community regards Canada as its home, especially because its children and grandchildren are here. Note the comment of a fifty-four-year-old Sikh man:

> When we came we had one goal – to earn money. Many of us worked hard and bought several houses. We value land, coming from a predominantly farming culture. We also worked hard to send money back home to buy more land. We may have had the idea of returning back to the Punjab. Now Punjab is prospering, the value of land is high, and some people now are selling or thinking of selling their land to help them pay for their mortgage here. People are starting to question the purpose of too much stress on money. People while living here actually think of Punjab as their home. Now we are starting to see that Canada is our home. It is the place where our children and grandchildren are. (Singh 2.5)

These Sikhs realize that Canada is their home and that cultural change is inevitable. However, this acceptance of the inevitability of cultural change is conditional: it is all right for others to change their culture 'so long as it is not for my own children.'

As for the third generation, those among it who have children belong to the third and fourth phases. Those of this generation who do not have children may not have moved to phase 4, but they often express the desire to achieve it in contrast to their own parents. The Sikhs of this generation see Canada as their home – many have not even visited the Punjab – and believe that cultural change is inevitable (even though it may come more slowly than they wish). The acceptance of change ranges from conditional (i.e., 'so long as it is not for my own children') to whole-hearted (i.e., even for 'my own children'). Thus, Canadian-born Sikhs who are children of immigrants do not precisely fit the often conceived three-generation cycle of ethno-cultural adaptation. Immigrant parents (the second generation, according to this study's typology) are concerned about maintaining ethnic identity and cultural practices; meanwhile, their Canadian-born children generally do not reject their religious and cultural heritage. Generally, they experience a great deal of ethnic insularity when, in fact, they would like to preserve the broader Punjabi culture and religion while doing away with those customs they dislike (such as *izzat*) and inter-acting more with the mainstream (discussed in chapter 7).

Conclusion

As the predominantly traditional Sikh community encounters moder-nity in Canada, tensions invariably arise between the three generations – tensions that are related to the gap between tradition and modernity. The first generation practises community honour as a means of social control. Although it experiences change in its modern environment, it retains a diffuse orientation; for them, the *gurdwara* is a place for social networking and activities. The second generation continues to follow tradition but has somewhat redefined community honour as cultural preservation and material achievement. Second-generation Sikhs have distanced themselves somewhat from the collectivity but have main-tained their clan loyalties as the determining factor in their community behaviour. This is most evident in *gurdwara* affairs. Third-generation Sikhs are generally critical of community *izzat*, because this value as it is practised does not correspond to modern notions of universalism. Third generation Sikhs, with some exceptions (e.g., those who have left home or who have been ostracized), feel ensnared in their commu-nity's traditions, and this gives rise to a profound sense of ethnic insu-larity. They want to move away from the clannish mentality of the community and to soften the socio-political impact of the *gurdwaras*.

Tensions within the Sikh community in Canada are generated by the social contradiction that Canadian-born children who live in a modern society with its own cultural ethos are being raised according to tradi-tional mores inside the family and are expected by their parents and by the broader family networks to operate in conformity with traditional norms of community honour and clan loyalty. Meanwhile, the *gurd-waras* – the traditional Sikh community centres – are perceived by young Sikhs as suffering from serious limitations, chief among them being their overinvolvement in clan politics and their inability to impart knowledge about the Sikh tradition and religion in an idiom that young Sikhs can understand. The consequent dissatisfaction has resulted in young Sikhs drifting away from the *guardwaras*.

7 Community Honour among Three Generations: Social Control, Cultural Preservation, and Ethnic Insularity, Part 2

As the predominantly traditional Sikh community encounters modernity in Canada, it must come to terms with Canada's official policy of multiculturalism. This policy was adopted in 1971 as a means to manage the country's ethnic and racial diversity. So it is important to examine the development of the Sikh community not only as an isolated religio-ethnic group, but also with regard to how it relates to the country's diversity and its policy of multiculturalism. That is, it is pertinent to investigate the external influences that have affected the Sikh community's adaptation process. While the manner in which a given generation of the Sikh community relates to and interacts with the mainstream society and its diversity undoubtedly reflects that generation's particular stage of adaptation and the mode of thinking, this does not negate the question the present chapter addresses: How does multiculturalism policy further or hinder the community's adaptation to and integration[1] with Canadian society?

This chapter has three parts. The first provides an overview of the main events relating to the Canadian policy on multiculturalism and of the various multicultural agencies used by the community. The second analyses how each generation of the Sikh community relates to and interacts with the mainstream in the light of Canada's social diversity and its orientation toward multiculturalism. This part also examines the role of the media. The third part discusses the tensions between the three generations of the Sikh community as a result of the different approach each takes to mainstream society in British Columbia. In general terms, the chapter tries to show what Canada can learn about itself in the light of the Sikh experience with multiculturalism.

Multiculturalism and the Punjabi Community

During its formative years in the 1970s, the Canadian government's multicultural policy focused mainly on preserving the cultures of the country's various communities. Then in 1985, the Charter of Rights and Freedoms was adopted. The following year, the Employment Equity Act was enacted. These put into law the right to preserve one's culture and the right against discrimination in federal institutions. Finally, in 1988, the policy of multiculturalism was formally incorporated in the form of the Canadian Multiculturalism Act. This act was an attempt to ensure, and manage, cultural diversity and cultural preservation through affirmative action and institutional 'mainstreaming' (i.e., the integration of minority groups into the mainstream so as to guarantee minorities equality in representation and treatment). Over time, however, the act came to be perceived as a resource for political and economic pursuits; for instance, the major political parties have used it to appeal to the 'ethnic vote,' to mobilize support from ethnic organizations, and to advance international business interests.[2]

Significant 'Multiculturalism' Developments for B.C.'s Punjabi Community

Canada's multiculturalism policy has had several highly significant effects on the Sikh community in British Columbia:

1 Khalsa School was established in Vancouver in 1986. This is a full-time private school that follows the prescribed curriculum but also provides instruction in Sikh religion and Punjabi language. A second Khalsa school was opened in Surrey in 1992.
2 On 23 May 1990, as a joint act of the municipal, provincial, and federal governments, a plaque commemorating the *Komagatu Maru* incident was unveiled at Portal Park in Vancouver.
3 The Solicitor General of Canada announced in 1990 that the RCMP dress code would be amended to allow turbaned Sikhs to join the force. In 1990, Constable Baltej Singh Dhillon became the first turbaned Sikh to join the RCMP.
4 In 1993, five Sikh war veterans were invited to participate in the 11 November Remembrance Day parade. Unfortunately, they were denied entry into the Royal Canadian Legion in Newton (Surrey), B.C., because of their turbans.

5 In July 1993, the Punjabi market at Main Street and 49th Avenue, Vancouver, with bilingual signs in English and Punjabi, received official recognition.
6 On 29 November, 1994, a seniors centre for Sikhs was opened in Surrey, B.C.
7 In 1995, the B.C. government officially recognized the Baisakhi parade.
8 In 1996, B.C. schools began offering Punjabi language in the regular curriculum from grades five to twelve.

The commemoration of the *Komagatu Maru* incident was an acknowledgment of the unjust treatment of Sikhs (and other East Indians) during the early 1900s. The other items listed above reflect the influence of Canada's multiculturalism policy as well as a recognition of the Sikh community's separate identity in Canada.

Important Multicultural Organizations Serving Punjabis in British Columbia

Canada's multiculturalism policy facilitated the growth of organizations on the Vancouver Mainland with various roles and goals. Many of these organizations depend for their funding on both government and private sources. The following are the most prominent ones patronized by members of the Sikh community:

1 Multilingual Orientation Service Association for Immigrant Communities (MOSAIC) (Vancouver) deals with new immigrants and social issues.
2 Progressive Intercultural Community Services Society (PICS) (Vancouver/Surrey) attends to labour and employment issues.
3 Rainbow Project (Surrey) concerns itself with health issues.
4 Options (Surrey) operates as a resource and referral centre for immigrants, especially adults.
5 Surrey-Delta Immigrant Services Society (Delta/Surrey) handles problems faced by new immigrants, especially adults.

Besides all this, government institutions are paying more attention to the language barrier in order to ensure that immigrant groups have access to mainstream institutions such as hospitals and social (including immigration) services. Literature about immigration, racism, health, and social services offered by the different ministries is printed in Punjabi; more and more interpreters have been hired by health and social institutions. Likewise, multicultural agencies – both governmental ones and NGOs such as MOSAIC and PICS – are providing services in Punjabi to various segments of B.C.'s Sikh community.

Ethnic Media in the Punjabi/Sikh Community

There has also been a burgeoning of ethnic media organizations providing radio programs, TV shows, and newspapers. These multicultural offerings are run as businesses and depend on sponsors. The TV shows are broadcast through the Shaw multicultural channel, the Now TV channel, and the Vision multifaith channel. Ethnic newspapers and radio programs have emerged under the umbrella of multiculturalism, which encourages ethnic minorities to preserve their culture.

There are five Punjabi radio stations based on the Greater Vancouver Mainland:

- Rim Jhim (interreligious, for East Indians; broadcasts talk shows about social, gender, and health issues; popular among second-generation women).
- Punjab Radio (Punjabi culture; talk shows about social, religious, and political issues; popular among the first and second generations).
- Gurbani Radio (Sikh religion; talk shows about mainly religious and religio-political issues; popular among the first and second generations, especially those who favour an independent Khalistan).
- Radio Punjabi Akashwani (Punjabi culture; talk shows about social, religious, and political issues; popular among the first and second generations).
- Radio India (Indian culture, religion and politics; mainly for the first and second generations).

All radio shows except for Gurbani Radio play religious, classical, and popular Bollywood (Hindi film) music. They also have hosts who interview people about political, religious, social and health issues. All of these radio shows in considerable part function as 'talk shows,' which people in the community can call to express their opinions or ask questions. Many of them are connected to the Internet and thus can reach out to the Punjabi community beyond British Columbia.

The following Punjabi television programs are shown either on Shaw (Rogers) Multicultural or on Vision TV:

- *Punjabi Profile* (religious music, music videos; viewed mainly by the first and second generations).
- *Kamal's Top Five* (music videos; popular among the third generation).
- *Phulkari* (music videos and interviews about political and social issues; popular among the second generation).
- *Gurbani* (religious music and interviews about the Sikh religion; popular among the first and second generations).
- *Apna Desh Apni Boli* (Punjabi folk music, dance; viewed predominantly by the second generation).
- *Ashirwad* (music videos; viewed mainly by the second generation).
- *Zindagi* (discussions about movies, screening of Bollywood music videos, interviews with celebrities; viewed mostly by the third generation).
- *Desi Rythmns* (skits, discussions about health issues, music videos; popular mainly among the third generation but also viewed by the older generations).
- *Tamana* (modelling, business, Punjabi culture; viewed mostly by the third generation).
- *Des Pardes* (Punjabi folk music, dance; viewed mainly by the first and second generations).

There are also two non-profit shows on the Shaw mainstream channel: *Kuldip Singh Chaggar* ('Face to Face') and *Manpreet Kaur Grewal* ('Cross-Cultural'). Both deal with broader Canadian social issues as well as local Vancouver issues, and include discussions about ethnic minority groups.

The following are the main Indo-Canadian papers published in British Columbia:

- *Indo-Canadian Voice* (in English; interreligious)
- *The Link Newspaper* (in English; interreligious)
- *Chardi Kala* (in Punjabi; Khalistani)
- *Indo-Canadian Times* (in Punjabi; interreligious)
- *Sach di Awaaz* (in Punjabi; interreligious)
- *Punjabi Tribune* (in Punjabi; Sikh minority politics)

These papers are published in Vancouver but focus mainly on

events in the Punjab and/or India. However, some of their articles relate to Canadian events.

Each generation of the Sikh community has adapted to Canadian society in its own way. Likewise, each has its own way of orienting itself toward Canada's multiculturalism policy. The specifics of this are discussed below.

The First Generation and 'Little Punjab'

First-generation Sikhs have continued to live in accordance with kinship loyalties and community *izzat* since being 'transplanted.' While adopting to Canadian society, they have embraced multiculturalism in their efforts to re-create a Punjabi 'home.' The re-creation of a 'little Punjab' has been achieved in part through interaction with the *gurdwaras*. It follows that *gurdwaras* are where social organizations come to reach out to the first generation. The *gurdwaras* serve as the structural centres of the community; however, radio shows are the most important medium for the first generation in its efforts to maintain a connection with the Punjab.

Living in 'Little Punjab'

The *gurdwaras* are where first-generation Sikhs gather to relive their memories of village Punjab. Indeed, the *gurdwaras* are where they create in a foreign environment a network or 'home' based on tradition. An important feature of the orality mode of thinking is the strongly held notion that there is *only one way to do something*; this makes social change a very slow process. Many first-generation Sikhs believe that they are incapable of change. Having been raised in the traditional environment of the Punjab, they intend to remain traditional for the rest of their lives, whether they live in the Punjab or in Canada.

One result of all this is that first-generation Sikhs have transplanted their traditional clan and particularistic mentality from the Punjab into Canada. Thus, the traditional Punjabi community in Canada is oriented toward the collectivity, which operates according to kinship relations and loyalties. Even though diversity exists in the community (some Sikhs live in joint family households, whereas others live in nuclear households), kinship is the principal feature of the informal community networks and social organizations. Since members of the first generation identify with their kin group and caste, in their social interactions they give primary importance to the village or region and the caste from which they have come. As a consequence, the first generation's social interaction with Canada's mainstream and even with other South Asians is often very limited where it exists at all.

This limited interaction with mainstream society is partly a result of the language barrier. Many of the first-generation Sikhs I interviewed, especially the women, had been living in the West (England or Canada) for over ten years but were still unable to understand or speak English (Singh 1.5, 1.6, 1.9; Kaur 1.8, 1.10, 1.11, 1.13, 1.14). Most often, facility with English was directly related to the level of education received in India prior to arrival in Canada; those who could speak English had learned it at school in India (Singh 1.1, 1.15, 1.16; Kaur 1.4). No one I interviewed from the first generation had successfully learned English since coming to Canada.

Multiculturalism and Its Sanction of 'Little Punjab'

Given their orality mode of thinking, it is no surprise that first-generation Sikhs have a limited ability to critique or comment on the role of multiculturalism in Canada. That said, all of those I interviewed said that multiculturalism is necessarily 'good' on the basis of its impact on their life situation. For example, as a result of multiculturalism they were able to wear Punjabi clothing, their children or grandchildren were being taught Punjabi, there were street signs in Punjabi at the Punjabi market, and they had Punjabi radio and television shows. A sixty-four-year-old Sikh man commented: 'It [multiculturalism] is good for our community. *My* children know Punjabi. Speaking Punjabi is the culture ... My son was taught Punjabi but did not like to speak [it]. When he started playing soccer on an Indian team, he started speaking very well from playing with the other Indians ... The children also need a recreational centre. The recreational centre for the young has to be geared to what they like for sports' (Singh 1.17).

Those who remember living in Canada during the earlier, racially intolerant times, when Sikhs were required to take on the Western lifestyle, regard multiculturalism as a positive development. For more recent immigrants, multiculturalism is good simply because they can live as if it is 'just like India.'

Also consistent with their orality mode of thinking, first-generation Sikhs express themselves with regard to only that which refers to their immediate life situation – the 'here and now.' In effect, because they lack any sense of the future, they have nothing to say regarding the direction the community should take or the impact of multiculturalism on the community. Similarly, the first generation does not voice any theoretical critique of multiculturalism. In the interviews, their only criticism of multiculturalism related to the abuse of funds. Only one first-generation interviewee, who was educated and thus tended toward the literacy mode of thinking, provided a critique of multiculturalism: 'Racism and life was very hard at the beginning for Sikhs in B.C. Now it is not as difficult. Racism still exists. Multiculturalism helped a little at first. Now it is not doing much because it is being used for personal things, to get benefits' (Singh 1.16).

The first-generation Sikhs who possessed the literacy mode of thinking did speak of how multicultural funding was being filtered through the *gurdwaras* and was not being properly distributed among the people. They saw funds as being misused by community leaders (e.g., Singh 1.16; Kaur 1.4).

First-generation Sikhs tend to lack analytical thinking and to be unable to conceptualize issues abstractly. This is all too evident in the area of mainstream politics. Politicians who wear Punjabi clothing at functions or who say a few words in Punjabi tend to create a favourable impression among first-generation Punjabis, who believe, accordingly, that these politicians are necessarily good. First-generation Sikhs equate speaking a few words in Punjabi with being good, and make this connection with little or no inquiry as to what benefits will follow for the community. They are not likely to ask these politicians more general questions, such as 'How are you helping our community progress?' For the first generation, inquiry is limited to concrete ideas connected to the present life situation (i.e., whether or not they will be granted bus passes and a pension).

It is interesting that even though first-generation Sikhs have brought with them from the Punjab a particularistic mentality and therefore have a limited capacity to comment on multiculturalism, they nonetheless appreciate the universalistic social welfare system, which offers them government-provided health care and pensions. Indeed, Sikh immigrants, like many other immigrants, came to Canada solely for economic reasons – to earn a better income. However, while their motives for immigration may have been economic, many first-generation Sikhs have readily taken to the universalism associated with the social safety net provided by modern society (Singh 1.1, 1.5, 1.6, 1.7, 1.9, 1.12, 1.15, 1.17; Kaur 1.4, 1.8, 1.10, 1.11, 1.14). According to a Sikh man of sixty-four: 'When we came to Canada, our main concern was to make quick money. Now as we are older, we appreciate the social system, like pensions and health care. In India, there are none of these kinds of social benefits, unless you work for the government' (Singh 1.17).

While first-generation Sikhs have learned to appreciate Canada's universal social programs, they don't understand the basic values connected with them. This illustrates yet again that the formal structures of modern institutions are much easier to embrace than the values underpinning them (such as confidentiality, neutral affectivity, and specificity). The community continues to operate within a traditional value system that is basically incongruent with Canada's broader social system, and its members therefore face serious difficulties in negotiating that system. For example, it is not uncommon for first-generation Sikhs to hide key information from care workers or to seek traditional solace from modern institutions. For example, one first-generation woman commented: 'My doctor is good. I like him. He says 'Sat Sri Akal' [Punjabi greeting: 'truth is eternal'] and he gives me an injection when I go to see him' (Kaur 1.10, trans.). This Sikh woman had chosen the doctor (who is not East Indian) based simply on the fact that he greets her in Punjabi. She learned about the doctor by word of mouth from other Punjabi women. Through the traditional Punjabi greeting, the doctor created for her a feeling of familiarity, thus breaking the barrier – however slightly – between 'Little Punjab' and the mainstream.

Briefly, the first generation is networked mainly according to kinship and clan relations; nevertheless it recognizes and appreciates the government's universalistic practices. The language barrier prevents many of them from interacting with the mainstream; it also reinforces their tendency to remain among their own people. As a result, they are apt to meet only with other seniors, at *gurdwaras* or seniors centres for Punjabis. This suggests how social organizations need to reach out to members of the first generation.

Multicultural Organizations: Language and Communication Barriers

Because many first-generation Sikhs are illiterate or have received little education, they must contend with a serious language barrier. Government institutions and social service organizations have paid attention to this, especially with regard to making mainstream institutions (e.g., hospitals and social services) accessible to immigrant groups. *Gurdwaras* offer classes (through MOSAIC) for the elderly to learn 'survival'

English. One community service worker commented that although the elderly need to learn English, it is difficult to motivate them to do so (social service 1).

Government literature is printed in Punjabi. Also interpreters are available for immigrant groups in many mainstream institutions such as hospitals and immigration offices. However, printed Punjabi literature is of little use to most first-generation Sikhs, most of whom are illiterate (this literature is used more by the second generation). Furthermore, there are issues beyond the language barrier that require attention. Because the first generation possesses the orality mode of thinking, most of its members are unable to get, and do not have the habit of seeking, information from organizations. They traditionally learn through word of mouth and feel more comfortable when information comes from people they know.

The solution to the challenge of reaching out to the first generation with regard to education and guidance in social affairs therefore lies within the community. The system of seeking resources and support from the social system is foreign to the first generation. This generation does not feel comfortable in going out and seeking help, especially with regard to taboo subjects. First-generation Sikhs prefer to get to know people in the community with whom they can talk about their problems. Therefore, in order to break the cultural gap between the traditional orientation and modern society, ethno-specific or language-specific organizations must go out to the *gurdwaras* and seniors groups. A counsellor who provides services to Punjabis at an NGO commented: 'The elderly people don't have the habit to seek out help, nor can they read. We give workshops and hand out pamphlets at the *gurdwara* in Punjabi to inform people about the resources they can use. If one person is able to read in the family they can become informed by him or her, otherwise they hear by word of mouth in the *gurdwara* or seniors centres' (counsellor 1).

A social worker for Punjabis at a government organization that provides multicultural services offered a similar comment: 'New seniors do not come to [...]. They only appear when they find out about the organization, about three or four years after arrival. They often hear about it through word of mouth or friend. Most resources are learned about that way. They often hear about seeking help from others and get ideas about independent living on welfare' (social service 2).

Indeed, the first generation, which is rooted in oral culture, must be sought out through the *gurdwaras* and their seniors groups. Otherwise, awareness of useful or necessary social programs will only be through 'word of mouth,' even when organizations have Punjabi-language facilities.

Punjabi Radio as a Link with the Home Country

Being illiterate or minimally educated, first-generation Sikhs most often listen to Punjabi radio as the medium of choice for engaging with the community or society. The radio is well suited to those who cannot read and who are accustomed to learning through oral transmission; also, Punjabi radio shows are similar to the *gurdwara* in that they enable the first generation to emotionally re-create their traditional Punjabi community in Canada. The favourite shows for the first generation are related to religious discussions or *kirtan* (chanting of scriptural hymns); these are often directly broadcast from *gurdwaras*. Indeed, the first generation is oriented toward 'mentally living in the Punjab and physically living in Canada' (Singh 2.11). In this generation's efforts to re-create and live in a Punjabi environment within Canada, the Punjabi radio shows are immensely helpful.

First-generation Sikhs are preoccupied with the local *gurdwara* politics and events involving Sikhs. Except for those who possess the literacy mode of thinking, they have little to say about the mainstream media or about how the Sikh community is portrayed by it. This is, no doubt related to the language barrier; but at the same time, it highlights the fact that the first generation tends to deal with cultural barriers by creating a little Punjab for itself. This is most evident in the first generation's dislike of mainstream shows; they see these as simply a bad influence on their children or grandchildren in that they teach Western values (Singh 1.1, 1.2, 1.6, 1.7, 1.9, 1.12, 1.15, 1.17; Kaur 1.4, 1.8, 1. 10, 1.11, 1.14). The same assessment also explains why radio is preferred over television – for the latter is overwhelmingly dominated by Western content.

A distinguishing feature of the orality mode of thinking is that it tends to agglomerate thoughts without much prioritization. The first-generation Sikhs I interviewed gave unfocused answers to my questions and needed constant redirection. Interestingly, some well-educated interviewees of the second generation commented on the lack of focus in the questions asked by callers. As a second-generation Sikh woman remarked: 'I find that the radio shows are good for discussing important issues but that they often go off the subject' (Kaur 2.12).

The lack of focus is apparent when radio hosts are asked questions like 'Which village are you from?' These questions demonstrate a concrete thought form based on one's own personal life situation; they are also particularistic and expressive of a collectivity-orientation.

The Second Generation and the Punjabi Community

Second-generation Sikhs have largely adapted themselves to the universalistic institutions of a modern society. Yet for the most part, they have not been able to take on that society's corresponding value system, including features such as universalism. There is some continuity between the second generation and the first generation; however, the second has distanced itself somewhat from the collectivity by increasing its (economic) participation in mainstream Canadian society even while living physically in the Punjabi community. The second generation perceives multiculturalism as endorsing Punjabi culture. For these Sikhs, kinship relations continue to provide the foundation for social interaction. One example is that they use *gurdwaras* as social centres. However, even though the second generation lives in the Punjabi community, it maintains an interest in events outside that community in Canadian society, predominantly through Indo-Canadian and mainstream newspapers.

Living in the Punjabi Community

Adaptation is a complex process, and is inevitably affected by interactions with the host country. For reasons of linguistic and cultural familiarity, second-generation Sikhs tend to stay within the Sikh community, more specifically within their kinship group, even down to the level of their home village in the Punjab. This is a consequence of the pattern of immigration (which is predominantly through the sponsorship system): from the very start, people get connected with the local Sikh community through their kinship relations. Note the response of a Sikh woman who arrived here through an arranged marriage: 'When I lived in the Punjab I went to the Hindu temple, the Sikh *gurdwara*, and the Christian church. Here, I only go to *gurdwaras* because I don't know Hindus and Christians here to invite me ... In Surrey, I only know the *gurdwara* from my family' (Kaur 2.13). Her social networking in the new country was thus dependent on the family and the larger ethnic community.

The social interaction that second-generation Sikhs have with the mainstream or with other ethnic communities is closely related to community size and the length of residence of its members. Sikhs who live in small towns are likely to interact more with the mainstream than those in a city with a large Sikh community. Sikhs who have been in Canada for over thirty years are likely to have more interaction than those who arrived only ten years ago. In contrast to Sikhs in Vancouver, which has a large Sikh community, Sikhs in small towns throughout British Columbia interact far more with other communities. As one second-generation Sikh woman remarked:

Surrey [B.C.] is the opposite of [...] [a town on Vancouver Island]. India is like [...] [a town on Vancouver Island]. All villagers are like family. People are old immigrants in [...] [a town on Vancouver Island], they have assimilated to Western lifestyle. In Surrey, the two races don't get along. East Indians don't have consideration for others: East Indians do their Punjabi [things], whites do their things. Separation [exists between the two]. (Kaur 2.20)

Another second-generation Sikh woman also underlined the difference:

In Surrey, all Indians hang around together, stick together. Indian people backstab each other and are jealous, but white people accept others as individuals. Groups of only Indian people look like a gang of hoodlums. In [a town in Northern B.C.], kids are with white kids. It is a safe community. In Surrey, there is bad relations between whites and browns. [For example,] neo-Nazi group kills Sikh caretaker of the Guru Nanak Gurdwara [Nirmal Gill]. Multicultural programs are not working. The government money is not being used properly. It is corrupt. Nothing for the youth. The old people get money, but it is not used efficiently. (Kaur 2.19)

It is important to note that although second-generation Sikhs interact far more with the mainstream, it does not follow that they emphasize traditional customs and values any less. Even in smaller towns, many third-generation Sikhs experience great pressure to conform to traditional norms although they may have friends from other racial or religious backgrounds (Sikh 3.12, 3.14, 3.15, 3.26, 3.29, 3.30; Kaur 2.19).

In the smaller towns there is more interaction between the two cultures. The Vancouver Sikh community is more insulated from the mainstream and is networked according to village and clan ties (particularism). Note the response of a Canadian-trained schoolteacher who, although belonging to the second generation, reflects the analytics mode of thinking:

> The 'ghettoized effect' makes the community insular. There has to be a fine balance between the Punjabi community and the mainstream. The people don't really think in terms of religion, very little, but more in terms of clan and family alliance. We have to promote mixed interaction. I proposed at the [...] Gurdwara that for the Baisakhi parade there should be [the practice to] 'bring a friend with you' to expose others about the celebrations about the Khalsa. They said 'thank you' and dropped the idea. There is merit to being in the mainstream. I think there needs to be an attempt at building a bridge. One has to start at the personal level with mainstream. It is with personal connections that one can influence people's thinking. (educator 2)

However, most of the second-generation interviewees did not recognize or believe that there is too much segregation; rather, many endorsed the separate existence of a larger Punjabi community. Nonetheless, I was occasionally told that the Sikh community needs to pay attention to the broader community beyond itself. For example, a fifty-four-year-old Sikh man commented: 'Our people go to the *gurdwara*, take *langar* and socialize with each other and then they come home and feel *razi* ["fulfilled"]. Yet they don't teach anyone about themselves ... The root is [lack of] education' (Singh 2.11).

This man was concerned about the lack of interaction between the Sikh community – as defined by the *gurdwara* social organizations – and the Canadian mainstream. For him, the *gurdwaras* have a role to play as social centres, but they also need to go beyond the boundaries of the Punjabi community as it exists in Canada.

Multiculturalism and Its Endorsement of Punjabi Culture

The second generation is able to provide more elaborate comments about the role of multiculturalism in Canada. However, like the first generation, most second-generation Sikhs see multiculturalism as necessarily good on the basis of concrete ideas; for example, it allows them to have Punjabi taught in schools and to watch Punjabi TV shows. They view multiculturalism as a positive change, in contrast to the racism of the earlier days, during which the pressure on Sikhs to become 'modern' or 'Western' was strong. A second-generation Sikh woman commented: 'One should be able to communicate with anyone but should be strong enough with one's background so that one does not lose it. The older generation is happy with multiculturalism because it has allowed them to keep something of their own, unlike before, when the women had to wear Western dresses to the *gurdwara*. People before had to struggle' (Kaur 2.18).

Likewise, another Sikh woman stated: 'It [multiculturalism] is good. People are coming from different cultures and can be part of the society. They can keep their own identity ... It is good to have values with your own kind ... This way they will have good personalities' (Kaur 2.16).

Members of the second generation view multiculturalism as a positive thing in that it allows ethnic groups to carry on their culture. They also see it as a necessary phase for immigrant groups – that is, it provides them with a sense of security while they integrate with mainstream society. A Sikh police official commented:

Sikhs need to feel secure with their own culture before they become part of a larger community or group. It is harder for an immigrant to change his value system. I do not feel as if I am 'other' ... I came to Canada sixteen years ago. I was aware of who I was before coming to Canada. Upon arrival, I had to deal with racism, but I did not let it control me. There needs to be a forum to educate the youth regarding the language barrier and the difference in values: role modelling to step forward. It is difficult to educate parents about this. It is not realistic to teach them. (police 1)

While most second-generation interviewees strongly embraced multiculturalism, several had some criticisms or concerns regarding Canadian policy. The main criticism was that multiculturalism reinforces racism instead of discouraging it. A Sikh social service worker commented:

Multiculturalism is fine to a certain degree but it is reinforcing racism ... we have placed too much emphasis on multiculturalism. It reinforces racist views on both sides – the English Canadians and the ethnic communities. There are racist views within the Indian community about Westerners, too ... It is not addressed. Multiculturalism has created the notion [that] we have to accept the other cultures, but there is no understanding of either culture or how people adapt. Indians mostly don't understand Western values, and Westerners don't really understand Indian values and customs. And the Indian culture needs to become more tolerant of difference. (social service 1)

Regarding the effects of the 'ghettoization' of the Sikh community, a middle-aged Gora Sikh commented: '[Because of multiculturalism] there is a "pickling" effect ... The Punjabi community now does not trust the outside culture. The "not secure" sentiment is turned inward. It is redirected because of multiculturalism. Its intent is to empower the minority groups and new immigrants, but now it is dangerously keeping the community in the victim mode' (Gora Sikh 2.1).

One second-generation interviewee even suggested that the federal and provincial governments should not be responsible for ethnic communities to keep their culture or religion; rather, the ethnic communities should be responsible for promoting their culture or religion: 'It is not the responsibility of the government to make sure that we as a community maintain our culture. The ones who will do it will do it regardless. Those who don't or won't, so let them be. This is the consequence of being in Canada. It is the responsibility of the home to teach values and [of] the priests in the body of churches to reach out to the young to make them learn about the religion' (Kaur 2.23).

Some second-generation Sikhs voiced concern over the lack of religion in schools as a result of multiculturalism and the associated political correctness. According to them, the teaching of morality and the practice of a daily universal prayer are crucial for the younger generations in school. They contend that memorizing a prayer helps discipline children as it also provides them with something moral and spiritual to hold on to in their lives. Since the children in schools come from a diversity of religious backgrounds, it would be useful to have a prayer with which all can pray to their God and that contains the main virtues shared by all religions. A Punjabi social service worker commented:

There is a problem in the community – a lack of social control or discipline in the schools. Here the family has to do a lot of the disciplining but, even if this is done, then the kids go to school and hear about one's rights. Traditionally, we had to pray at the beginning of school all together on the field and then do stretches before studying. This was good because it was a ritual for discipline. We would pray – even if you don't believe, it gives you something to remember and then you carry it for life. People here talk about being concerned about religion once they get old, but it is necessary to have it from a little child. Here in the schools there is too much emphasis on multiculturalism and political correctness, making it counterproductive. Many people come from other religions; they should have a prayer to God and have the children pray to their own God. There should be a certain amount of morality and [universal] values taught in the schools. (social service 1)

Many second-generation interviewees voiced a similar concern. One fifty-nine-year-old Sikh man remarked: 'There needs to be concern about morality at school since religion has been removed. There is a need to teach about religion and values in the schools. However, this is not politically [correct], so it is not implemented. You can have a universal prayer with universal morality' (Singh 2.10).

Multicultural Organizations

We have already discussed how, in accordance with Canada's multiculturalism policy, government institutions are increasingly attending to the language barrier by making mainstream institutions accessible to immigrant groups. They are doing this by printing information in immigrants' languages and by providing interpreters. Like the first generation, the second generation tends to seek out mainstream institutions by word of mouth, even though it is able to benefit from Punjabi-language materials.

Multicultural agencies, besides assisting various segments of the Sikh community in the Punjabi language (mainly the first generation, but also some of the second generation), have also tried to inform mainstream institutions about South Asian or Punjabi culture so that they will relate better to Punjabi clients. However, according to one such NGO, this attempt to enhance cross-cultural understanding has not really succeeded. As one social service worker put it:

We did workshops to train health professionals regarding culture and networked with them so that they know of our existence [so they can seek our help], but it has not done much. We gave two hundred people in the health fields [doctors, nurses, social workers, community agency workers] a half-day training on South Asian culture. Even with the networking between the hospitals and health units, the people in the community are not being reached. (social service 3)

Because Sikh families tend to be close-knit, ethno-specific organizations are more successful in reaching them:

To reach out to the community it has to be done from within the community, in a place where trust can be cultivated ... The community health
units have certain programs that don't reach out specifically to the community. And then the community doesn't feel comfortable going and
seeking help, especially if it is regarding a taboo subject. They prefer getting to know people in the community to whom they can speak of problems when they arise, especially in a general place where no stigma is
attached as opposed to a specific AIDS centre, and so on. (social service 3)

Counter to this point of view that second-generation Sikhs are better
served by ethno-specific organizations, several of the second-generation Sikh women I interviewed said they found it difficult to discuss
marital, family, or health issues with Indian personnel, who maintain a
traditional mentality and who lack the modern values of affective neutrality (i.e., 'professionalism' and 'confidentiality') (Kaur 2.12, 2.19, 2.20,
2.21). Also, their experience had been that Canadian personnel had better communication skills, notwithstanding the cultural gap. These
women's desire for affective neutrality reflects some distancing from
the collectivity and represents a general move away from tradition
toward modernity.

Indo-Canadian Media

The multicultural media have provided the second generation with a
means to keep in touch with events in the Punjab and India as a whole.
For these Sikhs, the Indo-Canadian media, especially Indo-Canadian
newspapers, are a popular means for obtaining news about their
'homeland,' but are less useful when it comes to information about the
host society. Note the comment of a fifty-four-year-old Sikh man: 'The
multicultural shows and papers are relatively recent [two or three
years] and it will take time for them to evolve. Ethnic papers are keeping us attached to the Punjab. The ethnic papers should be concerned
with Canadian issues. The shows are new and will start bringing other
things' (Singh 2.11).
    While the Indo-Canadian media have been able to link the commu-
nity with events in the Punjab, many second-generation Sikhs think
there is too much emphasis on *bhangra* (Punjabi dance) and Bollywood
(as Hindi popular films are called) on the multicultural television
(Singh 2.11, 2.14; Kaur 2.20, 2.21, 2.23). These people recognize that the
multicultural shows are run as businesses and need sponsors (with
whom *bhangra* and Bollywood sells); even so; some second-generation

Sikhs want attention paid to social issues relating to the community in Canada, especially the youth (Singh 2.11, 2.14; Kaur 2.17, 2.20, 2.21, 2.23). Meanwhile, like the first generation generally, quite a few second-generation mothers say they dislike mainstream television shows because they are 'Westernizing' their children (Kaur 2.13, 2.16, 2.19).

The second generation has embraced the idea of living in a Punjabi community and entertaining itself through the ethnic media, but it also takes an interest in, and participates in, mainstream Canadian society, which is the second generation's 'new home.' It does pay close attention to the mainstream news, and it keeps up with current events in Canada and other parts of the world. As well, the mainstream television shows affect how second-generation Sikhs perceive themselves. The manner in which the Sikh community is portrayed by the mainstream news media is a highly problematic issue for the second generation.[3] A fifty-four-year-old Sikh man stated: 'The TV news is prejudiced about the Sikh community. They show wrong images of the community. For example, during the Baisakhi parade they will say 50,000 [participated] when there had been 70,000. They will interview people who look like they don't know about the festival when there are many people who do. [Reporter X] always blames everything on the fundamentalists. [X] does not go to see what is really going on' (Singh 2.11).

The comment most often made about how the news media portray the Sikh community is that they misrepresent orthodox Sikhs as 'fundamentalists' or even as terrorists. A Sikh woman of thirty-five observed: 'The media makes it sound like all *amritdharis* are Khalistanis. It is not so. The media does not understand Sikhism either. These categories of 'moderates' and 'fundamentalists' are not found in the Punjab. The media divides the community, and the Punjabi community is stupid to fall for it. They should really try to understand each other' (Kaur 2.17).

Many second-generation Sikhs contend that the mainstream news media are trying to divide the community by reporting the fighting among a few as representative of the whole. A middle-aged Gora Sikh commented: 'The media divides the community, but the Punjabi people are using the media for political pursuits. There is an unstable alliance between the minorities and the media ... [One reporter] plays with the dividing of the community and is hard on the 'fundamentalists,' equating them with terrorists. On the whole, [that reporter] contributes to the demonizing of the traditionalists. The youth are sick of the media and others are sucked into the rhetoric used by the politicians' (Gora Sikh 2.1).

The second generation endorses the Indo-Canadian media but is generally troubled by the way the mainstream media portray the Sikh community.

The Third Generation and the 'Punjabi Bubble'

The children of immigrants (third generation) have been raised in Canada and tend to interact more with mainstream society. As a consequence, they experience tension vis-à-vis the traditional approach of their second-generation parents. 'Punjabi bubble' is the term they use for the tension between ethnic insularity and mainstream culture. Because of their experience with the Punjabi bubble, many third-generation Sikhs see multiculturalism policy as encouraging segregation. They fail to see much benefit for the third generation from the *gurdwaras* and multicultural organizations. Some Indo-Canadian television programs appeal to the younger generations, but the mainstream media are their main source of entertainment and information.

Living in the Punjabi Bubble

Having been raised in Canada, third-generation Sikhs experience tension between multiculturalism policy, which sanctions Punjabi culture, and the modern values and practices they learn from interacting with the society at large. There are three basic dimensions to the Punjabi bubble that they experience: (1) the physical segregation of the Sikh community from mainstream Canadian society, (2) divisions within the community as a result of the traditional clannish mentality (such as the divisions relating to geographic regions like Doaba, Malwa, and Majha), and (3) the resulting limited interaction with or openness to other racial and religious groups on the part of the Sikh community. These three dimensions of the bubble are viewed by the third generation as encouraging racism and reinforcing prejudices on the part of both the Sikh community and the mainstream, as well as instilling in third generation Sikhs the idea that they are 'other' than the mainstream. A twenty-four-year-old Sikh woman commented:

> The pioneers [the very early Sikh immigrants] were not living in a bubble because they were forced to integrate. The elders live in a bubble as if in India. Change takes a lot of time and parents don't have a lot of education. A lot of kids have depression, emotional problems, drink alcohol excessively, are into drugs, and even running away from home because

the parents are too strict. I had very few Punjabi friends in elementary and secondary school. I was not raised in an Indian environment. My parents wanted to avoid the ghetto because they wanted us to be well-rounded. They wanted us to appreciate our culture and religion but not to be stuck in a ghetto ... I had a good opportunity to be exposed to other cultures. It eliminates racism. (Kaur 3.32)

Ethnic insularity offers the comfort of familiarity and a sense of community to immigrant parents; it does the same for the third generation. However, the children, who have been raised inside the bubble, face serious difficulties later. A twenty-two-year-old Sikh man talked about life inside the bubble: 'The Punjabi bubble encourages kids to be in the community. Kids like the bubble to a certain extent. It gives them a sense of a community. One can with ease be with friends of one's own kind. But there comes a point when they get sick of it; when they realize everyone behaves for *izzat* [in order to save face]. It is so strong with the bubble. Parents like the bubble because it is their community and they are not comfortable in any other than their own' (Singh 3.33).

Secure in the comfort of the Punjabi community, and fearful of contacts with the broader society, many second-generation parents do not comprehend the need to encourage their third-generation children to engage or socialize with the mainstream. Note the comment of a twenty-three-year-old Sikh woman: 'Punjabis still feel threatened by Caucasians. My father still encounters racism at the mill. Why would he want his daughter to enter the white community? The Punjabi, as a result, is also racist about the white community' (Kaur 3.27).

Second-generation parents fear that their children are becoming too Western. Several derogatory terms have emerged to describe Westernized third-generation Sikhs, 'coconut' and 'whitewashed' being two. These terms refer to those whose roots are Punjabi or Indian but who live as if they are 'white' (*gora*).

Sikhs who have lived in Britain, Hong Kong, or Singapore, or elsewhere in North America, are able to provide a more critical perspective in comparing the Vancouver community with those in other places. Interviewees from small B.C. towns and from other countries thought that the bubble was stronger in Vancouver (and in Toronto as well). A Sikh woman who had lived in California encountered a great deal of pressure to conform to traditional cultural norms in Vancouver, in part because of the size of the community: 'It is difficult living with the 5 Ks (*kakars*) when living in an area where there are not many

Sikhs – you become an odd one. In Vancouver, there is pressure to live strictly according to the precepts in comparison to other places like in California' (Kaur 3.9).

In discussing the Punjabi bubble, many third-generation Sikhs commented on its negative impact on the young as well as on the community as a whole. The Punjabi bubble as they have experienced it in Vancouver has raised concerns among them about young Sikhs' educational development. Some who were university students brought up the issue that ESL (English as a second language) is not as effective as it could or should be, because kids (who are often raised speaking mostly Punjabi before entering the school system) hang around together and thus reinforce one another's poor grammar, limited vocabulary, and slang: 'There is a problem with ESL – it is not working because the Punjabis stick together and do not improve speaking English' (Singh 3.17).

Educator 3 – who is not Punjabi – observed that college students with a Punjabi background had greater difficulty grasping abstract and conceptual thought than other students. Indeed, third-generation Sikhs are raised in a milieu where the analytics mode of thinking is not encouraged. This is mainly because most second-generation parents possess the literacy mode of thinking.

Some third-generation Sikhs have tried to break out of the Punjabi bubble by reaching beyond Punjabi circles: 'I try to find the best of both cultures. Parents don't want kids to be Canadian [because they believe] there is emphasis on looks – like, cut hair to be modern. There is a fear that kids will be too Canadian, but parents don't understand that some values in the West are good, like the work ethic versus Punjabi corruption. We are in a bubble and I see this a lot because of the crisis regarding a cousin who dated white girls and was thought of as "whitewash" and then married an Indian, and my sister who is ostracized for dating a white guy' (Kaur 3.27).

Similarly, a twenty-four-year-old Sikh man noted: 'I would like to see the Sikh community grasp and communicate with other communities. I would like to see more youth outreach about religion ... The community needs to open up to other groups' (Singh 3.12).

A rare but still significant example of an attempt to bridge the gap between the community and the mainstream was a speech given at a *kirtan* celebration on Remembrance Day, arranged by the Sikh Students Association at Simon Fraser University:

It [Remembrance Day] is a time to feel proud that, when Sikhs were needed on the war fronts, we went ... It is very important to remember those war heroes, but also we must look at ourselves, within our souls, and there we will find the passion that brewed inside *those* men all those years ago ... I am simply here to make you aware that on November 11th and every other day you are a Sikh. Therefore, brewing within you is the fire that brewed within those war heroes that represented us with courage and bravery. Now, it is up to us to make our contribution, not necessarily in war, but in daily life. You can start by learning to let go of boundaries that we have created around ourselves that prevent us from nurturing fruitful relationships with others. (10 November 2000)

This extract reflects the need to relate Sikh values to the broader society and to encourage people to move beyond the Punjabi Bubble.

Multiculturalism as Both Identity Enhancing and Divisive

Various opinions prevail among the third generation regarding life in a society with a policy of multiculturalism. A dividing line in attitudes toward multiculturalism exists on the basis of whether or not members of that generation have lived elsewhere (England, Singapore, Hong Kong, small B.C. towns). Those who have been raised in Vancouver, who have experienced the world basically confined to that city, view multiculturalism as 'how things are' and 'necessarily good' because it allows people to keep their culture (Singh 3.4, 3.5, 3.6, 3.10; Kaur 3.2, 3.8, 3.31). Note, for example: 'I do not think of it [multiculturalism] as something negative or positive. Rather, it is something that just exists where I live. I think that segregation [of ethnic communities] has [always] existed throughout time' (Singh 3.4).

In contrast, those who have lived elsewhere – be it in England, Singapore, Hong Kong, small B.C. towns, or the United States – assess multiculturalism more critically. They embrace it for protecting uniqueness, but they also criticize it for its divisiveness (Singh 3.12, 3.13, 3.14, 3.15, 3.21; Kaur 3.9, 3.18, 3.19, 3.22, 3.25). One of them commented:

Multiculturalism is unique. It is something I did not know about in England. It is positive in that there is the celebration of customs and culture, but it is negative because people don't talk about the issues, there is a denial of the negative. In England, there was a lot more talk about the problems and issues in the community. The men don't want to change, because it keeps them in the position of being in control. I think there need to be people to talk with, there need to be eyes open to see more than just roles. (media 2)

The same ambivalence emerged in the comments of a twenty-four-year-old Sikh man:

> It [multiculturalism] is good, because each community has support to keep its culture. It is bad, because everyone ends up sticking together in their own culture and not mingling with others. It should be transitional in order to help people assimilate. The youth don't want to be Punjabi, they don't know what they represent. Most Punjabis are unaware of their history. They are different and stand out, so they build a reputation and get proud too fast about their group. There needs to be education from the ones who are willing to help us to go in the right direction. (Singh 3.26)

A Sikh woman who had lived abroad as well as in Vancouver pointed out the positive *and* the negative consequences of multiculturalism:

> It [multiculturalism] is good for the community if one gets out of its bubble. In India, people are evolving. If that could happen here, that would be very nice. People should be allowed to be themselves, but they should be in an environment which allows them to progress ... There is a paradox to multiculturalism. Freedom of speech, dress, and so on, is allowed, but on the other hand, people have to think of the broader picture, which is being neglected. The community is not evolving in Canada. We are not interacting with others. We are not intermingling with others. Multiculturalism is tokenism. It is stereotypical, just bringing out superficial aspects of the culture. There has to be a balance. Paradoxically, the community could prosper more and advance if it was not in this bubble encouraged by multiculturalism. The community would have better resources to draw upon, have more knowledge of what is out there, if they were not in a bubble. (Kaur 3.32)

Some third-generation Sikhs go so far as to describe multiculturalism as a form of 'divide and rule.' They believe that it hinders upward social mobility and social integration (Singh 3.13, 21; Kaur 3.18, 3.27), and they especially dislike being called 'Indo-Canadian.' One Sikh woman remarked, 'Why call me Indo-Canadian? You don't hear "Euro-Canadian" used' (Kaur 3.19).

In Search of a Suitable Organization

The third generation manifests a variety of opinions and attitudes toward multiculturalism. For their part, people in the social and educational fields – who have hands-on experience with incorporating multiculturalism into mainstream institutions – are highly critical of multiculturalism. One Punjabi social worker observed: 'People are just being polite and not getting to the issues. [It is] political correctness ... The youth don't really know what is Punjabi besides the stereotypes and [intergenerational] pressures' (social service 1).

In voicing their criticisms, social and educational workers are careful to make sure their comments will remain confidential. The Punjabi workers offered their criticisms with some reluctance, out of fear for their jobs; the non-Punjabi workers were afraid their views might be misconstrued as racist when in fact they were speaking out of concern for their clients. In either case, both Punjabi and non-Punjabi social service workers and educators agreed that multiculturalism was both impractical and a form of tokenism. One non-Punjabi educator contended: 'In my experience with the students, it does not do anything good. It is just an industry. Multiculturalism is not practical. It makes them marginalized in a group, and does not give them choice. It makes it even harder for the women' (educator 3). This educator gave an example of how multiculturalism was impractical:

> I was asked to do a discussion with the class during multicultural week at [a postsecondary school]. I did not feel very comfortable with it from the beginning, but tried to do it because it was requested. I had to ask what the multicultural contribution characteristic of each community was, which would demonstrate cultural diversity. The kids became segregated and in less than five minutes I realized that the kids did not want this. Their heads were nodding, and one student said, 'This is the first time I noticed a difference.' I realized all of a sudden that there was no longer any connection in the class. (educator 3)

Likewise, a Punjabi educator, who also sees multiculturalism as impractical, commented:

> I feel multiculturalism is too superficial ... There needs to be a bigger approach to multiculturalism, like an antiracism movement. People need to learn what is behind these clothes and so on. Many kids feel a need to hide their culture. There is no attempt to deal with misconceptions and misperceptions ... What it has been up to now is an emphasis on what is different. Kids want to feel part of the mainstream but they don't. (educator 1)

· Ethno-specific and general community service groups cater mainly to recent immigrants or second-generation people. Third-generation Sikhs do not generally associate with organizations like PICS and OPTIONS, but other avenues are open to them. During the 1990s there was a burgeoning of Sikh and Punjabi clubs at colleges (Kwantlen, Douglas, Langara) and universities (SFU and UBC). These clubs serve as meeting places for third-generation Sikhs, who share a common background in terms of having been raised in Canada as Punjabi or Sikh.

Some third-generation Sikhs find that 'there is not enough for the youth, like the clubs at UBC and SFU' (Singh 3.4). A few contend that more resources are becoming available for the youth:

> The reason why there is no continuity in the community for the youth: you don't have enough initiative to take on projects [school, job]. A lot of people bitch and complain but don't do anything about it. There is SSA at UBC and SFU. There is Sikhnet and Sikhvision now starting a monthly *kirtan* [a sacred hymn-sing] for the youth at the [...]. The first Sunday of each month, there will be English *kirtan* for the youth where kids will be doing the *kirtan* and 'Ardas' [a Sikh prayer]. We are targeting the group of people who went to the Sikh camps.[4] (Kaur 3.31)

Although the above extract refers to the several initiatives that have been taken to engage young Sikhs, the clubs that exist tend to cater to opposite ends of the Sikh social spectrum. On the one hand, those Canadian-born third-generation Sikhs who tend to identify themselves as Punjabi are often heavily involved in the Punjabi folk dance (*bhangra*) scene; on the other hand, those who are baptized (*amritdhari*) and heavily involved in the *gurdwara* temple scene often identify themselves as Sikh first. The majority lie somewhere between the two groups. In fact, these clubs represent only a fraction of third-generation Sikhs. Those involved with the Sikh clubs and/or the Sikh camp represent a small minority. Typically, their families are involved in *gurdwara* politics. As a consequence, youth issues are not addressed sufficiently in terms of the modern values of universalism and personal choice. A twenty-four-year-old Sikh man commented:

> I consciously try to stay away from any Sikh organizations or groups, like *gurdwaras* and university clubs, because I find they all have hidden political agendas. I had a bad experience in the [...] Sikh club. I was approached and asked, 'Are you a moderate or a fundamentalist?' I said, 'I am Christian,

now don't you feel bad for asking?' ... I believe that there is a group of kids who are quiet but with a yearning to learn about their religion but don't really know where to go, as opposed to the group of kids who are interested in the political aspects they pick up from their parents. (Singh 3.15)

The question arises: Where do third-generation Sikhs go for help in personal growth and development? They identify with the main-stream, but they also realize that they are different from it, having been raised as Sikh. They want to be raised like other children in the West. The third-generation 'kids want to be raised like the Cosby kids, where the parents are involved and interact with the kids' (Singh 3.14). In order to learn more about life in the mainstream, some third-genera-tion Sikhs go to bookstores or libraries and get books on the subject, following the practice of the mainstream. But there are few resources for the younger Sikh generation regarding the special issues it faces. A third-generation Punjabi counsellor commented: 'The [Western self-help] books available are not going to answer their specific questions and needs. The books, for example, are for Western dilemmas and life-style, but the Sikh youth have other issues that they are dealing with – their heritage and how to fit in the West. Does it have a place in my life? How am I going to preserve it? What of my culture am I going to preserve?' (counselor 2).

Many members of the third generation are now approaching middle age. Once members of this generation become more established in mainstream society as professionals, perhaps, with their analytics mode of thinking, they will be able to help the younger generation more effec-tively than present-day Punjabi workers, who live in the Punjabi bubble and accept traditional mores.

The Media as a Source of Information and Entertainment

Third-generation members of the Sikh community use the mass media for entertainment and often get their news through mainstream outlets. It follows that the portrayal of the Sikh community in the media is a sensitive issue for them. Indeed, third-generation Sikhs are broadly dis-mayed about how their community is portrayed in the mainstream media. Their principal grievances are three: (1) The media always seem to report 'negative' events regarding the community, and never positive ones such as Sikh efforts to establish soup kitchens and their generosity in making charitable donations. For example, Daniel Igali (referred to as Toofan ['typhoon, storm'] among Punjabis) – winner of an Olympic Gold Medal in wrestling for Canada – was provided free room and board by a Punjabi family after he immigrated to Canada. (2) When reporting an event involving a Sikh family, the media make it a point to emphasize that the people involved are Sikh, even when religion has nothing to do with the crime (such as a drug-related murder or the murder of the girl from Maple Ridge).[5] (3) The media tend to associate orthodox Sikhs with terrorists. This last issue is the one most commonly voiced by members of the third generation. A twenty-year-old Sikh man commented:

> The media exploit the politics, and so on, and their presentation produces prejudices against the Sikh people. If they have a turban, they are fundamentalists and violent. The media never show the good things that the Sikhs are doing, never show them in a fair light. The media is very one-sided, which has a bad effect on the Sikh youth, especially for those who live in smaller communities where there are mostly white people. We have to deal with these prejudices that are reinforced by the media. (Singh 3.10)

Likewise, a Punjabi media person remarked:

> The British like to divide and rule. This happens here with the Indian community. People who are reporting like [...] should know about the religion and India if they are to report about the community. The media divides the community – moderates and extremists – which, then, some Indians buy into. (media 1)

Many third-generation Sikhs are dismayed that community divisions are shown in a highly exaggerated manner. Their concern is that some members of the Sikh community then go along with the news reported, as if the reports about the community are, in fact, correct. Third-generation Sikhs also wonder why reporters always seem to take for granted *gurdwara* administrators are the 'leaders' of the Sikh community.

In terms of the mainstream media's treatment of the Sikh community, third-generation Sikhs believe that the media must stop presenting ethnic communities in a biased way. It seems to them that when a negative event involving a Caucasian takes place, the media present it as an anomaly of the culture, group, or religion. When it reports on a similar negative event involving an ethnic minority group, it presents that event as the norm. Most Sikhs believe that the B.C. mainstream media, based in Vancouver, generally paint a negative picture of the Sikh community as a whole, and that reporting tends to be more balanced in cities where the Sikh community is small.

Ethnic insularity has generated tension between the three generations; not only that, but it has affected how the mainstream media (i.e., media directed toward the general public) perceive and interact with the Sikh community. As long as the community remains alienated from mainstream society, it is likely to be viewed as something 'other' or 'alien,' with corresponding negative connotations. One non-Punjabi media person commented: 'Yeah, it is true that the media presents the Sikhs through a stereotypical viewpoint – as terrorists – which reinforces the mainstream stereotype of the community. Change will come when minority groups begin to integrate and not exist separately' (media 2). Indeed, mainstream depictions of the Sikh community are related closely to the fact that the community is insular and is perceived as alien to the mainstream.

Television, both mainstream and Punjabi, is a source of entertainment for the third generation. Punjabi TV provides mainly Bollywood and *bhangra*. This service is inevitably profit-driven, and its content reflects this fact. Even so, some television producers agree that there is more to be conveyed to the young than just Bollywood and *bhangra*. Veeno Dewan, a TV producer and director with five years' experience at BBC-TV in the United Kingdom, commented: 'Perhaps the root of the problem is that many so-called "producers" of these programs are either makers of wedding videos or own video shops renting out Hindi movies ... It's time that the current generation of program makers embrace and try new ideas and improve their quality or make way for new people who want to make things better.'[6]

It seems that a more concerted effort must be made to deal with cultural issues – one that takes a more modern approach which encourages creativity and the analytics mode of thinking and creativity. Such an approach is evident in *Punjabi Vibes* (which was taken off the air) and the British sitcom *Goodness Gracious Me* (popular even among non-Punjabis).

Punjabi TV offers mainly Bollywood and *bhangra*. Quite a few third-generation Sikhs believe there should be more focus on youth issues. While the shows are entertaining, they seem to avoid the issues faced by the younger generation. TV interviews are mostly with high-profile people – the ones that can bring *izzat* to the community. In contrast, the problems of the younger generation are neglected or inadequately addressed.

As discussed in chapter 4, *Punjabi Vibes*, which provided skits about the tensions and problems experienced by young Canadian-born Sikhs, was popular among the third generation; it was also therapeutic, in the sense that it addressed intergenerational issues. However, some people had reservations about the show. According to one of its producers, many older Sikhs did not like seeing skits dealing with controversial issues (like alcoholism, physical abuse, double life) on public TV.[7] Some elders complained to Rogers (Shaw) Television that the show was offensive and that it portrayed the community in a bad light.[8] As a producer explained: 'We did a few skits regarding women's issues but it caused a problem for us ... People [from the community] don't want a particular woman acting or being associated with negative things on TV' (media 1).

Some members of the third generation have made a strong effort to shed light on the negative implications that traditional authoritarian parenting has on Canadian-born Sikh children, the older generations are uncomfortable about Sikh community problems being offered to the public gaze. This reaction of the first and second generations is related to the Punjabi value of *izzat*, which requires one to save face, whether the family's or that of the community. Moreover, they tend to treat the images they see enacted on TV at the literal level. Instead of acknowledging the problem that many young Sikhs lead double lives (which requires a conceptual and interpretive mode of thinking), they miss the point and simply take, for example, a woman talking to a man on the phone as something deserving disapproval because it violates the traditional norms of proper behaviour. The first and second generations are not intellectually prepared for the more analytical and conceptual portrayals offered as skits on shows like *Punjabi Vibes*.

The Vancouver Sikh community is relatively closed and has not yet aired its problems regarding family tensions. The Punjabi TV skits performed by the third generation have been a means to raise issues that are not otherwise discussed. Only recently however, have Punjabi radio programs begun to discuss family problems in the community. And only now is the community, after too many gang killings, suicides, and the like, showing a willingness to talk about these problems within its own 'safe' circles. The issues must be thoroughly debated within the community; only then can resolutions emerge. It will be difficult to solve such problems until they are acknowledged and understood by the Sikh community. During a forum on gang violence held in June 2002,[9] the discussion boiled down to the RCMP blaming Sikh culture for gang violence and Sikh activists accusing the RCMP of racism.

The Sikh Community as It Relates to Multiculturalism

This discussion of the tensions between the three generations of the Sikh community has attempted to explore the 'insular' nature of the community. No doubt the tensions between the three generations reflect the communication barriers associated with the different modes of thinking based on the broader historical development of society (from tradition to modernity). They are also related to the external influences from the broader society in which the Sikhs, as an immigrant community, are located. Even though assimilation as an ideology or policy may not be desirable, some level of integration with the larger society seems necessary if an immigrant community is to function smoothly. Broadly, there seem to be three main barriers to the integration of Sikhs, who have arrived in Canada as a predominantly illiterate (or not very educated) farming group: language, lack of education, and visibility. Of course, the linguistic and educational barriers can be overcome through appropriate policies; in any case, they are likely to attenuate with the passage of time as younger generations are raised in Canada. The element of visibility is likely to be more problematic.

As an immigrant group, the Sikhs must interact with three distinct entities: the homeland, the host country, and their own ethnic group within the host country. First-generation Sikhs maintain strong links with the Punjab (in part, through the radio), but have minimal interaction with Canadian society. Living in 'little Punjab,' they interact mainly with their own ethnic group. Second-generation Sikhs interact with Canadian society, mainly in the economic arena, yet they, too, remain rooted in the Punjabi community as it exists in Canada. Third-generation Sikhs find themselves living in a Punjabi bubble but desire to integrate more with the society beyond the Punjabi community. They have weak or non-existent links with the Punjab, yet find themselves having to identify with it, and as a result feel themselves to be 'other' than mainstream. The older generations (first and second) have trouble understanding the needs of the younger generation, because they see the younger generation as having a good life in a society with less racism, more food, and better shelter than they themselves had.

It is unavoidable that as an immigrant group the Sikhs are influenced by the social and political culture of the host country. A distinctive feature of Canada in recent decades has been the government policy of multiculturalism, and this policy has been of considerable significance to the Sikh community. However, the community does not have a single perspective on this policy. Rather, how it is viewed depends largely on the particular generation to which the individual Sikh belongs.

New Sikh immigrants readily embrace the policy's cultural preservation aspects, especially in light of the experience of the earlier immigrants during racially intolerant times, when assimilation was an expectation. However, because Sikh immigrants bring with them the traditional clan mentality, multiculturalism can also reinforce racial discrimination and divisions, especially when the immigrants resist adopting the modern values that go with the modern institutions (medicare and social welfare) of which they avail themselves.

Some of the second-generation Sikhs and a large majority of the third-generation Sikhs I interviewed referred to the Sikh community as being 'in a slump' and lacking organization and cohesion. As discussed in chapter 6, the particularistic clan mentality and the tendency toward factionalism have prevented the Sikh community from asserting itself as a unified and cohesive ethno-cultural group. As a consequence, the Sikh community has not been able to organize itself with long-term goals for its betterment, nor has it been able to meet its social and political needs. Buchignani and Indra discussed the problems that Canadian Sikhs are facing: '[It] is representative of a more deep organizational difficulty endemic to Sikhs in Canada: the structural inability to develop long term community planning, to institutionalize planning objectives, and to develop a broad-based community support for such institutions.'[10]

As noted earlier, this problem (one that other ethno-cultural groups in Canada, like the Jewish community, do not face) is related to the fact that the Sikh community behaves in a manner that is in between the fused traditional pattern and the fully differentiated modern one (i.e., it behaves in a manner more in accordance with a 'prismatic' social setup). Though it has distanced itself somewhat from the collectivity, the second generation continues to operate on the basis of clan loyalties. Also, the traditional mentality orients second-generation Sikhs toward their immediate life situation, and this makes planning for long-term objectives difficult.

The Sikh community's traditional culture contributes to its isolation as 'alien' or 'other' from the perspective of the mainstream (as evidenced in the portrayal of the Sikhs in the media). Furthermore, Canada's policy of multiculturalism raises it own barriers. It seems that the Sikh community's lack of socialization into the mainstream is partly a result of the policy's cultural preservation aspects. Also, that policy does not seem to sufficiently acknowledge the impact of being a *visible* minority on the community's isolation. In his comparative study of the Sikh communities in Canada and Singapore, Verne Dusenbury observed 'mixed messages' with regard to Canadian Sikhs and the policy of multiculturalism: the preservation of culture is sanctified by Canadian multiculturalism, but as a project, that cultural preservation is pursued quite divorced from the instrumental culture of Canada, that of liberalism.[11] Indeed, this contradiction is reflected in the conflict – which has emerged in this study – between cultural preservation and social integration, especially since the Sikh community has arrived in Canada as a predominantly traditional agricultural group rooted in oral culture (an issue that will be explored in chapter 8).

Being a visible minority (i.e, rather than an ethno-cultural group that can easily blend into the mainstream) poses a problem for the Sikhs. Racism still exists, even if only tacitly, both internally within the Sikh community and in the society at large. The first and second generations often regard Western culture negatively (an attitude that may or may not be carried over to their children and grandchildren). For their part, mainstream Canadians see the Sikh community as 'insular' and 'other.' Is the lack of adequate integration with the mainstream a problem particular to Vancouver because of its high concentration of Sikhs? Sikhs interact more with the mainstream in the small towns of B.C. than in Vancouver, but even in those small towns the first and second generations enforce considerable ethnic insularity. That said, multiculturalism seems to encourage concentrations such as Vancouver: funding for ethnic communities is provided where those communities are concentrated (i.e., in cities, not in smaller towns). The impact of multiculturalism is strongest where ethnic groups constitute important voting blocks.

Multiculturalism thus seems to have been a good thing to the extent that it has helped end the overt racism that existed before the 1970s. Yet at the same time, it now seems to be encouraging ethnic groups like the Sikhs to turn in on themselves. This is evidenced in the third generation's dislike of being referred to as 'Indo-Canadian,' which differentiates it from the mainstream even though it was born in Canada. Third-generation Sikhs no doubt want to learn about their heritage, but they want to do so in the context of increased interaction with the mainstream, not from within the Punjabi bubble, where it sees only community self-promotion and a lack of the cohesiveness that is necessary for the long-term advancement of the community.

Conclusion

As the predominantly traditional Sikh community encounters cultural diversity and multiculturalism in Canada, tensions have arisen between the generations. These tensions are related to the gap between tradition and modernity and to the nature of the community's interactions with the host country. The first generation has recreated a 'little Punjab' for itself. It has fully embraced those Canadian institutions which provide universal social services, but has done so without absorbing the modern values associated with them. In terms of customs and values, the first generation continues to maintain strong links with the Punjab.

The third generation is dismayed to find itself living in a Punjabi bubble. It wants to integrate more fully with the larger society. On the whole, third-generation Sikhs want the liberty to preserve their broader culture while shedding values they dislike, such as *izzat*. What distinguishes third-generation Sikhs is their desire to interact more with mainstream Canadian society. In this desire it feels constrained by the Punjabi community in Canada.

The second generation interacts with Canadian society, but mainly in the economic sphere. Its interactions, like those of the first generation, remain limited to the Punjabi community in Canada. On the whole, second-generation Sikhs approve of multiculturalism, but they also express disdain for how that policy is funded. (The grant monies are earmarked for Sikh social organizations.)

Ethnic insularity generates tensions between the generations; it also affects how the Canadian mainstream perceives and interacts with the community. So, how can the Sikh community become less alien to the mainstream? And how can the mainstream, with its orientation toward multiculturalism, enhance ethnic integration? In the next chapter I try to answer these questions.

8 Conclusion: Canadian Sikhs amid Modernity and Multiculturalism

Hailing largely as farmers from Punjabi villages, predominantly illiterate (or poorly educated), the Sikhs have settled in the modern industrial society of Canada. Rooted in oral culture and traditional society, they have essentially been 'transplanted' into a modern society, without having fully undergone the experience of modernization in their home society. The consequence of all this is conflict between, on the one hand, cultural preservation – which is sanctioned by the Canadian policy of multiculturalism – and, on the other, socialization into modern society, which is essential for the smooth functioning of Canada's Sikh community.

Canadian multicultural policy, which sanctions the preservation of traditional cultures, has been a worthwhile attempt to move away from the overt racism that existed in the past. However, multiculturalism has its drawbacks, especially when the ethno-cultural group involved is a *group with a religious identity rooted in traditional village society and faces pressure to adjust to a modern society.* In the inevitable clash between modernity and tradition, multiculturalism tends to obstruct – or at least prolong – the adjustment to modernity. At the same time, the community itself faces the problem as to what part of the traditional culture it ought to preserve and what changes it ought to accept.

The Inevitable Impact of Modernity on Tradition

When a traditional community is transplanting itself to Canada, there is inevitably a generational time lag while it 'learns' the new society. However, the pressures of modernity are relentless. Although most

Sikhs certainly continue to identify strongly with their cultural and religious heritage, an overwhelmingly modern society such as Canada's cannot help but have a transformative impact on their traditional patterns of behaviour.

The impact of modernity on the Sikh community in Canada can be seen in the differences that exist between the three generations. In this study I found that although second-generation Sikhs approve of *modern* 'economic' practices – such as being employed in the industrial sector – they disapprove of *Western* 'cultural' values – such as the orientation toward the individual. The second generation sees the former (e.g., earning higher wages) as 'good' and readily takes to them; it perceives the latter (e.g., self-orientation) as 'bad'. However, such an understanding of the values of modernity and Canadian society is overly simplistic, especially in the light of the tensions that exist between the generations and the issues that the Sikh community must deal with in order to function harmoniously as a community in Vancouver.

To at least some degree, many immigrant groups have failed to realize that the cultural values associated with Western society (such as self-differentiation, success by merit, the exercising of personal choice, and egalitarianism) are integral to the economic order and to the independence they gain from that order. This failure to take to the cultural values that underpin Canada's modern economy generates personal disorientation, especially for those who have been reared in or are now working in a modern environment. The inevitable impact of modernity on a traditional group is most evident in the different modes of thinking and communication patterns generated by the interaction of modernity and tradition. It is especially evident in the tension between generations and genders in the areas of household dynamics, child rearing and development, and religious and social practices.

Communication Patterns

Thought forms are expressive of the kind of society a person comes from. Traditional and modern societies have their own distinctive modes of thinking. The first generation of the Sikh community, which arrived in Canada mainly from village Punjab, reflects the mode of thinking particular to the oral culture found in traditional society (orality). Most first-generation Sikhs are either illiterate or had received minimal formal education, and thus reflect the orality mode of thinking. Accordingly, they tend to express themselves in concrete thought forms rather than abstract terms, also, their expression is based directly on their own life situation, and their basic orientation is toward the collectivity rather than the individual.

In contrast, the children of immigrants (third generation) have been raised in the modern host country, have been educated in Western schools, and are living amidst and interacting more with modern culture and its associated analytics mode of thinking. Thus, the general tendency among third-generation Sikhs is to move toward analytics, which is characterized by self-reflection, the ability to articulate analytical and conceptual thoughts, and self-orientation (rather than collectivity orientation).

Meanwhile, most second-generation Sikhs – that is, the parents of Canadian-born Sikhs – are somewhere along the continuum between orality and literacy. Although some of them were educated in India and thus were literate on arrival in Canada, most are rooted in traditional mentality or an oral culture. The literacy mode of thinking is a transitional mode in that it has some characteristics of orality (concrete thought form, traditional mentality) while moving toward analytics. The distinguishing features of literacy, which are the consequence of the ability to read and write, include the capacity of its bearers to distance themselves from the collectivity even while remaining rooted in traditional culture, and a shift toward *some* comprehension of the abstract (i.e, the capacity for *translation* and for *literal interpretation*).

These different thought forms, which are associated with the different stages in the historical development of society (tradition, modernity, and the transition from the former to the latter), shed light on the distinctive features of each of the three generations of the Sikh community. These particular modes of thinking illuminate the adaptation process for traditional immigrant groups to a modern host society, and demonstrate the inevitable impact of modernity on such groups. At the same time, these different modes of thinking, which are related to societal development, become a major communication barrier between the generations.

Third-generation Sikhs tend to ask many questions and to be self-reflective – qualities that the first and second generations view as undermining authority and tradition. Also, these qualities are rooted in the modern analytics mode of thinking as fostered in Western schools. In those schools, third-generation Sikhs are trained to exercise the analytics mode of thinking; at home, this mode is not encouraged at all and is even condemned. The analytics mode of thinking, an inevitable outcome of modernity, is a major source of tension between the generations.

The Effects of Economic Independence on the Traditional Household

The impact of modernity on socio-economic arrangements can be seen in relation to the household network. Much tension is experienced by the first generation, which functions according to the traditional Punjabi norms and customs of the extended family system. This tension is the result of (a) change in the locus of economic control within the family network, and (b) the reduction in household size to the 'modified extended family.' When both second-generation parents work outside the home (as they often do), members of the first generation – who do not have access to the full extended family structure as it exists in the Punjab – feel overworked in the household as grandparents. To make matters worse, they do not receive the respect or attention that they were accustomed to receiving 'automatically' in the traditional joint family household by virtue of their seniority (i.e., on an ascriptive basis).

Meanwhile, even though the second generation continues to endorse the traditional Indian values of duty and respect, it simultaneously experiences the double-edged effects of economic independence within the family household. Second-generation Sikhs are proud of their economic achievements, which are based on their own hard work, especially with regard to establishing the 'modified extended family'; indeed, they expect and demand respect for their success. But at the same time, second-generation women resent having to play the role of the obedient and dutiful wife (or daughter-in-law), since Canada has given them a taste of economic independence and exposed them to modern ideas of social equality.

With modern society comes economic independence, which leads to an expansion of choice for individuals. This is evident in the third generation's appreciation of the modern value of self-orientation, in its desire to exercise choice in life decisions, and in its search for respect within the family. But this quest for expansion of choice and individualism clashes with the traditional value of fulfilling one's duty in honour of and conformity with the collectivity of the family.

Tension between Self-Individuation and Collective Conformity in Child Rearing

Economic independence also leads to self-orientation. Even though second-generation Sikhs have generally succeeded in adapting to Canada's economy, they have not accepted modern attitudes toward the individual. As a consequence, their children are sometimes thwarted in fulfilling their individual potential in the modern milieu, which is oriented toward the individual.

Continuous with the parental roles traditionally performed by the first generation, second-generation Sikh parents in Canada have undoubtedly been able to provide their children with the necessary physiological and safety needs. However, they seem for the most part to have failed to satisfy the more abstract emotional and communicative needs that are essential for the personal development of their children, who are living in an individual-oriented milieu. The modern requirement of encouraging children to develop self-orientation and to internalize ethical standards tends to undermine the traditional norms of collectivity orientation, which depend on the outer social control of *izzat* as well as on conformity with the collectivity. Consequently, second-generation parents resist the individuation process associated with modernity. Moreover, fearing loss of control over their children, second-generation parents overindulge their children with material goods in order to maintain control over them within the household.

As they grow up, Canadian-born Sikh children are socialized at home to live in accordance with traditional mores. For example, they are for the most part raised to follow the wishes or orders of their parents (collective conformity), instead of being encouraged in the self-individuation process, a developmental stage that is necessary for functioning effectively in modern society. This results in ineffective coping mechanisms, with the children leading double lives in *outward* conformity to parental pressures. That, or they go off track in extreme rebellion and defiance.

The Expansion of Personal Choice in Religious Practice

The influence of the expansion of choice for individuals associated with modernity is evident in the third generation's quest for personal choice in religious practice. This clashes with the traditional approach to religion. The first and second generations express their faith through collective beliefs and customs (e.g., showing respect for sacred space and reciting prayers by rote), which have been passed down through oral transmission. Although second-generation Sikhs have undergone some distancing from the collectivity, their traditional mentality makes it difficult for them to intellectually accept the fact that their children want to choose whether to seek a personal relationship with God (as opposed to accepting the customs at face value). Parents expect their third-generation children to practise religion as it has been tradition-ally followed, without inquiry or questioning. Furthermore, because the second generation equates the practice of religion with maintaining the inherited culture, the third generation encounters confusion, since their analytics mode of thinking distinguishes between religion and culture (and, in fact, often views Sikhism as preached by the ten gurus as contradictory to Punjabi culture). Third-generation Sikhs do not seem to gain the sense of spiritual fulfilment that the elders (especially of the first generation) experience simply by following the traditional customs and rituals that have been transmitted orally. The modern mentality, which the third generation acquires at school in Canada, encourages a self-conscious approach to religion, including the right to question Sikh beliefs and practices. It also fosters the conceptual expression of religious notions, the desire for personal choice, and an emphasis on a personal relationship with God.

The Impact of Individualism on Traditional Communal Honour

The modern value of individualism tends to negate collectivity orien-tation. It also encourages action based on personal convictions. The first generation functions according to the traditional Punjabi custom of ascriptive status, and it embraces community *izzat* as a means of social control. In contrast, the second generation feels considerable pressure to accumulate material wealth for status, yet at the same time demands that its children continue with Punjabi customs in order to save face. Second-generation Sikhs are generally unable to adequately distance themselves from the collectivity or, more broadly, to concep-tualize the serious difficulties that arise when they attempt to function according to tradition in a modern context. Rather, they tend to cover up serious matters in order to save face for the family.

Third-generation Sikhs regard the traditional value of *izzat* nega-tively, because it contradicts the modern notion of individualism. They want to move away from the community's clan mentality (which they encounter in the *gurdwaras*), but they find this difficult because com-munity pressure is so strong. The experiences of individualism and at the same time of 'being caught in community tradition' have generated a sense of ethnic insularity among third-generation Sikhs.

Like many other immigrants, most Sikh immigrants have come to Canada mainly for a better economic life. Having succeeded economically, they now appreciate economic integration, but economic integration is not the same as social integration. Their initial motives may have been purely economic; nevertheless, the act of immigration to a modern society has generated social and psychological changes within the Sikh community. Notwithstanding the economic success of the Sikhs in Canada, a number of important issues that have been discussed in this study – such as role playing or double life, the double standard, the confusion between culture and religion, the refusal to countenance inquiry into the nature of religion, and the feeling of ethnic insularity – reflect personal disorientation and lack of success in social integration. All of these problems have, prevented the smooth functioning of the community in the modern Canadian milieu.

The Tension between Cultural Preservation and Social Integration

Multiculturalism policies have enabled immigrant communities to live according to their inherited customs and values. However, there has been much debate regarding the appropriateness of Canadian multiculturalism, since traditional values often clash with the modern values of individualism, success by merit, and equality of opportunity, which prevail in Canada.[1] At the same time, there can be no doubt that conflict is likely to arise if ethnic groups are made either to remain distinct or to assimilate into the mainstream involuntarily. The official 'sanction' of cultural preservation can itself become a source of conflict between the various generations – in particular, between Canadian-born children and their immigrant parents.

Multiculturalism and the Sikh Community

The preservation of culture is sanctioned by the Canadian policy of multiculturalism and is embraced by the first and second generations; however, this has given rise to conflict, since that culture is rooted in tradition and thus hinders social integration into modern society for Canadian-born third-generation Sikhs. First-generation Sikhs have created a 'little Punjab' for themselves in Canada and continue to maintain strong links with their homeland. They see multiculturalism as good because it promotes the preservation of their culture. On the other hand, although this generation has fully embraced the Canadian institutions that provide universal social programs, it has done so without absorbing the modern values associated with them.

The second generation interacts more than the first with Canadian society, but this interaction is limited mainly to work. Also, the second generation is similar to the first in that it remains largely rooted in the Punjabi community and maintains links with the Punjab. The second generation endorses the policy of multiculturalism but looks askance at funds being misused by social organizations. Some members of this generation perceive that their commmunity is in a 'slump' and lacks organization and cohesion, yet they have difficulty understanding why this is so, or how to correct matters. The first and second generations seem limited in this regard by their modes of thinking (orality and literacy), and are unable to visualize or conceptualize an alternative scenario that would serve the longer-term interests of the community.

In contrast, many third-generation Sikhs, who tend toward the analytics mode of thinking, feel constrained by the Punjabi community in Canada and by Canada's multiculturalism policy. They perceive themselves as living in a 'Punjabi bubble' and are distressed by this. Indeed, they ardently desire to integrate themselves more fully with the broader Canadian society. On the whole, third-generation Sikhs want the freedom to preserve the broader Punjabi culture while casting away those customs it dislikes, such as *izzat*. What especially distinguishes the third generation is its keen desire for more interaction with mainstream Canadian society and to be considered 'Canadian' (as opposed to 'Indo-Canadian').

In the light of the above findings, it would be reckless for policymakers to assume that Canadian-born children want to retain a traditional mentality while living and functioning in a modern society. Indeed, the tensions between the generations reflect a profound conflict between tradition and modernity. If the culture of certain immigrant groups is equated with the traditional mentality, then it certainly can impede social integration in Canada. On the other hand, such a view of culture itself may well be a mistaken one.

Multicultural studies often examine South Asian communities as if their cultures are static. That is, they take what is observed about these communities here in Canada and categorize it as 'the culture,' without comparing it to the present situation in the 'homeland,' where in fact the culture has been evolving under various influences and is undergoing vast changes. Immigrants themselves tend to perpetuate their culture as 'they remember it' back in the homeland. But culture is not static, whether back in the community's homeland or here in Canada. Culture is always changing. This more informed view of culture needs to be better appreciated if the former agricultural community from the Punjab is to adapt to its modern milieu.

Multiculturalism: Empowering or Disempowering Ethnic Communities?

Although ethnic insularity may generate tensions between the generations, partly because of their different modes of thinking, insularity is not entirely something that the ethnic minorities in Canada themselves have determined. Rather, some of the problems that ethnic minorities face are a consequence of the existing policies of the country. The discussion of these problems in the present study seems to suggest that the government need not assume the burden of responsibility for preserving the cultures of ethnic groups. The preservation of the culture ought to be strictly the concern of the community itself. Those who want to continue with their culture and religion, may then do so; those who do not want to need not do so.

Perhaps the government ought to focus more on helping communities integrate; that is, it ought to give priority to making resources available to those new immigrants or the elderly, who face language and cultural barriers, for the precise purpose of overcoming such barriers. Both the government and the mainstream public need to be aware that the Punjabi bubble is not necessarily the outcome of rational choices by individuals; in part, it is also the structural consequence of being a visible ethnic minority in a predominantly white society. At the same time, that bubble is also in some measure a result of the public policy of multiculturalism. Too much emphasis on multiculturalism seems to have made it harder for immigrants to familiarize themselves with the ways of the West, to have hindered their children from acquiring the ability to live in accordance with those ways, and to have generally blocked creativity in cultural development through the interaction of tradition and modernity.

It would perhaps be better to conceptualize multiculturalism as a necessary phase, but one that if it continues may hinder adaptation to modernity and integration into Canada. This problem is most visible in the third generation of the Sikh community. It may well be that multiculturalism policy is premised on an unstated assumption that the forces pushing toward the integration of ethnic groups into the main-stream in Canada are so overwhelming that it can confidently afford to be generous on the side of seeming to 'sanction' cultural preservation. In the meantime, however, the policy has resulted, perversely, in ex-cluding some (i.e., first and second generations) from fully interacting with the mainstream and in complicating the transition of others (third generation) to the mainstream. That being so, the policy seems to be in need of some modification, so that the balance of emphasis shifts from preservation of traditional culture to greater interaction and integration with a modern cohesive Canadian society.

The first and second generations need help to interact with the main-stream community and institutions. The third generation needs guid-ance in living as Canadians, no doubt with a grasp of their own cultural heritage but at the same time adapting to the values of modernity. Eth-nic communities can continue to be responsible for preserving their own culture and religion. However, multiculturalism needs to be reori-ented toward encouraging communities to interact with the Canadian mainstream. Integration should be the responsibility of the govern-ment; cultural preservation should *not* be. More emphasis on integra-tion will help new immigrants adapt to Canada as a modern society; it will also enable the various ethnic communities to contribute to the development of the Canadian mosaic.

The responsibility for breaking down barriers between the main-stream and an ethnic group belongs to both the government and the ethnic group itself. Since the interests of an ethnic group are the con-cern of the group itself, the Sikh community needs to work harder to interact with the mainstream. It is important to note that the notion of integration and interaction with people beyond one's immediate circle – family, clan, caste, ethnic group, religion – is not altogether foreign to the Sikh tradition; in fact, it is supported by its own scriptural litera-ture.[2] However, there has remained a vast gulf between rhetoric and practice in the Sikh community.

If tensions between the generations are to be eased and if the Sikh community is to adapt to Canadian society, there must be more atten-tion paid to programs that encourage the analytics mode of thinking and creativity, and more effort to deal with cultural issues using more modern approaches. For instance, third-generation Sikhs could benefit from help in striking a balance between the traditional orientation toward the collectivity and the modern value of personal choice, so that they can reach their full potential as creative and innovative individuals. As well, rather than being marginalized or tokenized, the Sikh community as a whole could benefit from moving away from its traditional village/clan mentality by interacting more with the mainstream and Canada's rich social diversity.

Summing Up

It should be clear from this study that the process of adaptation of the Sikh community, as it moves from Punjabi villages to a Canadian metropolis, is enormously complex. This complexity – which is characterized by contradiction – has been evident in the analysis of the three generations. Many of the tensions between the generations are a result of the clash between tradition and modernity. Communication barriers and social contradictions arise from the existential situation of Canadian-born children living in a traditional Punjabi household while being educated in schools encouraging the analytics mode of thinking and interacting more with the mainstream.

In exploring the relations and tensions between Sikh generations, we also see the broader processes of continuity and change in a traditional religio-ethnic group as it adapts to a modern society with an official policy of multiculturalism. The continuity in traditional customs, modifications in behaviour patterns, and changes in values and customs in the context of the broader Canadian social environment ought to indicate to Canadians that multiculturalism policy can hinder adaptation to modernity and integration in Canada as long as that policy remains focused exclusively on the sanctioning of cultural preservation.

Notes

1 From Punjabi Villages to a Canadian Metropolis

1 Diaspora was originally a term used for the Jewish community that was forced out of its homeland and thus became a displaced community. More recently, the word has been used somewhat more loosely to refer to any group that exists outside its homeland. Tatla takes the position that the initial Sikh migration does not fit the original criterion of a diaspora, since it was the Sikhs (and other Punjabis), who chose to leave the Punjab for economic reasons. See Darshan Singh Tatla, *The Sikh Diaspora: The Search for Statehood* (Seattle: University of Washington Press, 1999), 3–6. For a broader treatment of diasporas, see William Safran, 'Diasporas in Modern Societies: Myths of the Homeland and Return,' *Diaspora* 1(1) (1991): 83–99; and R. Cohen, *Global Diasporas: An Introduction* (Seattle: University of Washington Press, 1997).

2 Integration is a movement toward the maintenance of cultural integrity while simultaneously becoming an integral part of the larger society.

3 'East Indians' refers to people whose roots are specifically in India. Although there is no country called East India, the British gave and used the term 'East Indian.' The British and Canadians commonly used the term 'East Indian' during the early period of Indian migration to Canada.

4 'South Asians' is a very broad category as it refers to people originally in the geographical area of South Asia, including India, Pakistan, Bangladesh, and Sri Lanka. 'South Asians' also refers to Indians who have migrated to other parts of the world such as Fiji, Malaysia, Hong Kong, and East Africa.

5 Norman Buchignani and Doreen M. Indra, *Continuous Journey: A Social History of South Asians in Canada* (Toronto: McClelland and Stewart, 1985); Joseph T. O'Connell, Milton Israel, and Willard G. Oxtoby (eds.), *Sikh History and Religion in the 20th Century* (Toronto: Centre for South Asian Studies, University of Toronto, 1988); N. Gerald Barrier and Verne A. Dusenbery

(eds), *The Sikh Diaspora: Migration and the Experience beyond the Punjab* (Delhi: Chanakya Publications, 1989); and James Gaylord Chadney, *The Sikhs of Vancouver* (New York: AMS Press, 1984).

6 Tatla, *The Sikh Diaspora*; Pashaura Singh and Gerald Barrier (eds.), *Sikh Identity: Continuity and Change* (New Delhi: Manohar, 1999).

7 Harold Coward, John R. Hinnels, and Raymond Brady Williams (eds.), *The South Asian Religious Diaspora in Britain, Canada, and the U.S.A.* (Albany: State University of New York Press, 2000).

8 For example, Evelyn Nodwell, '"Integrating Indian Culture into our Life": The Construction of (East) "Indian Culture" in Vancouver, Canada' (PhD dissertation, University of British Columbia, 1993), 21; Buchignani and Indra, *Continuous Journey*; Josephine C. Naidoo, 'Women of South Asian Origins: Status of Research, Problems, Future Issues,' in *The South Asian Diaspora in Canada: Six Essays*, ed. Milton Israel (Toronto: Multicultural History Society of Ontario, 1987), 37–58; Anne Woollett et al., 1994, 'Asian's Women's Ethnic Identity: The Impact of Gender and Context in the Accounts of Women Bringing Up Children in East London,' *Feminism and Psychology* 4(1), 119–32; P.A.S. Ghuman, 'Canadian or Indo-Canadian: a Study of South Asian Adolescents, *International Journal of Adolescence and Youth*, 4 (1994): 229–43; Mary Stopes-Roe and Raymond Cochrane. 'The Process of Assimilation in Asians in Britain: A Study of Hindu, Muslim and Sikh Immigrants and Their Young Adult Children,' *International Journal of Comparative Sociology* 28 (1987): 43–56; Aziz Talbani and Parveen Hasanali, 'Adolescent Females between Tradition and Modernity: Gender Role Socialization in South Asian Immigrant Culture,' *Journal of Adolescence* 23(5) (2000): 615–27.

9 The term 'Indo-Canadians' came into use in the 1980s as a result of the Canadian government's policy and ideology of multiculturalism. It refers to Canadian-born people whose origins are on the Indian subcontinent. Although this term is often used in 'mainstream' Canadian circles, many Canadian-born South Asians dislike the term because it differentiates them from other Canadians.

10 Farah Ibrahim et al., 'Asian American Identity Development: A Culture Specific Model for South Asian Americans,' *Journal of Multicultural Counseling and Development* 25 (January 1997): 34–50.

11 For more information about Gora Sikhs, see Verne A. Dusenbery, 'Punjabi Sikhs and Gora Sikhs: Conflicting Assertions of Sikh Identity in North America,' in O'Connell et al. (eds.), *Sikh History and Religion in the 20th Century*, 334–55.

12 See P.N. Dhar, *Indira Gandhi, the 'Emergency' and Indian Democracy* (New Delhi: Oxford University Press, 2000), 224–5.

13 Ferdinard Toennies, *Community and Association* (New York: Harper and Row, 1963): the original (*Gemeinschaft und Gesellschaft*) was published in German in 1887.

14 Weber also isolated a third category of the structure of authority – charismatic domination – that is not relevant in the present discussion.

15 Max Weber, *Economy and Society: An Outline of Interpretive Sociology* (Berkeley: University of California Press, 1978): the original was published in German in 1921.

16 Talcott Parsons and Edward A. Shils, *Toward a General Theory of Action* (Cambridge: Harvard University Press, 1951), 77.

17 Francis X. Sutton, 'Analyzing Social Systems,' *Political Development and Social Change*, ed. Jason L. Finkle and Richard W. Gable (New York: John Wiley and Sons, 1966), 24.

18 Ibid., 25.

19 Alex Inkeles, *One World Emerging? Convergence and Divergence in Industrial Societies* (Boulder, CO: Westview Press, 1998).

20 Fred Warren Riggs, *Administration in Developing Countries: The Theory of Prismatic Society* (Boston: Houghton Mifflin, 1964).

21 Postmodernity has been much written about in a variety of fields (literature, history, religious studies, political science, etc.). For more information about postmodernity in the social sciences, see Richard J. Bernstein, *The New Constellation: The Ethical-Political Horizons of Modernity/Postmodernity* (Cambridge: MIT Press, 1992); Albert Borgmann, *Crossing the Postmodern Divide* (Chicago: University of Chicago Press, 1992); and Stephan Crook, Jan Pakulski, and Malcom Walters, *Postmodernity: Change in Advanced Society* (Newbury Park, CA: Sage, 1992).

22 Chadney, *The Sikhs of Vancouver*.

23 Will Herberg claimed that the Protestants, Catholics and Jews never melted, thus reinforcing the workings of pluralism. See Will Herberg, *Protestant, Catholic, Jew* (New York: Doubleday, 1955). Two other scholars have noted that the American melting pot was not achieved in New York City. It was found that the communities had not assimilated. The Jewish community had no interest in assimilating because of its pride as a distinct religious group. Afro-Americans were unable to assimilate because of the racism they experienced at the hands of the mainstream society. The Catholics and Puerto Ricans represented a combination of the two types. See Nathan Glazer and Daniel P. Moynihan, *Beyond the Melting Pot* (Cambridge: MIT Press, 1963). Also, see the more recent work by Arthur M. Schlesinger, Jr, *The Disuniting of America: Reflections on a Multicultural Society* (New York: W.W. Norton, 1992).

24 Statement by the prime minister in the House of Commons, 8 October 1971.

25 The debate regarding immigration and the process of adaptation can be traced back to the early twentieth century. In the 1920s, Robert Park put forward the notion that all immigrants eventually lose their ethnic identity because the dominant culture and language tend to prevail, and that the length of the assimilation process is dependent on whether immigrant groups enter with minimal resistance (contact, accommodation, and assimilation), or with a lot of resistance (contact, conflict, competition, accommodation, and assimilation) See C. Everenett et al. (eds.), *Race and Culture: The Collected Papers of Robert Ezra Park*, vol. 1 (Glencoe, IL: Free Press, 1950). Later, it was argued that assimilation occurs more easily in the areas of education, economics, and politics, whereas it is more difficult in the areas of family life. See Milton Gordon, *Assimilation in American Life* (New York: Oxford University Press, 1964). John Porter thought that assimilation was inevitable because of modern technology and urbanization, and that ethnicity was counterproductive because it hinders upward social mobility. See John Porter, *The Vertical Mosaic: An Analysis of Social Class and Power in Canada* (Toronto: University of Toronto Press, 1965), and John Porter, *The Measure of Canadian Society: Education Equality and Opportunity* (Toronto: Sage, 1979).

In an early critique of assimilation, Horace Kallen believed that many groups continue to retain a separate identity and never assimilate, and that pluralism should be supported because: (1) one is born in an ethnic group with its distinctive ancestry, (2) each ethnic group has valuable things to contribute to the mainstream society, and (3) the American constitution states that all are created equal. See Horace M. Kallen, *Culture and Democracy in the United States* (New York: Livernight, 1924).

26 Augie Fleras and John Leonard Elliot, *Multiculturalism in Canada: The Challenge of Diversity* (Toronto: Nelson, 1992), 53–67.

27 Ibid., 99–104, 179–82.

28 Ibid., 11.

29 Ibid., 129–44.

30 Neil Bissoondath, *Selling Illusions: The Cult of Multiculturalism in Canada* (Toronto: Penguin Books, 1994), 218–19.

31 Schlesinger, *The Disuniting of America*, 13.

32 Will Kymlicka, *Finding Our Way: Rethinking Ethnocultural Relations in Canada* (Toronto: Oxford University Press, 1998).

33 Porter, *The Vertical Mosaic*, and *The Measure of Canadian Society*.

34 Gurnam Singh Sanghera, 'The Male Punjabi Elderly of Vancouver: Their Background, Health Beliefs and Access to Health Care Services' (MA diss., University of British Columbia, 1991), 21; Badrinath Krishna Rao, 'The

Agony When East Meets West,' *Globe and Mail*, 17 May 1991, 17; Rekha Basu, 'Expatriate Indians: American Born Confused Desis,' *India Today* (Delhi: 30 August 1989), 106–9; Yogesh Atal 'Outsiders as Insiders: The Phenomenon of Sandwich Culture,' *Sociological Bulletin* 38 (1989): 23–42.

35 Evelyn Nodwell, '"Integrating Indian Culture into our Life": The Construction of (East) "Indian Culture" in Vancouver, Canada' (PhD diss., University of British Columbia, 1993), 21; Buchignani and Indra, *Continuous Journey*. This has also been pointed out by the literature specifically on the Sikh diaspora: Verne A. Dusenbery, 'Introduction: A Century of Sikhs Beyond Punjab,' in Barrier and Dusenbery (eds.), *The Sikh Diaspora*, 1–28: 17–18.

36 Sutton, 'Analyzing Social Systems,' 24–5; Geert H. Hofstede, *Culture's Consequences: International Differences in Work-related Values* (Beverly Hills, CA: Sage, 1980); Harry Charalambos Triandis, *Individualism and Collectivism* (Boulder, CO: Westview Press, 1995).

37 Jean Piaget, *The Child's Conception of the World* (Paterson, NJ: Littlefield Adams, 1965).

38 Erik H. Erikson, *Identity and the Life Cycle: Selected Papers* (New York: International Universities Press, 1959), and *Identity, Youth and Crisis* (New York: W.W. Norton, 1968).

39 Hofsteade, *Culture's Consequences*; Triandis, *Individualism and Collectivism*.

40 Sutton, 'Analyzing Social Systems,' 24–5.

41 H. Tajfel, *Social Identity and Ethnic Group Relations* (New York: Cambridge University Press, 1982), 255.

42 Fleras and Elliot, *Multiculturalism in Canada*, 49.

43 Kamaljit Kaur Sidhu, 'Second Generation Sikh Adolescent Males: A Grounded Theory Model of Self and Identity Construction' (PhD diss., University of British Columbia, 1999); Michael Angelo, *The Sikh Diaspora: Tradition and Continuity in an Immigrant Community* (New York: Garland, 1997); and Nodwell, '"Integrating Indian Culture into our Life."'

44 An overview of the Sikh religion is provided in chapter 3.

45 Hindoo was commonly the term given, referring to those who came from 'Hindustan'. See the newspaper *Days in the Sun* (11 September 1907) as an example of the press reporting about the Hindoos/Hindus arriving in Canada.

46 Tatla, *The Sikh Diaspora*, 51.

47 James Gaylord Chadney, 'The Formation of Ethnic Communities: Lessons from Vancouver Sikhs,' in O'Connell et al. (eds.), *Sikh History and Religion in the 20th Century*, 185–199, 193.

48 Tatla, *The Sikh Diaspora*, 51.

49 Chadney, *The Sikhs of Vancouver*, 33; Hugh Johnston 'Patterns of Sikh Migration to Canada 1900–1960,' in O'Connell et al. (eds.), *Sikh History and Religion in the 20th Century*, 296–313.
50 Chadney, *The Sikhs of Vancouver*, 33.
51 For a thorough analysis of the *Komagata Maru* incident, see Buchignani and Indra, *Continuous Journey*, 50–70; Hugh Johnston, *The Voyage of* Komagata Maru: *The Sikh Challenge to Canada's Colour Bar* (Delhi: Oxford University Press, 1979).
52 Chadney, *The Sikhs of Vancouver*, 33.
53 James G. Chadney, 'The Formation of Ethnic Communities,' 190.
54 Narinder Singh, *Canadian Sikhs: History, Religion, and Culture of Sikhs in North America* (Ottawa: Canadian Sikhs' Studies Institute, 1994), 73.
55 John Wood, 'East Indians and Canada's New Immigration Policy,' *Canadian Public Policy*, 4(4) (1978): 547–67.
56 Ted Palys, *Research Decisions: Quantitative and Qualitative Perspectives* (Toronto: Harcourt Brace Jovanovich, 1992), 148–9.

2 Communication among Three Generations: Reflections on Orality, Literacy, and Analytics

1 For example, Merry Wood, *Cross-Cultural Communication*. Vancouver: Vancouver Hospital and Health Services Center, 1994.
2 Three scholarly works were influential in this conceptualization: Talcott Parsons and Edward Shils, *Toward a General Theory of Action* (Cambridge: Harvard University Press, 1951), which looks at the essential characteristics of the polar types of traditional society and modern society; Benjamin S. Bloom, *Taxonomy of Educational Objectives: The Classification of Educational Goals. Handbook 1, Cognitive Domain* (New York: David McKay, 1956), which discusses cognitive development, differentiating the stages in development of intellectual abilities and skills through the categories of knowledge, comprehension, application, analysis, synthesis, and evaluation; and Walter J. Ong, *Orality and Literacy: The Technologizing of the Word* (London: Routledge, 1982), which is a literary analysis that looks at the changes in the human thought process stemming from the creation of the written and print form in contrast to the earlier oral tradition. Ong identifies three stages (orality, 'residual orality,' and literacy), reflecting the changes of the human thought process as a result of the 'technologizing of the word.'
3 Ong, *Orality and Literacy*, 37–49.
4 Ibid., 37–49.
5 Ibid., 37–49.

6 Bloom, *Taxonomy of Educational Objectives*, 89–91.

7 Ibid., 93.

8 Ong, *Orality and Literacy*, 37–49.

9 Parsons and Shils, *Toward a General Theory of Action*, 77.

10 Ong, *Orality and Literacy*, 37–49.

11 Ibid., 37–49.

12 One *bigha* is roughly 5/8 of an acre.

3 Family Relations among Three Generations: Duty, Role Playing, and Independence, Part 1

1 Francis X. Sutton, 'Analyzing Social Systems,' *Political Development and Social Change*, ed. Jason L. Finkle and Richard W. Gable (New York: John Wiley and Sons, 1966), 24–5; Geert H. Hofstede, *Culture's Consequences: International Differences in Work-related Values* (Beverly Hills, CA: Sage, 1980); and Harry Charalambos Triandis, *Individualism and Collectivism* (Boulder, CO: Westview Press, 1995).

2 The ancient sacred Hindu text, the *Bhagavad Gita*, which has had a wide and profound influence on Indian thought and culture, refers to *dharma* as action that affects both the mundane social level and the spiritual level. Since the ultimate goal is salvation (*moksha*), one is required to strive toward the religious ideal of performing one's duty but to be detached from its fruits (*nis-kama-karma-yoga*). One ought to follow both the social and religious law as a means to *moksha*; one should follow the prescribed customs and rituals, but within the framework of detachment and the pursuit of higher spiritual attainment.

3 *Guru Granth Sahib*: Asa 3, 349; Var Siri Ragu, Pauri 3.1, 83; *Sikh Rahit Maryada* Article XVIII. a. *Adi Sri Guru Granth Sahib* (Sri Damdami Bir, Amritsar: Sri Gurmat Press, original work published in 1706).

4 *Bhagavad Gita* 18.41–44; *Manusmrti* 1.87–91, 5.154. According to the Hindu tradition, there are four social classes (*varna*): (1) *brahmin*, the priestly class, (2) *kshatriya*, the warrior class, (3) *vaishya*, the trader class, and (4) *shudra*, the class which serves the other three classes.

5 Baldev Raj Nayar, *Minority Politics in the Punjab* (Princeton, NJ: Princeton University Press, 1966), 22ff; W.H. McLeod, *The Evolution of the Sikh Community* (Oxford: Clarendon Press, 1976), 45–52.

6 Nayar, *Minority Politics in the Punjab*, 57.

7 Harjot Singh Oberoi, *The Construction of Religious Boundaries: Culture, Identity and Diversity in the Sikh Tradition* (Chicago: University of Chicago Press, 1994).

8 *Sikh Rahit Maryada*, Article III.

9 Murray J. Leaf, *Information and Behavior in a Sikh Village: Social Organization Reconsidered* (Berkeley: University of California Press, 1972), 72.

10 India's independence from British rule (August 1947) was accompanied by the partition of the country through the creation of Pakistan as a separate state for Muslims. During this time, many Muslims left India to live in Pakistan, while most Hindus and Sikhs had to migrate from the newly created Pakistan to India. Partition was marked by extensive communal bloodshed, especially in the border regions, during which many families were split apart and many more were killed..

11 Leaf, *Information and Behavior in a Sikh Village*, 186–92.

12 Ibid., 187.

13 James Gaylord Chadney, *The Sikhs of Vancouver* (New York: AMS Press, 1984).

14 Chadney, *The Sikhs of Vancouver*, 69

15 Norman Buchignani and Doreen Marie Indra, 'Key Issues in Canadian-Sikh Ethnic and Race Relations: Implications for the Study of the Sikh Diaspora,' in *The Sikh Diaspora: Migration and the Experience Beyond the Punjab*, ed. N. Gerald Barrier and Verne A. Dusenbery (Delhi: Chanakya Publications, 1989), 141–184: 155; Norman Buchignani and Doreen M. Indra, *Continuous Journey: A Social History of South Asians in Canada* (Toronto: McClelland and Stewart, 1985).

16 Michael M. Ames and Joy Inglis, 'Conflict and Change in British Columbia Sikh Family Life,' *B.C. Studies* 20 (Winter 1973): 15–49.

17 Leaf, *Information and Behavior in a Sikh Village*, 189.

18 Ames and Inglis, 'Conflict and Change in British Columbia Sikh Family Life,' 25.

19 Josephine C. Naidoo, 'Women of South Asian Origins: Status of Research, Problems, Future Issues,' in *The South Asian Diaspora in Canada: Six Essays*, ed. Milton Israel (Toronto: Multicultural History Society of Ontario, 1987), 37–58; Josephine C. Naidoo, 'Contemporary South Asian Women in the Canadian Mosaic,' *International Journal of Women's Studies* 8 (Sept.–Oct. 1985): 338–50; Josephine C. Naidoo and J. Campbell Davis, 'Canadian South Asian Women in Transition: A Dualistic View of Life,' *Journal of Comparative Family Studies* 19 (Summer 1988): 311–327.

20 James Gaylord Chadney, *The Sikhs of Vancouver* (New York: AMS Press, 1984), 42, 73–4.

21 Although the study is of South Asians in general, none of the twenty-two participants were Sikh.

22 Aziz Talbani and Parveen Hasanali. 'Adolescent Females between Tradition and Modernity: Gender Role Socialization in South Asian Immigrant Culture,' *Journal of Adolescence* 23(5) (2000): 615–27, 621.

23 Michael Angelo, *The Sikh Diaspora: Tradition and Continuity in an Immigrant Community* (New York: Garland, 1997), 111.

24 Sutton, 'Analyzing Social Systems,' 24–5.

25 B.B. Hergenhahn, *An Introduction to the History of Psychology* (Pacific Grove, CA: Brooks Publishing, 1997), 522–3.

26 See Abraham H. Maslow, *Toward a Psychology of Being*, 2nd ed. (New York: Van Nostrand Reinhold, 1968), and Abraham H. Maslow, *Motivation and Personality*, 2nd ed. (New York: Harper and Row, 1970).

27 Maslow, *Motivation and Personality.*

28 See Maslow, *Toward a Psychology of Being* and *Motivation and Personality.*

4 Family Relations among Three Generations: Duty, Role Playing, and Independence, Part 2

1 Francis X. Sutton, 'Analyzing Social Systems,' *Political Development and Social Change*, ed. Jason L. Finkle and Richard W. Gable (New York: John Wiley and Sons, 1966), 24–5; Geert H. Hofstede, *Culture's Consequences: International Differences in Work-related Values* (Beverly Hills, CA: Sage, 1980); and Harry Charalambos Triandis, *Individualism and Collectivism* (Boulder, CO: Westview Press, 1995).

2 *Adi Sri Guru Granth Sahib* (Sri Damdami Bir) (Amritsar: Sri Gurmat Press, original work published in 1706).

3 Jaswinder Singh (Sandhu), *Discovering Divine Love in the Play of Life: The Teachings from Guru Arjun's Bhawan Akhri* (Surrey, BC: Journal of Contemporary Sikh Studies, 2001), 13–24.

4 Ibid., 13–24.

5 Ibid., 24.

6 The discussion of the phases of personal development according to the Sikh scripture is based on Guru Nanak, *Sri Guru Granth Sahib*, 74–8, 137–8; Guru Ram Das, *Sri Guru Granth Sahib*, 76; Guru Arjun, *Sri Guru Granth Sahib*, 78.

7 The discussion of the phases of spiritual development according to the Sikh scripture is based on Guru Nanak, 'Japji-sahib,' in *Sri Guru Granth Sahib*, 7–8.

8 *Sikh Rahit Maryada*, Articles XVII–XIX, XXIV.

9 *Sri Guru Granth Sahib*, 75.

10 See Abraham Maslow, *Toward a Psychology of Being*, 2nd ed. (New York: Van Nostrand Reinhold, 1968).

11 *Sri Guru Granth Sahib*, 77.
12 Similar to the first generation, the second generation expects its children to be made fit primarily for married life: the man should have a 'government' or 'well-paying' job, and the woman should have the necessary skills for running the household and possibly having a job. This was the orientation often expressed indirectly in the interviewees' biographical accounts about their children's careers (Singh 2.1, 2.2, 2.8, 2.10, 2.14), and daughters' relations with their in-laws (Singh 2.8, 2.9). It was also expressed by way of negation as to what their children are not but *should* be doing with regard to pursuing a career or getting married (Singh 2.22; Kaur 2.6, 2.19). The understanding of growing up remains basically to learn one's duty and to fulfil it.
13 John W. Santrock, *Adolescence* (Boston: McGraw-Hill, 1998), 327.
14 *Sri Guru Granth Sahib*, 76.
15 See Maslow, *Toward a Psychology of Being* and *Motivation and Personality*.
16 *Sri Guru Granth Sahib*, 75–78.
17 Anand C. Paranjpe, *Self and Identity in Modern Psychology and Indian Thought* (New York: Plenum Press, 1998), 151.
18 *Sri Guru Granth Sahib*, 76.
19 Aziz Talbani and Parveen Hasanali, 'Adolescent Females between Tradition and Modernity: Gender Role Socialization in South Asian Immigrant Culture,' *Journal of Adolescence* 23(5) (2000): 615–27.
20 See Kamaljit Kaur Sidhu, 'Second Generation Sikh Adolescent Males: A Grounded Theory Model of Self and Identity Construction' (PhD diss., University of British Columbia, 1999). See also Michael Angelo, *The Sikh Diaspora: Tradition and Continuity in an Immigrant Community* (New York: Garland Publishing, 1997) and Evelyn Nodwell, '"Integrating Indian Culture into Our Life": The Construction of (East) "Indian Culture" in Vancouver, Canada' (PhD diss., University of British Columbia, 1993).
21 *Guru Granth Sahib*, 76.
22 Erik H. Erikson, *Identity and the Life Cycle: Selected Papers* (New York: International Universities Press, 1959) and *Identity, Youth and Crisis* (New York: W.W. Norton, 1968).
23 Baldev Raj Nayar, *Minority Politics in the Punjab* (Princeton, NJ: Princeton University Press, 1966), 103–105.
24 Nayar, *Minority Politics in the Punjab*, 103–5.
25 Tara Singh Bains and Hugh Johnston, *The Four Quarters of the Night: The Life Journey of an Emigrant Sikh* (Montreal: McGill-Queen's University Press, 1995), 172.
26 *Sri Guru Granth Sahib*, 76.

27 See Sidhu, 'Second Generation Sikh Adolescent Males'; Angelo, *The Sikh Diaspora*; Nodwell, 'Integrating Indian Culture into Our Life.'" Sidhu's study looks at the construction of Sikh identity among adolescents. Its limitations should, however, be noted. It is based on a limited sample of baptized (*amritdhari*) children (twenty-two respondents) and focuses more on the traditional Sikh ideal, rather than analysing the pertinent issues experienced by the youth regarding personal development or the problems surrounding the youth going off track. See section 'Double Life and Role Playing' in this chapter. Angelo's study is based on a limited sample of Sikh white-collar professionals, managerial and scientific personnel in upstate New York, United States (thirty-five respondents). While many Sikhs in the United States are professionals, there is nevertheless also a large Sikh working class, a consideration of which would have highlighted the problems in adaptation. Furthermore, the study measures integration without analysing the underlying process of adaptation in its discussion of continuity and change. Nodwell's study is based on Indo-Canadian youth who attend a particular youth group. While it is a good starting point for entry into the community, it is limited in that the youth who participate in this youth group would typically come from educated or professional families (thus ignoring many issues, especially regarding the Sikh youth from blue-collar families).

28 Anne Woollett et al., 'Asian's Women's Ethnic Identity: The Impact of Gender and Context in the Accounts of Women Bringing Up Children in East London,' *Feminism and Psychology* (1994) 119–132; Angelo, *The Sikh Diaspora*; and Mary Stopes-Roe and Raymond Cochrane. 'The Process of Assimilation in Asians in Britain: A Study of Hindu, Muslim and Sikh Immigrants and Their Young Adult Children,' *International Journal of Comparative Sociology* 28 (January/April 1987): 43–56.

29 Gurnam Singh Sanghera, 'The Male Punjabi Elderly of Vancouver: Their Background, Health Beliefs and Access to Health Care Services' (MA diss., University of British Columbia, 1991), 21; Badrinath Krishna Rao, 'The Agony When East Meets West,' *Globe and Mail*, 17 May 1991, 17; Rekha Basu, 'Expatriate Indians: American Born Confused "Desis,"' *India Today* (Delhi) 30 August 1989, 106–9; and Yogesh Atal, 'Outsiders as Insiders: The Phenomenon of Sandwich Culture,' *Sociological Bulletin* 38 (March 1989): 23–42.

30 For example, employment in the Canadian workforce, or having children acquire a good education so that they can get well-paying jobs.

31 Interestingly, the tension between the generations in regard to discussion of the issues that the community faces, which is revealed in the manuscript,

recently received some attention from prominent leaders in the community: B.C. Supreme Court Justice Wally (Taru) Oppal said, 'This is a community that protects itself through denial' (*Macleans*, 23 December 2002, 32). Similarly, speaking at a community forum on Punjabi youth gang violence, former B.C. Premier Ujjal Dosanjh stated that there is a 'conspiracy of silence' in the community (*The Province*, 16 June 2002, A4).

32 Adam Blatner, 'Psychodrama,' in *Current Psychotherapies*, ed. R. Corsini and D. Wedding (Itasca, IL: F.E. Peacock 1995), 399–408

33 The show *Punjabi Vibes* was started in January 1999 by Jassa Randhawa and Jassi Gill for the Shaw TV network (multicultural non-profit channel). *Punjabi Vibes* consisted of a doctor's corner, comical skits, and music videos. It was inspired by the success of the cultural shows at the University of British Columbia, where a host for the shows in between the acts or skits would entertain the audience while the groups prepared for the following show. The UBC cultural shows also marked the beginning of the tradition of Punjabi clubs performing annual cultural shows meant for people of all ages.

34 The other three goals of *Punjabi Vibes* are (1) for the younger generation not to lose Punjabi language and culture (festivals, events), (2) to educate the Punjabi community about medical problems, and (3) to make people laugh because they are stressed out and don't really have peace of mind.

5 Religion among Three Generations: Oral Transmission of Customs, Reading about the Sikh Tradition, and Inquiry into Sikhism

1 Darshan Singh Tatla, *The Sikh Diaspora: The Search for Statehood* (Seattle: University of Washington Press, 1999); Pashaura Singh and Gerald Barrier (eds.), *Sikh Identity: Continuity and Change* (New Delhi: Manohar, 1999); and Harold Coward, John R. Hinells and Raymond Brady Williams (eds.), *The South Asian Religious Diaspora in Britain, Canada and U.S.A.* (Albany: State University of New York Press, 2000).

2 Khushwant Singh, *A History of the Sikhs*, Vol. 1 (Princeton, NJ: Princeton University Press, 1963), 17.

3 The general survey of Sikhism here draws on the following works: J.S. Grewal, *The Sikhs of the Punjab* (Cambridge, U.K.: Cambridge University Press, 1998); W.H. McLeod, *The Sikhs: History, Religion and Society* (New York: Columbia University Press, 1989); and Harbans Singh, *The Heritage of the Sikhs* (Delhi: Manohar Publishers, 1994).

4 *Sati* is the act of a widow throwing herself on her husband's funeral pyre in order to reunite with her husband. *Garuda Purana* 11.91–100.

5 Guru Amar Das, *Guru Granth Sahib*, 787; *Sikh Rahit Maryada* Articles XVIII.d and n.

6 The Harimandir is now known as the Golden Temple. During the Mughal rule, the Harimandir was destroyed. It was then rebuilt under the rule of Maharaja Ranjit Singh with a gold dome.

7 Grewal, *The Sikhs of the Punjab*, 64.

8 Prior to Jehangir, the Mughal ruler was Akbar; he favoured the unity of Hindus and Muslims in general.

9 Grewal, *The Sikhs of the Punjab*, 64–8. Another theory explaining Guru Hargobind's decision to adopt militancy in the Sikh Panth was the influence of the Jats who are believed to have had the tradition or custom of bearing arms. See, W.H. McLeod, *The Evolution of the Sikh Community* (Delhi: Oxford University Press, 1975), 1–50.

10 For a general overview of Sikh religious beliefs, see W. Owen Cole and Piara Singh Sambhi, *The Sikhs: Their Religious Beliefs and Practices* (London: Routledge and Kegan Paul, 1978); and, W.H. McLeod, *Guru Nanak and the Sikh Religion* (Delhi: Oxford University Press, 1976).

11 *Ek Onkar satnam kartapurakh nirbhau nirvair akal murat ajuni sabang gurprasad.* For a theological discussion of Sikh *dharam*, see Jaswinder Singh (Sandhu), *Discovering Divine Love in the Play of Life: Guru Arjun's Bhavan Akhri* (Surrey, BC: Journal of Contemporary Sikh Studies, 2001).

12 *Sri Dasam Granth: Text and Translation*, trans. Dr Jodh Singh and Dr Dharam Singh, 2 vols. (Patiala: Heritage Publications, 1999).

13 *Manas ki jat sabhai ekai pahchanbo.*

14 On the historical development of the *Sikh Rahit Maryada*, see W.H. McLeod, *Textual Sources for the Study of Sikhism* (Chicago: University of Chicago Press, 1984) and Harjot S. Oberoi, *The Construction of Religious Boundaries: Culture, Identity and Diversity in the Sikh Tradition* (Chicago: University of Chicago Press, 1994).

15 Baptized Sikhs are also referred to as the Khalsa Sikhs.

16 There are also three different sects that grew out of the Sikh Panth ('path') during the mid-nineteenth century and that would be categorized as heterodox because they have followed living human gurus since Guru Gobind Singh: (1) *Namdhari*, a sect founded by Bhai Balak Singh (1799–1862) that had as its objective the return back to the way of life in keeping with the teachings of the Sikh gurus. This sect, especially under the leadership of Baba Ram Singh (1816–85), also fought against the British and thus had a place in India's freedom movement. This sect is known for its austere lifestyle and for observing a rigid code of conduct. Although it embraces the teachings of the Sikh gurus, it follows a human guru, which goes against

orthodoxy. (2) *Radhaswami beas*, a sect founded by a Hindu, Shiv Dyal (1818–78), who described God as the union of *radha* ('soul') and *swami* ('Master'). This sect has attracted both Hindus and Sikhs. However, in contrast to orthodox Sikhism, it does not keep the *Guru Granth Sahib* in the temple. Rather, there is simply a platform, where the guru sits and engages in discourse. The human guru is believed to be the means to the Guru (as in God). (3) *Nirankari*, a sect that emerged as a reform movement in northwest Punjab, was founded by Baba Dyal (1783–1855) with the objective of getting rid image worship in the Sikh tradition and returning to the worship of *nirankar* ('the formless One'). The founder, however, acquired the status of guru; after him there has been a succession of human gurus. Harbans Singh, *The Heritage of the Sikhs*, 190–202, and Khushwant Singh, *A History of the Sikhs*, Vol. 2, (Princeton: Princeton University Press, 1966), 123–135.

17 For more information about Gora Sikhs, see Verne A. Dusenbery, 'Punjabi Sikhs and Gora Sikhs: Conflicting Assertions of Sikh Identity in North America,' in Joseph T. O'Connell et al. (eds), *Sikh History and Religion in the 20th Century* (Toronto: Centre for South Asian Studies, University of Toronto, 1988), 334–55.

18 Willard G. Oxtoby (ed.), *World Religions: Eastern Traditions*. 2nd ed. (Don Mills, ON: Oxford University Press, 2002), 155.

19 Jaswinder Singh, *Discovering Divine Love*, 36–38.

20 Harold Coward, 'Hinduism in Canada,' in *The South Asian Religious Diaspora in Britain, Canada, and the U.S.A.* (Albany: State University of New York Press, 2000), 151–72, esp. 161–3.

21 Ibid., 161–3.

22 Baisakhi (or Vaisakhi) is the Punjabi festival celebrating the harvest at the advent of the month Baisakh (between April–May). The people in the villages participate in Baisakhi by organizing a local fair and participating in the festivities of feasting, singing and dancing. Although Baisakhi is a traditional agricultural festival for Punjabis, it has greater importance for Sikhs. According to tradition, Guru Gobind Singh created the Khalsa Order on Baisakhi day in 1699. In the Punjab, many Sikhs go on pilgrimage to Anandpur (the place of the birth of the Khalsa) to celebrate the occasion. In Vancouver Lower Mainland, the Sikhs hold a parade that starts and ends at the *gurdwara*; along the parade route, many Sikhs put up tables and give away food, refreshments, and books.

23 Gurinder Singh Mann, 'Sikhism in the United States of America,' in *The South Asian Religious Diaspora in Britain, Canada and U.S.A.*, edited by Harold Coward, John R. Hinells, and Raymond Brady Williams (Albany: State University of New York Press, 2000), 259–76, esp. 273–4.

24 As noted in chapter 4, the *Guru Granth Sahib* teaches that most adolescents cannot internalize religion and spirituality because they are drawn to sensual pleasures. Kamaljit Kaur Sidhu, 'Second Generation Sikh Adolescent Males: A Grounded Theory Model of Self and Identity Construction' (PhD diss., University of British Columbia, 1999).

25 Harjot Singh Oberoi, *The Construction of Religious Boundaries: Culture, Identity and Diversity in the Sikh Tradition* (Chicago: University of Chicago Press, 1994).

26 Owen Cole, 'Sikh Diaspora: Its Possible Effects on Sikhism,' in *Sikh History and Religion in the 20th Century*, 338–402.

27 Norman Buchignani, 'Conceptions of Sikh Culture in the Development of a Comparative Analysis of the Sikh Diaspora,' in *Sikh History and Religion in the 20th Century*, 276–295.

28 Dusenbery, 'Introduction: A Century of Sikhs Beyond Punjab,' in *The Sikh Diaspora: Migration and the Experience Beyond the Punjab*, ed. N. Gerald Barrier and Verne A. Dusenbery (Delhi: Chanakya Publications, 1989), 1–28, exp. 17–18.

29 Tatla, *The Sikh Diaspora*, 3–6.

30 See, chapter 1.

6 Community Honour among Three Generations: Social Control, Cultural Preservation, and Ethnic Insularity, Part 1

1 Francis X. Sutton, 'Analyzing Social Systems,' in *Political Development and Social Change*, ed. Jason L. Finkle and Richard W. Gable (New York: John Wiley and Sons, 1966), 24–5. See also Fred Warren Riggs, *Administration in Developing Countries: The Theory of Prismatic Society* (Boston: Houghton Mifflin, 1964).

2 Although there is no country called East India, the British used the term 'East Indian' for all immigrants from India during the early period of Indian immigration to Canada, in order to distinguish them from the Indians of Canada's First Nations. Since then, the term has been commonly used by Canadians.

3 Bela Singh and Harnam Singh worked as informants for W.C. Hopkinson, whose duty was to spy on the nationalist Ghadar Party. When Harnam Singh vanished on 17 August 1914 and was found dead, and another spy – Arjun Singh – was shot and killed by Ram Singh, Bela Singh took revenge. Turning up at Arjun Singh's funeral on 5 September, he shot two priests (Bhag Singh and Battan Singh). The Sikh community was enraged at these killings. Because the killings had taken place in the *gurdwara* (Khalsa

Diwan Society), many Sikhs believed that the government was behind Bela Singh's attack. Although Bela Singh was tried, Hopkinson argued that his actions had been taken in self-defence, and he was acquitted on that basis. On the day of Bela Singh's trial, Mewa Singh murdered Hopkinson, and then surrendered. Mewa Singh was convicted and sentenced to death. He was hanged on 11 January 1915, and has since then been revered as a martyr in the Sikh tradition.

4 In 1969 the *gurdwara* and the headquarters of the Khalsa Diwan Society moved to 8000 Ross Street, Vancouver.

5 Norman Buchignani and Doreen M. Indra, *Continuous Journey: A Social History of South Asians in Canada* (Toronto: McClelland and Stewart, 1985), 53.

6 Norman Buchignani and Doreen Marie Indra, 'Key Issues in Canadian-Sikh Ethnic and Race Relations: Implications for the Study of the Sikh Diaspora,' in *The Sikh Diaspora: Migration and the Experience beyond the Punjab*, ed. N. Gerald Barrier and Verne A. Dusenbery (Delhi: Chanakya Publications, 1989), 141–84.

7 Darshan Singh Tatla, *The Sikh Diaspora: The Search for Statehood* (Seattle: University of Washington Press, 1999), 92–5.

8 James G. Chadney 'The Formation of Ethnic Communities: Lessons from Vancouver Sikhs,' in Barrier and Dusenbery (eds), *The Sikh Diaspora*, 190.

9 Tara Singh Bains and Hugh Johnston, *The Four Quarters of the Night: The Life Journey of an Emigrant Sikh* (Montreal: McGill-Queen's University Press, 1995), 113–14.

10 Tatla, *The Sikh Diaspora*, 92–5.

11 Bains and Johnston, *The Four Quarters of the Night*, 149–64.

12 Akhand Kirtani Jatha Sikhs are followers of Randhir Singh who, held prisoner for participating in the Ghadar struggle for independence, sang the hymns of the Guru as the sole form of worship. Although this group emerged in the early 1900s in the Punjab, its presence was felt in Vancouver only during the early 1970s.

13 Tatla, *The Sikh Diaspora*, 120–1.

14 The Nirankaris, a sect founded by Baba Dayal (1783–1855), believe in a living human guru. They held a big convention in 1978 in the holy Sikh city of Amritsar. A number of Sikhs marched in protest against their belief in a human guru as the 'true guru' (*sat-guru*). A clash occurred in which several people were killed. Harbans Singh, *The Heritage of the Sikhs* (New Delhi: Manohar Publishers, 1983), 190–191, 347–348.

15 Tatla, *The Sikh Diaspora*, 120.

16 Tatla, *The Sikh Diaspora*, 116–123.

17 'Akalis' refers to the members of the dominant Sikh party in the Punjab – Shiromani Akali Dal – which was founded in 1920 during British rule. This political group had at that time sought to protect and represent the rights of the Sikhs in the political domain in India as well as to preserve the Sikh religion and heritage through the Akali movement (even as it supported the Indian National Congress Party). After independence, it opposed the Congress Party and is policies.

18 Tatla, *The Sikh Diaspora*, 116–23.

19 Hardial Singh Bains, *The Call of the Martyrs: On the Crisis in India and the Present Situation in the Punjab* (London: Workers' Publishing House, 1985).

20 *Vancouver Sun*, 28 October 2000, D3.

21 See House of Commons, *Debates*, 10 March 1988 ('Sikh Organizations: the Government Position'); 11 November 1988 ('India: Sikh Community'); 22 March 1990; 22 July 1993.

22 Augie Fleras and John Leonard Elliot, *Multiculturalism in Canada: The Challenge of Diversity* (Toronto: Nelson, 1992), 179–82.

23 Punjabi politicians from B.C. have succeeded in mainstream politics. At the federal level, Harbans Dhaliwal (Vancouver South–Burnaby) was elected as a Liberal MP in 1996 and 2000. Gurmant Grewal (Surrey Central) has served as an Alliance MP since 1996. At the provincial level, Manmohan Sihota (Esquimalt-Metchosin), Ujjal Dosanjh (Vancouver-Kensington), and Harbhajan Lalli (Yale-Lillooet) all served as NDP MLAs in between 1991 and 2001; of the first two, the former was associated with the 'fundamentalists' and the latter with the 'moderates'. In 2001, Dave Hayer (Surrey–Tynehead), Gulzar Cheema (Surrey-Panorama Ridge), Tony Bhullar (Surrey-Newton), Patti Sahota (Burnaby-Edmonds), Karan Manhas (Port Coquitlam–Burke Mountain), and Rob Nijjar (Vancouver-Kingsway) were elected as Liberal MLAs.

24 Sant Nand Singh (1872–1943) attracted a considerable following during his life. His sermons emphasized both the recitation of the Divine Name (*simran*) and the singing of sacred hymns (*kirtan*). He traveled extensively and established preaching centres called *thaths*. There has since been a lineage of living human *sants* to whom the followers submit.

25 Riggs, *Administration in Developing Countries*.

26 Murray J. Leaf, *Information and Behavior in a Sikh Village: Social Organization Reconsidered* (Berkeley: University of California Press, 1972), 166.

27 Riggs, *Administration in Developing Countries*. The concept, which describes the transitional stage between tradition and modernity, is based on the analogy of the prism. Light enters one side of the prism and is somewhat diffracted inside it but not as completely as it appears on the other side.

28 'Questions and Answers with Giani Sant Singh Maskeen,' *Mehfil Magazine*, vol. 2, no. 5 (1994), 97.

29 Joyce Pettigrew, *Robber Noblemen: A Study of the Political System of Sikh Jats* (Boston: Routledge and Kegan Paul, 1975), 57, 187–98.

30 Arthur W. Helweg, 'The Sikh Diaspora and Sikh Studies,' in *Studying the Sikhs: Issues for North America*, 69–93, esp. 76.

31 Joseph T. O'Connell, 'Sikh Religio-Ethnic Experience in Canada,' in *The South Asian Religious Diaspora in Britain, Canada and U.S.A.*, ed. Harold Coward, John R. Hinells and Raymond Brady Williams (Albany: State University of New York Press, 2000), 191–209, esp. 195.

32 For example, before the consolidation of the Federation of Sikh Societies (an umbrella consisting primarily of *gurdwara* societies), attempts at unity were undermined by the rise of several pro-Khalistani organizations.

33 Verne A. Dusenbery, 'The Poetics and Politics of Recognition: Diasporan Sikhs in Pluralist Polities,' *American Ethnologist*, 24(4) (1997): 738–62, esp. 742–3.

34 See 'Mainstream and Gurdwara Political Relations (1985–present)' for a list of the Punjabi-Sikh MLAs and MPs from British Columbia.

35 Dusenbery, 'The Poetics and Politics of Recognition,' 751.

36 Martin E. Marty and R. Scott Appleby (eds.), *Fundamentalisms and the State* (Chicago: University of Chicago Press, 1993), 3.

37 Karen Armstrong, *Battle for God* (New York: Ballantine, 2000).

38 Harjot Oberoi, 'Sikh Fundamentalism: Translating History into Theory,' *Fundamentalisms and the State*, ed. Marty and Appleby 256–85.

39 The Damdami Taksal or the Damdama School of Sikh Learning was founded by Baba Deep Singh Shahid (1682–1757), who studied the sacred texts under Bhai Mani Singh (under the supervision of Guru Gobind Singh) and who also trained in the martial arts. This school of Sikh learning specializes in the religious discourse (*katha*) of the fundamental tenets of Sikhism. Harbans Singh (ed.), *The Encyclopaedia of Sikhism*, vol. 1 (Patiala: Punjabi University, 1995), 587–8.

40 See Baldev Raj Nayar, *Minority Politics in the Punjab* (Princeton, NJ: Princeton University Press, 1966).

41 An ethnic-national movement is a secessionist movement based on discriminatory practices directed against an identifiable ethnic group (based on any distinctive attribute, e.g., race, religion, language and custom). Raymond Corrado and Eric Tompkins, *Terrorism* (Burnaby, B.C.: Simon Fraser University, 1992), 20–1.

42 In the case of anti-state terrorist movements for an independent state, there are two basic types: (1) ethnic-national (see previous footnote), and (2) reli-

gious, which occurs when religious scripture or doctrine can be identified as the fundamental motivating and unifying factor (e.g., the Islamic concept of *jihad*). Corrado and Tompkins, *Terrorism*, 19–21.

43 The three fundamental principles for a Sikh are: (1) meditation on God's name (*nam japo*), (2) hard work and honest living (*kirt karo*), and (3) sharing one's earnings with the needy (*wand chako*). *Sikh Rahit Maryada* Article III.

44 Edward N. Herberg, *Ethnic Groups in Canada: Adaptations and Transitions* (Scarborough, ON: Nelson Canada, 1989), 243–56.

45 The models that have been used to understand the change that occurs when two cultures meet are as follows: assimilation, acculturation, integration, separation, marginalization, and fusion. See Leo Driedger, 'Toward a Perspective on Canadian Pluralism: Ethnic Identity in Winnipeg' *Canadian Journal of Sociology* 2(1) (1977): 77–95; John W. Berry, 'Finding Identity: Separation, Integration, Assimilation or Marginality?' in *Ethnic Canada*, ed. Leo Driedger (Toronto: Copp Clark Pitman, 1987), 223–39.

46 For example, see W.W. Isajiw, 'The Process of Maintenance of Ethnic Identity: The Canadian Context,' in *Sounds Canadian*, ed. P.M. Migus (Toronto: Peter Martin Associates, 1975), 129–38.

47 Arthur W. Helweg, 'Sikh Identity in England: Its Changing Nature,' in Joseph T. O'Connell et al. (eds.), *Sikh History and Religion in the 20th Century* (Toronto: Centre for South Asian Studies, University of Toronto, 1988), 356–75, esp. 372.

48 Verne A. Dusenbery, 'Introduction: A Century of Sikhs Beyond Punjab,' *The Sikh Diaspora: Migration and the Experience Beyond the Punjab*, ed. N. Gerald Barrier and Verne A. Dusenbery (Delhi: Chanakya Publications, 1989), 1–28, esp. 19.

7 Community Honour among Three Generations: Social Control, Cultural Preservation, and Ethnic Insularity, Part 2

1 For a definition of integration, see chapter 1.

2 Augie Fleras and John Leonard Elliot, *Multiculturalism in Canada: The Challenge of Diversity* (Toronto: Nelson, 1992), 99–104, 179–82.

3 A longstanding problem has been the news media's negative and unbalanced portrayal of South Asians. See Doreen M. Indra, 'South Asian Stereotypes in the Vancouver Press: 1905–1976,' *Ethnic and Racial Studies*, 2(2) (1979), 166–89.

4 The Sikh youth camp (for children ranging from nine to sixteen) in British Columbia has been operating for six years. The camp is held for two weeks each year. According to one of the founders, 'it is the youth teaching the

youth'. The goal is to talk with the younger generation, not at them; there are discussions of Sikh history and *gurbani*. Elders are not allowed. The oldest counsellor is twenty-eight. Most are between twenty-two and twenty-five.

5   In 2000, a girl from Maple Ridge was murdered in the Punjab. It is alleged that she was murdered for having married a rickshaw driver against the wishes of her family; that is, the murder was an act of retribution for having dishonoured the family. Although this event reflects the importance of *izzat*, it is not an acceptable Sikh or Indian custom to kill your children in order to save face. See 'To Love, Honour and Obey,' Vancouver: David Paperny Films, 2001.

6   Veeno Dewan, 'South Asian T.V.: A Time for Change,' *U Magazine*, 2(1) (2000): 12–15.

7   Because of the show's success, some competitors from other multicultural shows allegedly also complained about the skits. (media 1)

8   *Punjabi Vibes* was taken off Shaw TV in September 2000. After that, many people called Shaw Multicultural TV complaining about its cancellation. Shaw then called Jassa and Jassi back and gave them another time slot for a music show. In their new show, they provide humorous commentary in between music videos.

9   *The Vancouver Province*, 16 June 2002, A4.

10   Norman Buchignani and Doreen Marie Indra, 'Key Issues in Canadian-Sikh Ethnic and Race Relations: Implications for the Study of the Sikh Diaspora,' in *The Sikh Diaspora: Migration and the Experience Beyond the Punjab*, ed. N. Gerald Barrier and Verne A. Dusenbery (Delhi: Chanakya Publications, 1989), 141–84, 167–8.

11   Verne A. Dusenbery, 'The Poetics and Politics of Recognition: Diasporan Sikhs in Pluralist Polities,' *American Ethnologist* 24(4) (1997): 751. According to Dusenbury, this differs from the Singaporean nationalist approach to pluralism, wherein the Sikhs have advanced as a unified ethno-cultural group and are regarded as a model minority. It is important to note that the Singaporean nationalist 'collective' orientation and authoritarian approach, wherein there is little choice, is perhaps in some ways more characteristic of Sikh culture, making social adaptation easier for Sikhs.

8 Conclusion: Canadian Sikh amid Modernity and Multiculturalism

1   Augie Fleras and John Leonard Elliot, *Multiculturalism in Canada: The Challenge of Diversity* (Toronto: Nelson, 1992), 11; John Porter, *The Vertical Mosaic: An Analysis of Social Class and Power in Canada* (Toronto: Toronto University Press, 1965).

2 See, for example, *Dasam Granth*: 'Akaal Ustat,' vs 85–86. Also, Guru Nanak took on the clothing, behavioural practices, and language of the places to which he travelled in order to blend in with the people (*Varan Bhai Gurdas*, Var 1.32, 38). Besides, the army under Maharaja Ranjit Singh – the last great Sikh ruler – was a composite one, comprising people from different religious and ethnic groups.

Glossary

Adi Granth	the initial compilation of Sikh scriptural hymns by Guru Arjan Dev (later referred to as the *Guru Granth Sahib*)
ahankar	ego or the sense of being separate from others
Akal	eternal or timeless; epithet for God
Akali Dal	dominant political party of the Sikhs in the Punjab; founded in the 1920s
Akal Takht	the 'throne' of the Guru at the Golden Temple, Amritsar; one of the five seats of Sikh secular authority
akhand-path	'continuous reading' of the *Guru Granth Sahib*
amrit	'nectar'; sacred water
Amritdhari	'one who has taken *amrit*'; baptized Sikh; also referred to as Khalsa Sikh
Amrit sanchar	initiation into the Khalsa order, marked by taking *amrit*
antahkaran	mind
atma	eternal soul
ayurveda	traditional system of Indian medicine
Baisakhi	traditional agricultural festival for Punjabis on the first day of the month of Baisakh; for Sikhs, Guru Gobind Singh created the Khalsa Order on Baisakhi in 1699; also known as Vaisakhi
bani	hymns
bhagat	devotional poet-saint
brahmin	the priestly class in the Hindu *varna* order
buddhi	intellect

cit	memory
dadaji	father's father
dadiji	father's mother
Darbar Sahib	'house of the *Guru Granth Sahib*'; prayer hall
Dasam Granth	'the Tenth Sacred Book'; collection of writings attributed to Guru Gobind Singh
desi	'indigenous'; refers to Indian or Punjabi
dharam	duty or righteousness; the performance of right action according to the moral and ethical regulations of nature and society; *dharma* in Sanskrit
Doaba	area between two rivers; region of the central Punjab plains between the Sultej and Beas rivers; includes Hoshiarpur and Jullundur districts
Ek Onkar	Sikh mantra; meaning 'God is One'
fateh	conquest or victory
GGB	'Giani Gone Bad,' used in Western Canada to refer to young Sikhs who were raised in an orthodox family, but have since moved away from living according to the Sikh code of conduct
ghadar	mutiny or revolt
gian	knowledge; one of the five *khands*
giani	'learned one'; religious teacher or Sikh scholar
gidda	traditional folk singing and dancing by Punjabi women
Gora Sikh	a white Sikh, primarily affiliated with the 3HO under the leadership of Harbhajan Singh (Yogi Bhajan)
granth	sacred book
granthi	reader of the *Guru Granth Sahib*
grhasthi	householder; *grhasthin* in Sanskrit
gup shup	gossip
Gurbani	sacred hymns of the gurus
gurdwara	'the door to the Guru'; Sikh temple; place where Sikh scripture is kept
gurmat marg	the path of the spiritual one
Gurmukhi	'from the mouth of the Guru'; Punjabi script
guru	spiritual teacher or enlightened one; there are ten gurus in the Sikh religion; an epithet for God
Guru Granth Sahib	the 'Great Guru-Scripture'; Sikh scripture
Harimandir	the house of God; Sikh temple

hukam	order
hukam-nama	edict
izzat	honour or respect
jagat	transient or material world
japji	morning prayer composed by Guru Nanak
jat	one of the agricultural castes
ji	honorific term
jiv	psyche; *jiva* in Sanskrit
kachcha	shorts for underwear; one of the five *kakars*
kakar	consonant K in the Punjabi alphabet, referring to the five Sikh symbols (5Ks); See *kachcha, kanga, kara, kesh, kirpan*
kal yug	dark age
kanga	comb; one of the five *kakars*
kara	steel bangle; one of the five *kakars*
karah prasad	Guru's food offering given at the gurdwara
karam	action, merit, and demerit; *karma* in Sanskrit
karam	grace
Kaur	'princess'; name taken by all female Sikhs
kesh	uncut covered hair; one of the five *kakars*
Keshdhari	non-baptized Sikh who follows the principal requirement of wearing uncut covered hair (*kesh*) along with the other *kakars*
Khalistan	'Land of the Pure'; nation of the Khalsa; name for independent Sikh homeland
Khalsa	'pure' or 'elect'; Guru's community
khand	5 realms to move through to attain ultimate spiritual wisdom; See *dharam, gian, saram, karam,* and *sach*
khanda	double-edged sword; Sikh emblem
khatri	one of the mercantile castes
kirpan	steel dagger; one of the five *kakars*
kirtan	hymn singing
kismat	fate
kshatriya	the warrior class in the Hindu *varna* order
langar	community dining hall
Majha	area of Punjab between Beas and Ravi rivers; includes Amritsar district
Malwa	area of Punjab south of the Sultej river; includes Patiala, Ludhiana and Ferozepur districts

manas	perception
manmat marg	the path of ego reasoning
mansakh	mental action
maya	illusion
mool-mantar	root-mantra
mukti	liberation from the cycle of rebirth; *mukti* or *moksa* in Sanskrit
nad	sound current
nam	divine name
Namdhari	heterodox sect founded by Bhai Balak Singh (1799–1862)
nam simran	recitation of the Divine Name
nanaji	mother's father
naniji	mother's mother
Nirankar	the formless One; epithet for God
Nirankari	heterodox sect founded by Baba Dyal (1783–1855)
nirgun	without attributes or formless; an epithet of God
nit nem	'daily prayers'
panth	path or community
param-atma	Supreme Universal Soul
pardah	'veil'; the custom for women to place a scarf low over their heads making eye contact impossible in public
parsad	grace of God
path	reading of scripture
piri-miri	the combination of 'spiritual' and 'worldly' affairs in the Sikh religion
Radhaswami beas	heterodox sect founded by a Hindu, Shiv Dyal (1818–1878)
rag	classical musical measure; *raga* in Sanskrit
ramgarhia	one of the carpenter castes
razi	fulfilled
sach	truth; *satya* in Sankrit
sadharan path	'intermittent reading' of the *Guru Granth Sahib*
Sahajdhari	'slow adopters'; Sikhs who do not follow the five *kakars* but accept the spiritual teachings of the gurus
sansar	cycle of birth, death and rebirth; *samsara* in Sanskrit
samskar	rites of passage; *samskara* in Sanskrit

sangat	religious assembly or congregation
sant	holy person or saint
Sarab-loh	'all-Steel'; epithet for God
saram	effort
sarir	physical body
sarirak	physical action
sat	truth
Sat Sri Akal	Punjabi greeting 'truth is eternal'
sati	the Hindu act of a widow throwing herself on her husband's funeral pyre in order to reunite with her husband
seva	volunteer service
SGPC	Shiromani Gurdwara Parbandhak Committee; set up in 1925 by the Sikh electorate to administer the principal gurdwaras
shabad	'word'; sacred word of the ten human gurus or God
shahid	martyr
sharam	sense of shame
sher	lion
Sikh	'learner'; followers of the Sikh tradition
Sikh Rahit Maryada	Sikh Code of Conduct
Singh	'lion'; name taken by all male Sikhs
stridharam	duty of the wife
takht	'throne' of Sikh secular authority at the five places: Amritsar, Patna, Nander, Anandpur, and Damdama
tirath	pilgrimage place; *tirtha* in Sanskrit
vaishya	the merchant class in the Hindu *varna* order
varna	literally means 'colour'; Hindu social division or class
vasakh	verbal action
Waheguru	'Infinite Light that dispels darkness'; Sikh mantra used in devotion to God

Bibliography

Primary Sources

Adi Sri Guru Granth Sahib (Sri Damdami Bir). Amritsar: Sri Gurmat Press.
   (Original work published 1706.)
Bhagavadgita. Trans. F. Edgerton. Cambridge: Harvard University Press, 1944.
Manusmrti. Trans. M.N. Dutt. Varanasi: Chowkhamba Press, 1979.
Sikh Rahit Maryada. Amritsar: Shiromani Gurdwara Parbhandak Committee,
   1982.
Sri Dasam Granth: Text and Translation. Trans. Dr Jodh Singh and Dr Dharam
   Singh. 2 Vols. Patiala: Heritage Publications, 1999.
Sri Guru Granth Sahib. Trans. and annotated by Gopal Singh. 4 Vols. New
   Delhi: World Book Centre, 1993.

Secondary Sources

Ames, Michael M., and Joy Inglis. 'Conflict and Change in British Columbia
   Sikh Family Life,' *B.C. Studies* 20 (Winter 1973): 15–49.
Angelo, Michael. *The Sikh Diaspora: Tradition and Continuity in an Immigrant
   Community.* New York: Garland Publishing, 1997.
Armstrong, Karen. *Battle for God.* New York: Ballantine Books, 2000.
Bains, Tara S., and Hugh Johnston. *The Four Quarters of the Night: The Life Jour-
   ney of an Emigrant Sikh.* Montreal: McGill-Queen's University Press, 1995.
Ballard, Roger. 'The Growth and Changing Character of the Sikh Presence in
   Britain.' In *The South Asian Religious Diaspora in Britain, Canada, and U.S.A.,*
   ed. Harold Coward, John R. Hinnels and Raymond Brady Williams, 127–44.
   Albany: State University of New York Press, 2000.
Barrier, N. Gerald, and Verne A. Dusenbery (eds). *The Sikh Diaspora: Migration
   and the Experience beyond the Punjab.* Delhi: Chanakya Publications, 1989.

Berry, John W. 'Finding Identity: Separation, Integration, Assimilation or Marginality?' In *Ethnic Canada*, ed. Leo Driedger, 223–39. Toronto: Copp Clark Pitman, 1987.

Bissoondath, Neil. *Selling Illusions: The Cult of Multiculturalism in Canada.* Toronto: Penguin Books, 1994.

Bloom, Benjamin S. *Taxonomy of Educational Objectives: The Classification of Educational Goals. Handbook 1, Cognitive Domain.* New York: David McKay, 1956.

Buchignani, Norman. 'Conceptions of Sikh Culture in the Development of a Comparative Analysis of the Sikh Diaspora.' In *Sikh History and Religion in the 20th Century*, ed. Joseph T. O'Connell, Milton Israel, and Willard G. Oxtoby, 276–95. Toronto: Centre for South Asian Studies, University of Toronto, 1988.

Buchigrani, Joseph, and Doreen M. Indra. *Continuous Journey: A Social History of South Asians in Canada.* Toronto: McClelland and Stewart, 1985.

– 'Key Issues in Canadian-Sikh Ethnic and Race Relations, Implications for the Study of the Sikh Diaspora.' In *The Sikh Diaspora: Migration and the Experience Beyond the Punjab*, ed. N. Gerald Barrier and Verne A. Dusenbery, 141–84. Delhi: Chanakya, 1989.

Chadney, James Gaylord. 'The Formation of Ethnic Communities, Lessons from Vancouver Sikhs.' In *Sikh History and Religion in the 20th Century*, ed. Joseph T. O'Connell, Milton Israel, and Willard G. Oxtoby, 185–99. Toronto: Centre for South Asian Studies, University of Toronto, 1988.

– *The Sikhs of Vancouver.* New York: AMS Press, 1984.

Cohen, R. *Global Diasporas: An Introduction.* Seattle: University of Washington Press, 1997.

Cole, W. Owen. 'Sikh Diaspora: Its Possible Effects on Sikhism.' In *Sikh History and Religion in the 20th Century*, ed. Joseph T. O'Connell, Milton Israel, and Willard G. Oxtoby, 338–402. Toronto: Centre for South Asian Studies, University of Toronto, 1988.

Cole, W. Owen, and Piara Singh Sambhi. *The Sikhs: Their Religious Beliefs and Practices.* London: Routledge and Kegan Paul, 1978.

Corrado, Raymond, and Eric Tompkins. *Terrorism.* Burnaby: Simon Fraser University, 1992.

Coward, Harold. 'Hinduism in Canada.' In *The South Asian Religious Diaspora in Britain, Canada, and the U.S.A.*, ed., Harold Coward, John R. Hinnels, and Raymond Brady Williams, 151–72. Albany: State University of New York Press, 2000.

Coward, Harold, John R. Hinnels, and Raymond Brady Williams (eds.). *The South Asian Religious Diaspora in Britain, Canada, and the U.S.A.* Albany: State University of New York Press, 2000.

Dewan, Veeno. 'South Asian T.V.: A Time for Change.' *U Magazine* 2(1) (2000): 12–15.

Driedger, Leo. 'Toward a Perspective on Canadian Pluralism: Ethnic Identity in Winnipeg.' *Canadian Journal of Sociology* 2(1) (1977): 77-95.

Dusenbery, Verne A. 'Introduction: A Century of Sikhs Beyond Punjab.' In *The Sikh Diaspora: Migration and the Experience Beyond the Punjab*, edited by N. Gerald Barrier and Verne A. Dusenbery, 1–28. Delhi: Chanakya, 1989.

– 'The Poetics and Politics of Recognition: Diasporan Sikhs in Pluralist Polities.' *American Ethnologist* 24(4), (1997): 738–62.

– 'Punjabi Sikhs and Gora Sikhs: Conflicting Assertions of Sikh Identity in North America.' In *Sikh History and Religion in the 20th Century*, ed. Joseph T. O'Connell, Milton Israel, and Willard G. Oxtoby, 334–55. Toronto: Centre for South Asian Studies, University of Toronto, 1988.

Fleras, Augie, and Jean Elliot. *Multiculturalism in Canada*. Scarborough: Nelson, 1992.

Ghuman, P.A.S. 'Canadian or Indo-Canadian: A Study of South Asian Adolescents.' *International Journal of Adolescence and Youth* 4 (1994): 229–43.

Grewal, J.S. *The Sikhs of the Punjab*. Cambridge: Cambridge University Press, 1998.

Hawley, John S., and Gurinder Singh Mann (eds). *Studying the Sikhs: Issues for North America*. Albany: State University of New York Press, 1993.

Helweg, Arthur W. 'The Sikh Diaspora and Sikh Studies.' In *Studying the Sikhs: Issues for North America*, ed. John S. Hawley and Gurinder Singh Mann, 69–93. New York: State University of New York Press, 1993.

– 'Sikh Identity in England: Its Changing Nature.' In *Sikh History and Religion in the 20th Century*, ed. Joseph T. O'Connell, Milton Israel, and Willard G. Oxtoby, 356–75. Toronto: Centre for South Asian Studies, University of Toronto, 1988.

– *Sikhs in England: The Development of a Migrant Community*. 2nd ed. Delhi: Oxford University Press, 1987.

Herberg, Edward N. *Ethnic Groups in Canada: Adaptations and Transitions*. Scarborough: Nelson Canada, 1989.

Hofstede, Geert H. *Culture's Consequences: International Differences in Work-related Values*. Beverly Hills, CA: Sage, 1980.

Ibrahim, Farah, Hifumi Ohnishi, and Daya Sandhu. 'Asian American Identity Development: A Culture Specific Model for South Asian Americans.' *Journal of Multicultural Counseling and Development* 25 (January 1997): 34–50.

Indra, Doreen M. 'South Asian Stereotypes in the Vancouver Press.' *Ethnic and Racial Studies* 2(2) (1979): 166–89.

Inkeles, Alex. *One World Emerging? Convergence and Divergence in Industrial Societies*. Boulder, CO: Westview Press, 1998.

Israel, Milton (ed.). *The South Asian Diaspora in Canada: Six Essays*. Toronto: Multicultural History Society of Ontario, 1987.

Jain, S. *East Indians in Canada*. The Hague: Klop Press, 1971.

Johnston, Hugh. *The Voyage of Komagata Maru: The Sikh Challenge to Canada's Colour Bar*. Delhi: Oxford University Press, 1979.

– 'Patterns of Sikh Migration to Canada 1900–1960.' In *Sikh History and Religion in the 20th Century*, ed. Joseph T. O'Connell, Milton Israel, and Willard Oxtoby, 296–313. Toronto: Centre for South Asian Studies, University of Toronto, 1988.

Kanungo, Rabindra N. (ed.). *South Asians in the Canadian Mosaic*. Montreal: Kala Bharati Foundation, 1984.

Kymlicka, Will. *Finding Our Way: Rethinking Ethnocultural Relations in Canada*. Toronto: Oxford University Press, 1998.

La Brack, B. *The Sikhs of Northern California, 1904-1986*. New York: AMS Press, 1988.

Leaf, Murray J. *Information and Behavior in a Sikh Village: Social Organization Reconsidered*. Berkeley: University of California Press, 1972.

Mann, Gurinder Singh. 'Sikhism in the United States of America.' In *The South Asian Religious Diaspora in Britain, Canada and U.S.A.*, ed. Harold Coward, John R. Hinells and Raymond Brady Williams, 259–76. Albany: State University of New York Press, 2000.

Marty, Martin E., and R. Scott Appleby (eds.). *Fundamentalisms and the State*. Chicago: University of Chicago Press, 1993.

Maslow, Abraham H. *Motivation and Personality*. 2nd ed. New York: Harper and Row, 1970.

– *Toward a Psychology of Being*. 2nd ed. New York: Van Nostrand Reinhold, 1968.

McLeod, W.H. *The Evolution of the Sikh Community*. Oxford: Clarendon Press, 1976.

– *Guru Nanak and the Sikh Religion*. Delhi: Oxford University Press, 1976.

– *The Sikhs: History, Religion and Society*. New York: Columbia University Press, 1989.

Minhas, Manmohan Singh. *The Sikh Canadians*. Edmonton: Reidmore, 1994.

Naidoo, Josephine C. 'Contemporary South Asian Women in the Canadian Mosaic.' *International Journal of Women's Studies* 8 (Sept.–Oct. 1985): 338–50.

– 'Women of South Asian Origins: Status of Research, Problems, Future Issues.' In *The South Asian Diaspora in Canada: Six Essays*, ed. Milton Israel, 37–58. Toronto: Multicultural History Society of Ontario, 1987.

Naidoo, Josephine C., and J. Campbell Davis. 'Canadian South Asian Women in Transition: A Dualistic View of Life.' *Journal of Comparative Family Studies* 19 (Summer 1988): 311–27.

Nayar, Baldev Raj. *Minority Politics in the Punjab*. Princeton, NJ: Princeton University Press, 1966.

Nodwell, Evelyn. "'Integrating Indian Culture into our Life": The Construction of (East) "Indian Culture" in Vancouver, Canada.' PhD dissertation, University of British Columbia, 1993.

Oberoi , Harjot S. *The Construction of Religious Boundaries: Culture, Identity and Diversity in the Sikh Tradition*. Chicago: University of Chicago Press, 1994.

– 'Sikh Fundamentalism: Translating History into Theory.' In *Fundamentalisms and the State*, ed. Martin E. Marty and R. Scott Appleby, 256–85. Chicago: University of Chicago Press, 1993.

O'Connell, Joseph T. 'Sikh Religio-Ethnic Experience in Canada.' In *The South Asian Religious Diaspora in Britain, Canada and U.S.A.*, ed. Harold Coward, John R. Hinells, and Raymond Brady Williams, 191–209. Albany: State University of New York Press, 2000.

O'Connell, Joseph T., Milton Israel, and Willard G. Oxtoby (eds.). *Sikh History and Religion in the 20th Century*. Toronto: Centre for South Asian Studies, University of Toronto, 1988.

Ong, Walter J. *Orality and Literacy: The Technologizing of the Word*. London: Routledge, 1982.

Oxtoby, Willard G. (ed). *World Religions: Eastern Traditions*. 2nd ed. Don Mills, ON: Oxford University Press, 2002.

Paranjpe, Anand C. *Self and Identity in Modern Psychology and Indian Thought*. New York: Plenum Press, 1998.

Parsons, Talcott, and Edward A. Shils. *Toward a General Theory of Action*. Cambridge: Harvard University Press, 1951.

Pettigrew, Joyce. *Robber Noblemen: A Study of the Political System of Sikh Jats*. Boston: Routledge and Kegan Paul, 1975.

Porter, John. *The Vertical Mosaic: An Analysis of Social Class and Power in Canada*. Toronto: University of Toronto Press, 1965.

'Questions and Answers with Giani Sant Singh Maskeen.' *Mehfil Magazine* 2(5) (1994): 40–43, 93–97.

Riggs, Fred Warren. *Administration in Developing Countries: The Theory of Prismatic Society*. Boston: Houghton Mifflin, 1964.

Safran, William. 'Diasporas in Modern Societies: Myths of the Homeland and Return.' *Diaspora* 1(1) (1991): 83–99.

Scanlon, T. Joseph. *The Sikhs of Vancouver: A Case Study of the Role of the Media in Ethnic Relations*. Ottawa: Carleton University Press, 1975.

Schlesinger, Arthur M., Jr. *The Disuniting of America: Reflections on a Multicultural Society*. New York: W.W. Norton, 1992.

Sidhu, Kamaljit Kaur. 'Second Generation Sikh Adolescent Males: A Grounded

Theory Model of Self and Identity Construction.' PhD dissertation, University of British Columbia, 1999.

Singh, Harbans. *The Heritage of the Sikhs.* Delhi: Manohar, 1994.

– (ed.). *The Encyclopaedia of Sikhism.* 4 vols. Patiala: Punjabi University, 1995.

Singh (Sandhu), Jaswinder. *Discovering Divine Love in the Play of Life: The Teachings from Guru Arjun's Bhawan Akhri.* Surrey, BC: Journal of Contemporary Sikh Studies, 2001.

Singh, Khushwant. *A History of the Sikhs.* 2 Vols. Princeton, NJ: Princeton University Press, 1963.

Singh, Narinder. *Canadian Sikhs: History, Religion, and Culture of Sikhs in North America.* Ottawa: Canadian Sikhs' Studies Institute, 1994.

Singh, Pashaura, and Gerald Barrier (eds.). *Sikh Identity: Continuity and Change.* New Delhi: Manohar, 1999.

Singh, Sarjeet. *An Oral History of the Sikhs in British Columbia, 1920-1947.* Vancouver: University of British Columbia, 1991.

Stopes-Roe, Mary, and Raymond Cochrane. 'The Process of Assimilation in Asians in Britain: A Study of Hindu, Muslim and Sikh Immigrants and their Young Adult Children.' *International Journal of Comparative Sociology* 28 (January–April 1987): 43–56.

Sutton, Francis X. 'Analyzing Social Systems.' In *Political Development and Social Change,* ed. Jason L. Finkle and Richard W. Gable, 19–31. New York: John Wiley and Sons, 1966.

Tajfel, H. *Social Identity and Ethnic Group Relations.* New York: Cambridge University Press, 1982.

Talbani, Aziz, and Parveen Hasanali. 'Adolescent Females Between Tradition and Modernity: Gender Role Socialization in South Asian Immigrant Culture.' *Journal of Adolescence* 23(5) (2000): 615–27.

Tatla, Darshan Singh. *The Sikh Diaspora: The Search for Statehood.* Seattle: University of Washington Press, 1999.

Triandis, Harry Charalambos. *Individualism and Collectivism.* Boulder, CO: Westview Press, 1995.

Wood, John. 'East Indians and Canada's New Immigration Policy.' *Canadian Public Policy* 4(4) (1978): 547–67.

Wood, Merry. *Cross-Cultural Communication.* Vancouver: Vancouver Hospital and Health Services Centre, 1994.

Woollett, Anne, Harriette Marshall, Paula Nicholson and Neelam Dosanjh. 'Asian's Women's Ethnic Identity: The Impact of Gender and Context in the Accounts of Women Bringing Up Children in East London.' *Feminism and Psychology* 4(1) (1994): 119–32.

Index

abstract thought form. *See* analytics

adaptation: phases in, 185–6; process of, 3; by Sikhs in Vancouver, 186–8, 223–5, 229

Adi Granth. See Guru Granth Sahib

adolescence, 14, 93, 95–7, 103–5

Air India bombings, 162–3

Akal Takht, 164–5, 184, 257

Akali Dal, 163, 251n17, 257

Akali Gurdwara, 165

AKJ (Akhand Kirtani Jatha), 162, 250n12

Ames, Michael, 62, 242n16

amritdhari. See Sikhs, *amritdhari*

analytics: description, 28; third generation, 38–44, 77, 94, 105–6, 143–9, 153, 209, 218, 225, 228, 230, 232. *See also* modern society; tradition/ modernity dichotomy, pattern variables

Angelo, Michael, 72, 239n43, 243n23

Anglo-conformity. *See* assimilation

anti-Asian riots in Vancouver, 16

Appleby, Scott, 183, 252n36

Armstrong, Karen, 183, 252n37

assimilation, 10, 160–1, 285n25; critique of, 238n25

Babbar Khalsa, 162, 184

Bains, Hardial S., 163, 251n19

Bains, Tara Singh, 160, 244n22, 250n9

Baisakhi, 142, 190, 207, 248n22, 257

Bissoondath, Neil, 12, 238n30

Bhindranwale, Jarnail Singh, 183–5

B.C. Organization for Fighting Racism, 18, 161

B.C. Societies Act, 159

British Crown, 17, 158–160, 182

British Honduras, 17

Buchignani, Norman, 59, 154, 220, 235n5, 236n8, 239n35, 242n15, 249n27, 250n6, 254n10

Canadian-born children. *See* third generation

Canadian Charter of Rights and Freedoms, 11, 164, 190

Canadian Employment and Equity Act, 11, 164, 190

Canadian Farm Workers Union, 161

Canadian Multiculturalism Act, 11, 190. *See also* multiculturalism

caste, 122–3, 126, 136; *jat*, 15, 48, 123, 125, 154, 247n9, 259; *khatri*, 48, 259; marriage, 48

Maple Ridge murder, 166, 216, 254n5
marriage: arranged, 71–2, 131, 200; love, 72; migration, 15; pressure for, 76, 101–3; semi-arranged, 72–3. *See also* divorce
Marty, Martin, 183, 258n
Maskeen, Giani Sant Singh, 173, 252n28
Maslow, Abraham, 80–2, 243n28, 244n15
media: critique of, 207–8, 215–17, 253n3; mainstream, 207, 215–17; *See also* ethnic media
migration. *See* Sikhs in Vancouver, waves of migration
minority group. *See* ethnic minority group
moderates. *See* Sikh, moderates
modern society: achievement in, 7–8, 12, 14, 46, 61, 84, 224; characteristics of, 7–8, 224; globalization and, 8; knowledge in, 8; social change in, 8; universalism in, 196–7, 230. *See also* analytics; tradition/modernity dichotomy
modernity, impact of, 9, 46, 59, 80, 223–4, 226–9, 230–1
multiculturalism: critique of, 11–12, 196, 203–5, 211–13, 220–2, 229–33; ethnic vote, 10, 169, 173–4; first generation, 195–9, 219, 229–30; second generation, 202–6, 219, 230; Sikh community, 161, 163–4, 189–92, 229–33; Theory of, 10–12; third generation, 12–13, 211–3, 219, 230
MOSAIC (Multilingual Orientation Service Association for Immigrant Communities), 191–2, 197–8
Mughals. *See* Islam
Muslims, 48, 127. *See also* Islam

Naidoo, Josephine, 66, 242n19
Nanak-sar Gurdwara, 165
Nayar, Baldev Raj, 184, 241n5, 244n23, 252n40
Nietzsche, Friedrich, 14
nirankari. See Sikhs, *nirankari*
NGOs, multicultural, 191–2, 197–99, 205–6, 214

Oberoi, Harjot Singh, 48, 153, 183, 241n7, 247n14, 252n38
O'Connell, Joseph, 181, 235n5, 236n11, 252n31
Ong, Walter, 27, 240nn2–3, 241nn8, 10
Operation Bluestar, 18, 139, 151, 153, 162, 184
orality: definition, 26–7; first generation, 28–33, 42, 51–2, 57, 58, 113, 117, 128–31, 137, 142, 165, 167, 195–7, 199–200, 218, 224–5, 230. *See also* traditional societies; tradition/modernity dichotomy, characteristics
orthodoxy. *See* Sikhism, orthodoxy; Sikhs, *amritdhari*; Sikhs, fundamentalists
Oxtoby, Willard, 127, 248n18

pardah, 50
Parmar, Talwinder Singh, 162
Parsons, Talcott, 7, 237n16, 240n2
Pettigrew, Joyce, 175, 252n29
Piaget, Jean, 14, 239n37
PICS (Progressive Intercultural Community Societies Services), 191–2, 214
Porter, John, 12, 238n25, 254n1
postmodernity, 8–9, 237n21
psychodrama: *gidda*, 117–18; skits,

unorthodoxy, 98–9, 109–10; warrior culture, 48
Sikhs: *amritdhari*, 126–7, 139, 150–1, 214, 245n27, 257; fundamentalists, 130, 136–7, 149, 151–2, 165, 184–5; Gora, 5, 22, 127–8, 248n17, 258; identity. *See* Punjabi, Sikh identity; *keshdhari*, 127, 130, 237; moderates, 130, 149, 136–7, 151–2, 165, 184–5; *nirankari*, 248n16, 250n14, 260; *sahajdhari*, 127, 260
Sikhs in Vancouver: description of, 18; distinctive features of, 4–5, 223; fundamentalism; insular nature of, 13, 218–9 (*see also* third generation: ethnic insularity); identity among, 154–5 (*see also* Punjabi, Sikh identity; Sikh, moderates; Sikhism); lack of cohesion among, 220–2, 254n11; origins of, 3, 15–16; orthodox vs unorthodox, 161–5; research on, 4; waves of migration, 15–18
SSA at SFU (Sikh Students Association at SFU, 210–11
Sikhnet, 214
Sikhvision, 214
Simon Fraser University (SFU), 214
Singh, Bela, 159, 182, 249–50n3
Singh, Gurdit, 17
Singh, Mewa, 159, 182, 250n3
Singh Sabha, 153
Singh, Sant Nand, 165
Singh, Sant Teja, 16–17
Singh, Shahid Bhagat, 182
Singh, Shahid Udham, 182
South Asian. *See* diaspora, South Asian
storytelling. *See* orality; first generation
Surrey-Delta Gurdwara, 164–5

Sutton, Francis, 7–8, 237n17, 239n36, 241n1, 243n24, 249n1

tables and chairs. *See gurdwara*: controversy
Talbani, Aziz, 72, 102, 236n8, 243n22, 244n19
Tat Khalsa, 48
Tatla, Darshan S., 235n1, 236n6, 239n46, 246n1, 249n29, 250n10, 250–1nn10, 13, 15, 16, 18
tensions. *See* intergenerational tension; gender tension
third generation: confusion between religion and culture, 141–4, 228; coping mechanisms, 73 (*see also* psychodrama); definition, 21–2; desire for more social integration, 208–11, 214–15, 230–3; earning respect, 73–5, 77–8, 82, 226; ethnic insularity, 178–81, 228–9, 230; going off track, 99–100, 108, 227 (*see also* GGB); increase in emotional needs, 80–2; maladaptive behaviours, 112–14, 227 (*see also* double life; role playing); parental pressure, 99–103, 227, 244n12; personal choice, 77, 84, 141, 149–53, 226–8; questioning by, 73, 76–7, 141, 144–9, 228. *See also* analytics; double standard; gender issues
Toennies, Ferdinard, 6, 237n13
tradition/modernity dichotomy, 5–10; critique of, 8–9, 237n21; framework for study, 8–9; pattern variables, 7
traditional societies: ascription in, 7, 12, 14, 46, 77, 84; characteristics of, 7; diffuseness in, 7, 84, 120, 128, 157, 165, 170–3; knowledge in, 8,